Pacifists in Chains

YOUNG CENTER BOOKS IN ANABAPTIST & PIETIST STUDIES

Donald B. Kraybill, *Series Editor*

Pacifists in Chains

The Persecution of Hutterites during the Great War

Duane C. S. Stoltzfus

JOHNS HOPKINS UNIVERSITY PRESS
Baltimore

Johns Hopkins University Press
2715 North Charles Street
Baltimore, Maryland 21218-4363
www.press.jhu.edu

Library of Congress Cataloging-in-Publication Data
Stoltzfus, Duane C. S., 1959–
Pacifists in chains : the persecution of Hutterites during the Great War /
Duane C. S. Stoltzfus.
pages   cm. — (Young center books in Anabaptist and
Pietist studies)
Includes bibliographical references and index.
ISBN 978-1-4214-1127-9 (pbk. : alk. paper) — ISBN 978-1-4214-1128-6
(electronic) — ISBN 1-4214-1127-X (pbk. : alk. paper) —
ISBN 1-4214-1128-8 (electronic)
1. Bruderhof Communities—History. 2. World War, 1914–1918.
3. Persecution. 4. Pacifism—Religious aspects—Bruderhof
Communities. I. Title.
BX8129.B63S76 2014
289.7'73—dc23   2013006918

A catalog record for this book is available from the British Library.

Special discounts are available for bulk purchases of this book.
For more information, please contact Special Sales at 410-516-6936 or
specialsales@press.jhu.edu.

Johns Hopkins University Press uses environmentally friendly book
materials, including recycled text paper that is composed of at least 30
percent post-consumer waste, whenever possible.

Contents

Contents

Preface

On July 27, 1918, while American and Allied soldiers fought German forces along the Western Front in Europe, four young Hutterite farmers from South Dakota arrived at the prison on Alcatraz Island. Weeks earlier they had been found guilty of failure to obey military orders. The farmers had refused to line up and drill alongside other recruits who were training as infantrymen at Camp Lewis in Washington State. The Hutterites said they could do nothing to aid the war effort, not even clean the dishes of the men who would carry guns into battle. And so the four men found themselves chained in the dungeon at Alcatraz, each sentenced to twenty years of hard labor. They were filled with foreboding.

One of the four Hutterites, Michael Hofer, wrote to his wife, Maria: "We are now in the military prison of Alcatraz behind iron and locks. We don't know what will become of us."[1] His younger brother, David, also wrote home: "We all do not expect to see each other in this world anymore."[2] Likewise, a third brother, Joseph, sent dire word back to their communal colony: "It is very clear that we are not destined for better days ahead and that our lives will endure for only a short while."[3]

During the day, the men were strung up by their wrists so that their toes scarcely touched the cold and wet floor, a technique known as "high cuffing," well established in the history of torture. The cells measured six feet high at the uppermost point, six and a half feet wide, and eight feet deep. For drink, they had water; for food, bread; and for company, the rats that scurried around the clock. Guards left uniforms on the cell floors, but the men remained in their underwear, unwilling to wear anything that carried a military label. In this dank, windowless basement, they lived in darkness, by day and by night.

In that summer of war, scarcely anyone but South Dakota relatives paid much mind to the Hutterites locked away. World War I brought a mountain of suffering to the people of many nations. Americans focused their attention, and sympathy, on the fighting along the Western Front, where tens of thousands of their young men would be buried in blood-soaked fields before the war ended. That was one true measure of the cost of war: simply counting the dead. More than nine million combatants in all died as the fighting raged between 1914 and 1918. Even after the armistice was signed early on the morning of November 11, 1918, but before it took effect, commanders continued to offer up their men in an eleventh-hour sacrifice.

The United States came late, and reluctantly, to the war. President Woodrow Wilson won reelection in 1916 by reminding voters that he had kept the nation far from the killing. Only a few months later, citing German provocations, he asked Congress to declare war. The president warned that conformity would become a virtue and dissent a vice. True to those words, the United States woke up on April 7, the morning after Congress had declared war, as if to put on the armor of a different country.

For its part, the federal government introduced an expansive military draft and vast measures of control like the Espionage Act. Amid an outpouring of government propaganda about war being waged at home as well as abroad, a hyperpatriotic fever swept across the land, turning neighbor against neighbor in a relentless search for traitors. When these neighbors formed mobs, they set about their business with hanging rope, whip, tar and feathers, yellow paint, and midnight fires.

South Dakotans targeted the Hutterites who lived in sixteen communities, which they referred to as colonies, in the southeastern part of the state. The Hutterites had several strikes against them. As speakers of a Germanic language, they broadcast their ancestry while the United States waged war against Germany. Moreover, they belonged to a Christian community that held all property in common in a nation that prized private enterprise and personal accomplishment.

Most troubling of all, they rejected military service at a time when young men were expected to eagerly put on uniforms to protect the home country, support the Allies, and advance democracy. As the war effort in the United States gained urgency in the spring of 1918, patience with the Hutterites was running thin. On May 15, when members of the Jamesville Colony in South Dakota refused to buy war bonds, the mayor and a mob of prominent citizens from nearby Yankton rounded up the Hutterite cattle and sheep and sold them at auction. The cash went for bonds.

The four imprisoned Hutterites were from nearby Rockport Colony, which consisted of about twenty-five families who together farmed four thousand acres. That same month, the Hutterite draftees, all husbands and fathers, left their home colony for induction into the U.S. Army. They packed Bibles and little else in their satchels, determined to remain faithful to their pacifist convictions whatever the cost. On board a special military train bound for Camp Lewis, a group of rowdy fellow soldiers pushed their way into the compartment where the four men—the Hofer brothers and Jacob Wipf, who was Joseph's brother-in-law—were riding. The soldiers grabbed the men, one by one, and used clippers to cut off their hair and beards, the first of many efforts to force the Hutterites to exchange religious markers for military values.

At Camp Lewis, where tens of thousands of soldiers were being trained for combat on the front lines, the Hofer brothers and Jacob Wipf refused to fill out personal information cards (which were titled "Statement of Soldier"), to put on military uniforms, or to accept work assignments. Their first night was spent in a guardhouse. There they would stay until their court-martial, when they were found guilty on all charges and sentenced to hard labor at Alcatraz.

Until now, their story—in which two returned home in caskets and two returned home to resume farming—has been told only in brief accounts. By drawing on a wide variety of unpublished sources, including letters that the men wrote while in prison, a more vivid picture emerges of their harrowing journey through the military prison system. The letters were kept by family members, Hutterites all, who today live in colonies in Montana and in Saskatchewan.

The Hofer brothers and Jacob Wipf were among 504 conscientious objectors who were court-martialed during the war. The experience of the four men contributes significantly to one of the darker chapters of this period of American history, when a wartime patriotic fever and a widespread suspicion of all things German fueled attacks on conscientious objectors and others who did not rally to the cause. For the National Civil Liberties Bureau (to be renamed the American Civil Liberties Union after the war) and other advocates for the objectors, the Hutterites from Rockport became the most compelling evidence of a pattern of mistreatment at military camps and prisons.

Though the National Civil Liberties Bureau pointedly accused the federal government of torture in its treatment of the men, the charge was never fully taken up in the court of public opinion, let alone a court of law. To the military, Joseph and Michael Hofer were slackers who died of influenza before they had completed their terms of imprisonment. Americans as a whole had little patience for any sign of what they saw as coddling men who had refused to serve in the military (the release of 113 conscientious objectors two months after the armistice created a fierce backlash).

Rather than call attention to the mistreatment, the Hutterites, the Mennonites, and the other historic peace churches that accounted for many of the conscientious objectors resolved to put the difficult times behind them. The Hutterites, including the Rockport colonists, moved en masse to Canada. They never received nor expected an apology from the federal government, but in their own quiet way they issued an indictment. The grave markers for Michael and Joseph Hofer, who were buried at home in South Dakota, identify them as "martyrs" (see chapter 9). The men chose to accept death at the hands of the state rather than to renounce their faith.

Their tale, distressing as it is, does not follow a simple script, neatly dividing the cast into heroes and villains. As the narrative unfolds, observers a century later can grasp why the Hutterites became absolutist objectors during the war and feel empathy for the men in the face of their sufferings. At the same time, followers of the story can appreciate the challenges set before military commanders and guards who followed a different set of orders and, by their worldview, could not understand why these men would not contribute to the national cause, if only by pushing a broom.

Even so, the federal government can be held to account these many years later. In the face of that apparent obstinacy on the part of the Hutterites, some military officials responded harshly, resorting to torture. President Woodrow Wilson and Newton Baker, the secretary of war, were convinced that every American should contribute to the war effort and would eventually do so, through the power of peer pressure and reason. When reason failed to persuade the conscientious objectors to get on board, Wilson and Baker ignored the mounting signs of mistreatment. Their default response was coercion, not compassion.

The Hutterites, for their part, harmed no one. Their only wrongdoing, if it can be counted as such, was refusing to support the war. They wanted to do right by the nation. They appeared to never lose faith in the good intentions of the federal government, especially embodied by Baker, who early on promised church leaders: "We'll take care of your boys."[4]

The story is made all the more poignant because of a series of ironies and ill-timed circumstances that form a striking subtext for this wartime account. President Ulysses S. Grant had personally appealed to the Hutterites to move from Russia to the United States in the 1870s, as the nation in that moment welcomed both their farming skills and pacifist convictions. So the Hutterites immigrated to the United States to escape military conscription in Russia. Then World War I arrived, and Washington had different expectations.

Throughout the war, so much depended on chance, beginning, of course, with the random selection of draft numbers. Timing, also, played unfair. To cite just one example, if the four Hutterite draftees had arrived at Camp Lewis only a few weeks later than they did, they would surely have stood before a newly formed panel of legal advisers and received a farm furlough instead of imprisonment. Other Hutterite young men followed that more desirable path.

But nearly a century later, with wartime passions having long since faded, the evidence suggests that the charges against the four men from Rockport were grievously misplaced. They faithfully followed in the religious footsteps of their ancestors; their conscience permitted them to go no further than they did in cooperating with the military system. But President Wilson and Secretary Baker, who presided over the war, determined that such pacifist beliefs were unreasonable and that conscientious objectors could be persuaded to line up with the majority of Americans in going to war.

In Washington the highest officials in the land set in motion a series of actions, carried out by subordinates, that in isolation may have seemed measured and appropriate. The cumulative effect was a miscarriage of justice that has never been acknowledged. Four men who sought neither to harm nor to injure anyone at any turn ended up hanging in chains, a treatment that in general terms President Wilson would later describe as "barbarous or mediaeval." The Hutterites were intended to be an example to deter other conscientious objectors. Instead, they became a shameful example of the failure of a government to stand by its constitutional guarantee of freedom to practice religion and promise to safeguard citizens from torture and other cruel and unusual punishments.

The inhumane treatment of the Hofer brothers and Jacob Wipf while in prison calls to mind the American response to suspected terrorists after the September 11 attacks. In an effort to defeat Al Qaeda and prevent future attacks on American soil, the United States subjected prisoners to waterboarding and other forms of torture. Human dignity and human rights became expendable—and for a highly suspect return. Many government officials and interrogators later said that the best intelligence information came from prisoners who were not tortured. The so-called enhanced interrogation techniques often yielded false information.

Americans carried out a similar pattern of fruitless coercion in World War I, this time with prisoners from within the national fold. No matter how violent the hand raised against them, hundreds of conscientious objectors remained true to their convictions. The memories of brutalities committed in military prisons during the war add an authoritative historical footnote to the case against torture: it erodes a nation's moral center just as surely as it dehumanizes the victims and in the end fails to achieve its stated goals.

The story that follows begins with a description of life on a Hutterite colony in 1918 and the religious faith that shaped the worldview of this communitarian people over the centuries. Succeeding chapters trace the arrival of the Hofer brothers and Jacob Wipf at Camp Lewis, their court-martial, their imprisonment at Alcatraz, and their subsequent transfer to Fort Leavenworth. The experiences of the four Hutterites are placed in the context of a nation at war. One chapter is devoted to recounting the formation of the American Army on deadline and another to examining the crackdown on dissent and the superpatriotism that raged across the country. The book brings current expertise to bear, including comments from medical and legal authorities on the government's treatment of the four men.

In remaining true to their religious convictions in the face of what they recognized as age-old persecution, Jacob Wipf and the Hofer brothers left behind a powerful Hutterite testimony and a reminder of how readily a country can cast aside its better angels during wartime. Joseph and Michael Hofer, the brothers who returned to the Rockport Colony in caskets, wrote home just days before they died. In his last letter, written while en route from Alcatraz to Leavenworth a week after the armistice had been signed, Joseph said: "Let us praise God that the bloodletting has now come to an end as we had hoped. But now is the time—as our Lord Jesus taught us that such a time would come—which has never been before as long as the world has stood, and will never be again."[5] Michael likewise signed off on the same day: "If we do not see each other again in this world, then we will see one another in the next world."[6]

Acknowledgments

A book more than five years in the making can still lay claim to a touch of research drama. The most suspenseful moment in the writing of this book happened at a Hutterite colony in Choteau, Montana, in 2009. I had traveled more than 1,500 miles to the Miller Colony to ask whether I might see copies of the unpublished letters written by four Hutterite men, all conscientious objectors who had been imprisoned at Alcatraz during World War I.

The daughter and three grandchildren of one of the men, Michael Hofer, welcomed me to the colony. Sarah Kleinsasser, a granddaughter, had answered my initial telephone call to the Miller Colony. On this day she provided introductions to her mother, Mary Hofer Kleinsasser, Michael's daughter, who was 90 at the time, and to her brothers Michael and Joseph Kleinsasser, both ministers at the Kingsbury Colony in nearby Valier.

After we visited for an hour or so, talking about the Hutterite and Mennonite branches of the Christian tree and whether I was the Stoltzfus who had caused some consternation by trying to convert Hutterites to the Mennonite side (thankfully, I wasn't), I asked about the letters. Did they have copies of Michael Hofer's letters? Would they be willing to share them? They would be pleased to, they said.

When they brought out the letters, I saw that the drama would be continued on another day. Most of the letters were written in a challenging German script, with touches of Hutterisch, a dialect distinct to the Hutterites, difficult to decipher even for a modern speaker of the German language. It would be weeks before two colleagues at Goshen College could provide the English translation. The waiting effort was yet another reminder that this wartime story would be told only through shared labor.

The Kleinsassers, in turn, introduced me to Anna Hofer Wurtz, who lives at the Miller Colony and shared copies of letters from her grandfather David Hofer. At the New Rockport Colony in Pendroy, Katie Jacob Waldner, a granddaughter of Joseph Hofer, said that she did not have copies of letters written by her grandfather, but she agreed to contact her cousin Joe Hofer, of the Kyle Colony in Saskatchewan. During my stay at the Kyle Colony, Joe Hofer kindly shared those letters.

There was still the matter of finding the linguistic key to the letter box. John D. Roth, editor of *The Mennonite Quarterly Review* and director of the Mennonite Historical Society at Goshen College, where he is a colleague who teaches in the history department, generously offered to transcribe and translate the Joseph and Michael Hofer letters. Gerhard J. Reimer, a professor emeritus of German at Goshen College, kindly agreed to do the same with the David Hofer letters.

Joe Springer, curator of the Mennonite Historical Library, initially noted the research potential in this wartime story; Daniel Hochstetler, a Mennonite who many years ago taught Sarah Kleinsasser when he was a grade school teacher among the Hutterites, introduced me to Sarah; Leonard Gross, a Hutterite scholar from Goshen, served as a guide to history and pointed the way to Hutterites who were also keenly invested in that history. They included Tony Waldner at the Forest River Colony in Fordville, North Dakota, and Patrick Murphy, who manages the James Valley Book Centre at the James Valley Colony near Winnipeg, Manitoba.

Victoria Waters and Carol Miller retrieved many a helpful source at the Mennonite Historical Library, as did Rich Preheim (who himself has written an article about the four Hutterite draftees) and Colleen McFarland at the Mennonite Church USA Archives in Goshen. Peggy Goertzen at the Center for Mennonite Brethren Studies at Tabor College, Kansas, and James Lynch from the Mennonite Library and Archives at Bethel College, North Newton, Kansas, both advanced the research.

Apart from handling numerous book and article requests, the Goshen

College Good Library staff arranged for microform reels to be delivered from several newspapers in South Dakota and from the American Civil Liberties Union. Adriane Hanson, a project archivist at the Seeley G. Mudd Manuscript Library at Princeton University, helped to navigate the ACLU collection.

Thanks to Norman Hofer, who mailed a folder of Hutterite materials to Goshen early on, and who let his tractor idle for a day to take a visitor on a tour of several colonies in the James River Valley, including Rockport, where the Hofer brothers and Jacob Wipf lived. Tim L. Waltner, the publisher of the *Freeman Courier*, suspended policy to lend several bound volumes of the weekly paper for research off site. Duane Schrag opened up the Heritage Hall archives at the Freeman Academy early, and kept the doors open late, extending the hours of a normal research day.

When doors did not open at Fort Lewis in Washington, Jean Fisher and the rest of the staff at the nearby Tacoma Public Library reached into the drawers of history. Down the coast, at Alcatraz, Jim Nelson of the Golden Gate National Parks Conservancy twice put on a hard hat to escort a visitor to the dungeon, which is officially closed to the public. John A. Martini, a former National Park Service ranger, led the way to helpful sources, including his own books on Alcatraz. Jean Grosser, chair of the art department at Coker College, Hartsville, South Carolina, shared information about her grandfather Philip Grosser, a conscientious objector who was imprisoned at Alcatraz and Fort Leavenworth.

Anita Stalter, the academic dean at Goshen College, gave her blessing to the book project from the beginning. Grants from the Mininger Center at Goshen College made possible research trips to California, Kansas, Montana, and South Dakota, as well as Saskatchewan. Support from the C. Henry Smith Peace Lectureship in 2011–2012 allowed for further research at the Library of Congress in Washington, D.C., where the Newton Diehl Baker papers are held, and in the state of Washington.

Goshen College colleagues, current and former students, and other readers critiqued early drafts of the book. Thanks to the following readers of the manuscript: Beth Martin Birky, Paul Boers, Andrew Clouse, Julia Spicher Kasdorf, Steve Nolt, John D. Roth, Chase Snyder, Donna Stoltzfus Neufeld, and Kelli Yoder.

As editor of the book series on Anabaptist and Pietist Studies, Donald B. Kraybill skillfully guided the manuscript preparation on behalf of Johns Hopkins University Press.

My best and closest readers remain my wife, Karen, and our daughters, Kate and Emily.

Timeline

Founding of the Hutterite Church and Immigration to the United States

1525	Conrad Grebel, Felix Manz, and Georg Blaurock perform adult baptisms in Switzerland
1533	Jacob Hutter joins the group that later became known as the Hutterites
1536	Hutter is burned at the stake, emblematic of the persecution of Hutterites, which at times forced them to relocate their colonies from shortly after their founding until the early twentieth century
1565–1592	Golden Age of the Hutterites, in which they enjoy a safe haven in Moravia (now divided into Slovakia and the Czech Republic)
1870	Czar Alexander II mandates the speaking of Russian in Hutterite homes and universal military service
1871	The Appropriations Act mandates taking land from Native Americans to allow settlement by pioneers
1873	Hutterites travel to the United States to decide whether to immigrate there and meet with President Ulysses Grant
1874–1879	Hutterites immigrate to the United States, settling in the Dakota Territory

World War I and the Hutterites

June 28, 1914	Archduke Francis Ferdinand is assassinated, setting the "Great War" in motion
April 2, 1917	President Wilson asks Congress to declare war
April 7, 1917	The Selective Service Act presented to Congress includes provisions for conscientious objectors
May 18, 1917	The Selective Service Act mandates enlistment for all men ages twenty-one to thirty
June 5, 1917	Michael, Joseph, and David Hofer and Jacob Wipf appear before the draft board
May 10, 1918	The men are inducted into the army
May 25, 1918	The four men are called up and requested to report to Camp Lewis in Washington State
	The German language is banned in South Dakota
May 28, 1918	The four men report to Camp Lewis and are put in the guardhouse for refusing to line up and follow other orders
June 10, 1918	The four men go on trial
June 27, 1918	The men are sent to Alcatraz and put in solitary confinement in the dungeon
November 11, 1918	The Armistice is signed, ending the Great War
November 14, 1918	The men are sent to Fort Leavenworth
November 21, 1918	The National Civil Liberties Bureau releases a report on the treatment of prisoners of conscience
November 29, 1918	Joseph Hofer dies at age twenty-four
November 30, 1918	John Wipf, Jacob's father, writes to U.S. Senator Edwin Johnson and asks him to intervene
December 3, 1918	Michael Hofer dies at age twenty-five
December 4, 1918	David Hofer released from Fort Leavenworth
December 7, 1918	The War Department promises to investigate Wipf's case
January 5, 1919	Jacob Wipf testifies at the Board of Inquiry
January 22, 1919	Enoch Crowder, the judge advocate general, affirms court-martial proceedings and sentence in Wipf's case

January 22, 1919	Secretary of War Newton Baker orders the release of 113 conscientious objectors
March 15, 1919	Peace activist Jacob Ewert telegrams Assistant Secretary of War Frederick Keppel requesting Wipf's release
March 17, 1919	John Wipf telegrams Keppel
March 18, 1919	Keppel's assistant advocates releasing Wipf; notes that Board of Inquiry had found him sincere in his beliefs at January 5 hearing
March 22, 1919	Army's Office of the Judge Advocate General orders Wipf's discharge
April 13, 1919	Jacob Wipf released from Leavenworth

Pacifists in Chains

Chapter One

Called to Duty

Thus saith the Lord: "Stand ye in the ways, and see,
and ask for the old paths, where is the good way, and walk therein,
and ye shall find rest for your souls."
—Jeremiah 6:16

All Talk Is of War

The wonder is that the United States Army even wanted four young Hutterite farmers from the Rockport Colony in South Dakota. The communal church to which they belonged had been resolutely set against all warfare since its inception during the Protestant Reformation nearly four hundred years earlier. And, when their grandparents immigrated to the United States in the 1870s, they did so by traveling thousands of miles, all to avoid conscription in the Russian army. Rather than agree to put on Russian uniforms, the Hutterites left their established farms in the breadbasket steppes to break sod in a state and a nation eager for settlers.

As part of the international courting process (Canada was in the bidding for these skillful immigrant farmers as well), President Ulysses S. Grant personally wooed emissaries for the Hutterites at his summer home on Long Island. While the president said that he couldn't promise that they would be free of military service in the United States, he made the prospect

of a draft sound highly unlikely—they could count on at least fifty untrou-
bled years, he assured them.

And yet here were four young farmers on the morning of May 25, 1918,
well short of the fifty-year mark, summoned by the army for service in
World War I. Three of the men were brothers: David, Michael, and Joseph
Hofer. As might be expected in their closed community, the fourth man,
Jacob Wipf, was a relative; he was Joseph's brother-in-law. All four were
leaving wives and young children at home on the colony.

On this day they were boarding a special military train for Camp Lewis in
Washington State, where tens of thousands of recruits from Western states
were already learning to salute, drill, and handle a bayonet. Jacob Wipf and
the Hofer brothers, as sheltered as any farmers, knew they would step off
that train to face sergeants who were eager to turn them into fighting soldiers as well. As the men packed Bibles in their bags that morning, they
were ready to assure officers of the highest rank that they were warriors only
in the sense of being soldiers for the one true commander in chief, Jesus
Christ, who said, "Love your enemies."[1]

At Rockport Colony near Alexandria, South Dakota, where the men were
raised, everyone followed a dress code that, with symmetry of design, set
them apart from their neighbors. Along with their homemade black jackets,
pants, and shoes, all of the men in the colony who were married, as were
these four, grew beards, a further testimony to their commitment to God
and the community.[2] The women, in turn, wore ankle-length skirts, often
plaid or speckled with flowers. Their hair, grown long, was covered at all
times by polka-dotted kerchiefs, in deference to their husbands, the head of
the household, and to God, the father of all. The children followed the lead
of their parents, looking like little adults (except for their bare feet in the
summer months). The people of Rockport, by any measure, cut a modest
appearance.

Their neighbors back in 1918 worried that looks could be deceiving. The
Hutterites appeared to be a secretive people, different in dangerous ways.
For one thing, the Hutterite farms dwarfed the properties of virtually every
other landholder along the fertile James River Valley in the southeastern
part of South Dakota, home to sixteen colonies. As a local newspaper re-

minded South Dakotans that spring, "their lands are among the richest in the state."[3] Even so, they were rumored to have intentionally reduced their planting that spring so they would have enough to feed themselves but nothing to spare for the military.

The Rockport Colony consisted of about twenty-five families, numbering 180 members; the colony owned four thousand acres, normally one field after another of wheat growing and cattle grazing. Besides five hundred head of cattle, the colonists owned about 130 horses and 1,500 sheep. They operated their own mill, blacksmith shop, and tannery. The Hutterites managed such large farms, as the neighbors well knew, because they were a communal society; at Rockport and the other colonies, joint corporations held title to the land. Everything, from the fields to the parallel rows of fieldstone houses of uniform dimensions, belonged to the community.

Even more worrisome to their neighbors, the Hutterites were a German-speaking people. They spoke the language of the enemy nation at a time when hundreds of thousands of American men were pouring into the Western Front to bolster the French and British lines, which were at risk of buckling under the thrusts of the German army. Though they knew English, the Hutterites seemed to prefer German.

In yet another strike against them, the Hutterites were longstanding pacifists, like the members of the Society of Friends and the Mennonites. When other Americans stood up patriotically during wartime, they stood apart. In the eyes of their neighbors, they were slackers of the first order— "Russian cloonies," as one local paper called them.[4] It bears repeating, one editorial writer said, that neighboring families who sent sons to the front lines were "equally as religious and God fearing."[5]

Every conversation seemed to circle back to the war, even the talk of weather. In this particular spring, South Dakota had reason to celebrate its good fortune in the fields. The state had broken large tracts of land that were being put into crops for the first time. Winter wheat and alfalfa, which had suffered damage over the cold months, were reseeded and coming along well; corn planting was nearly completed; even up in the northern reaches of the state, where the planting traditionally lagged, green shoots were showing through the ground. J.D. Deets, who had left his position as state immigration agent to take over those duties for the Minneapolis & St. Louis Railroad, proclaimed that the "prospects for a great crop were never better in the history of the state."[6]

The importance of planting was not lost on the farmers and townspeople of South Dakota. The federal government was calling on farmers across the country to cultivate all the land that they could, ensuring that the nation at war would have food supplies for the task at hand. The *Freeman Courier*, a weekly paper that circulated among the Hutterite colonies and their neighbors, made explicit the link between farmers and soldiers: "Let us not have even a backyard or vacant lot that is not producing something. Patriotism lies here just as strongly as it does on the battle line."[7]

The sentiment was widely shared by Americans. Across the country, posters proclaimed "Every Garden a Munitions Plant" and "Win the War with Wheat." By midsummer, the United States expected to double the number of its men fighting on the front lines in France; that would mean more than a million soldiers, among them thousands from South Dakota, sent to repel the Germans—and working up an appetite.

The state had already invested as directly as one could in the war campaign, by sending native sons abroad. An American colonel in France had just decorated two South Dakota boys for bravery after an overloaded ration cart broke down under a barrage of German fire.[8] They saw to the temporary repairs, allowing the supplies to be delivered in the dark, all without casualties. That same week fifty-three other Americans on their way to France, likely all asleep on a moonlit night, were not so lucky. The soldiers were reported lost when a German submarine torpedoed the armed merchant cruiser *Moldavia* while crossing the English Channel.

It was a reminder of the ultimate risks being undertaken by American soldiers on behalf of the nation and its European allies. The French and British troops desperately needed the American reinforcements. A German offensive had opened along the Chemin des Dames only days before the Hutterites' leave-taking, on May 22, smashing a hole in the British-French lines, whose retreating troops clogged the roads.

If there was any question about the magnitude of the stakes at this juncture in the war, the *Daily Argus-Leader*, based in Sioux Falls, the largest city in the state, had a ready reply: "There is no doubt whatever that the world has reached the point where certain antagonistic forces are meeting in a death grapple. Forces that are material, spiritual, and political, and the issue of this final conflict is to decide the destiny of the world."

Reluctant Draftees Pack for the Army

Jacob Wipf and the Hofer brothers had grown up together, attending grade school at the home colony until they were pulled away to work in the fields in their early teens. They were literate to be sure but, outside of the Bible, not very well read; the community put a premium on productivity in the field or in the workshop and not in book learning. On their draft cards each described himself as of medium height and build, with brown hair.

The Hutterites encouraged large families, and the men and their wives were well on the way. David, who was twenty-eight, and his wife, Anna, had five children, ages six, five, three, and two, and a newborn, three months old. Michael, who was twenty-four, had been married for only a year; his wife, Maria, had given birth to their first child, a daughter named Mary after her mother, two months earlier. Third in line was Joseph, twenty-three, who was saying goodbye to his wife, Maria, Jacob's sister, and their two children, ages two and one. Joseph's wife was pregnant with a third child, who would be born in eight months. The eldest member of the group, Jacob, thirty, and his wife, Kathrina, had three children, ages seven, five, and three.

On this day of departure, the Hutterite draftees likely had time for only two meals, in the morning and at noon. They would have sat down to breakfast at long wooden tables, the men and boys on one side of the room, and the women and girls on the other, in each row the men and women arranged in descending order of age. The minister or another colony leader offered a brief spoken grace in German, and then, the "amen" serving as a starting pistol, hands quickly reached for coffee, others for homemade bread with cheese or syrup, and maybe even some fresh radishes from the garden. Few people spoke during these mealtimes, a sign of reverence. Twenty minutes later, perhaps less, a prayer of thanks announced an end to the breakfast meal. Shortly before noon, they would have returned to the communal dining hall and once again sat down on benches, awaiting the prayer. Young Hutterite girls on kitchen duty for this meal might have brought in bowls of noodle soup followed by platters of chicken or pork, boiled potatoes, and freshly baked bread.

The four draftees left home dressed in black, as always.[9] If they followed the advice given to Michael A. Stahl, a Hutterite neighbor who left for Camp Funston in Kansas in September, they took only clothes not worth saving, anticipating that their personal belongings would be burned or thrown away once they arrived at camp. Their satchels held room for their Bibles but likely not two other books found in every Hutterite home: the Lehren, the readings, consisting of a corpus of hundreds of sermons, centuries old, intended to keep readers faithful, and the Lieder, the songs, a collection of hymns, many of them recalling ancestors who remained true to their faith in the face of relentless torture in the sixteenth century.

The people of the colony gathered around the men that afternoon. A team of horses stood ready to pull the buggy, with the men sitting abreast in benches. They were likely accompanied by the minister of the colony, David D. Hofer, and maybe a parent or two. Joseph Hofer's wife remembered that her son, then nearly three, ran along behind the buggy as the men pulled away, their wives, in their polka-dot kerchiefs, left standing in tears.

A Hutterite author recalled the leave-taking when other draftees from the South Dakota colonies were bound for Camp Funston eight months earlier, in September 1917. Their language sounds overwrought a century later, especially to an outsider, but it also makes clear how firmly the Hutterites had separated themselves from the world around them. The Hutterites saw themselves as a pure remnant of believers, a select group of Christians who had remained faithful to the biblical mandate to live holy lives in community. All around them, they saw others giving in to temptations—perhaps worst of all, to take up arms. This was the scene at the station: "And the time came when some of our brothers had to get ready and leave with the godless soldiers from Parkston (our city) to Camp Funston on the train. And as the horrible day arrived the whole community assembled before the Lord and begged our compassionate Lord under tears and sighs to protect them and make them steadfast even under the godless soldiers in the war camp."[10]

Bearing Witness through the Centuries

Whether the train was bound for Camp Lewis or Camp Funston, both those who left and those who stayed looked as if they might have been transported from a European village in the Old World. Walter G. Kellogg, an army major who interviewed hundreds of conscientious objectors on behalf of the government during the war, said it bluntly: "They remain now as their forefathers were three centuries ago. . . . Civilization, apparently, has passed them by."[11] The Hutterites were rooted in the Protestant Reformation, separated from their neighbors by more than large fields. When they worshipped, as they did each day, they used an archaic form of High German, the language of their sacred hymns and sermons (around the house, they switched to a German dialect called Hutterisch). During church services, the minister would not preach a sermon of his own but would instead read a text written in Europe centuries earlier.

Why share possessions? Peter Riedemann, a church leader in the 1500s, had answered that question plainly: "[At] the beginning God ordained that people should own nothing individually but should have all things in common with each other. . . . Therefore, whoever will adhere unwaveringly to Christ and follow him must give up acquiring things and holding property."[12] Why renounce war? Jakob Hutter, whose influence as an early leader would be known in part through the legacy of his name, said, "We do not want to hurt or wrong anyone, not even our worst enemy. . . . [W]e want to show by our word and deed that men should live as true followers of Christ, in peace and unity and in God's truth and justice."[13] When the words are true and clear, like these, the Hutterites would say, there's no need for a modern, updated version.

The Hofer brothers and Jacob Wipf were anxious over what awaited them at Camp Lewis, which was closer to the front lines than they had ever expected to go. As baptized members of the Hutterite community, they had pledged never to take up arms, not even in self-defense.[14] And the Hutterites kept that pledge across generations and centuries, as they sojourned eastward from Austria to Transylvania to Ukraine and then on to Russia. They kept the pledge when they moved to South Dakota during the time of President Grant. In Matthew 5, Jesus had commanded his followers to love without condition: "Ye have heard that it hath been said, Thou shalt love thy neighbor, and hate thine enemy. But I say unto you, Love your enemies, bless them that curse you, do good to them that hate you, and pray for them which despitefully use you, and persecute you." For the Hutterites there could be no just war. They took Jesus at his word: always turn the other cheek.

So, the four Hutterite men were obligated by their faith to refuse to serve in a war. And yet, in 1917 the Selective Service Act of the federal government of the United States had required all physically able men between the ages of twenty-one and thirty to prepare for duty. Provisions in the act allowed the Hutterites and other conscientious objectors to avoid combat on the battlefield, but, if drafted, they still had to report to a military camp to request noncombatant service and receive their assignment.

The four had appeared before the draft board in the little township of Beulah, west of their home colony, on June 5, 1917, in response to the act. Their answers to the twelve questions on the registration form were nearly identical. Each reported that he was a natural born citizen living in Alexandria, South Dakota. Each noted that he was born at Rockport. They were farmers by occupation, employed by the Hutterite colony at Rockport, officially known as the Hutterisch Brethren Church. When asked whether they had a parent, spouse, or child dependent solely on them for support, each answered no, and in doing so saw slip away an opportunity for an exemption from military service. The men knew that the community as a whole would take care of its members; no single person was indispensable; no family would be left uncared for.

By contrast, most draftees in the area with a dependent wife and children received an automatic exemption. In neighboring Hutchinson County, the draft board tried to take only hired hands or but one member of the same family when several sons were drafted.[15] Draft board members generally felt, and the public agreed, that bachelors should be sent to war first. For example, that was the practice in Elkhart County, Indiana, home to many Amish and Mennonites, where the board simply discharged all married men with children.[16] When the Hutterites were asked if they claimed exemption from the draft, each said that he was a member of the Hutterisch

Church, and added: "My creed forbids any military service." The draft board enjoyed latitude and could have granted the men exemptions from any military service (some boards supported the most dubious of claims for medical or dependency exemptions).

But the Hanson County board, perhaps infected by the widespread prejudice against the Hutterites in South Dakota, entered their four names on what President Woodrow Wilson called the "lists of honor."[17] Much later in the war, long after the four men had been shipped to Camp Lewis, Enoch H. Crowder, the head of the Selective Service System, said that local boards should not treat members of intentional communities any differently in deciding whether or not a man had dependents at home. He concluded: "membership in one of these societies neither establishes nor relieves dependency."[18] But Crowder did not revisit the induction of four Hutterites from Rockport.

The uniformity of the registration responses from the Hofer brothers and Jacob Wipf reflected the common counsel the men had received from church leaders. The colonies had agreed that their young men would register and complete their physical examinations.[19] The church understood this part of the process to be like participating in a census—the government was simply gathering information about its citizens. The moment of reckoning for any men who were drafted would come when they actually had to report to the military camps.

David Hofer, the youngest of the brothers, almost stayed home. On May 10, the *Alexandria Herald* published the names of thirty-four men who were being inducted from Hanson County. The list included Joseph Hofer, Michael Hofer, and Jacob Wipf. A week later, the newspaper published a revised list of thirty-four men. This time David Hofer's name appeared on the list. The local exemption board had to make last-minute changes because the War Department had just confirmed that it wanted farmers to remain at home. Nearly half of the men on the original induction list, sixteen, were told to stay home and farm. The exemption board decided that the Hutterites should go as planned.

On an overcast day, the four draftees traveled from the colony by dirt roads to Alexandria. The local paper reported that "one of the largest crowds ever seen in Alexandria" gathered that afternoon for a "patriotic demonstration" to honor the soldiers.[20] The Emery band played several rousing numbers. At three o'clock, a native son, Judge E.E. Wagner of Sioux Falls, rose to address the crowd. He said that when he arrived in town, someone had commented that "we are losing many of our boys today." Not so, Judge Wagner said. "They are merely going over the sea to participate in the fight for freedom and for humanity, and by so doing they are proving a loyalty to their country of which every citizen should be proud," he said.

As Wagner was speaking, a storm rolled in, and the crowd dashed for cover to wait out the downpour. A few minutes later, he resumed, urging the soldiers to beat the enemy "back to Berlin" and plant the "Stars and Stripes in the German capital." With the band leading the procession, the soldiers then marched to the train depot. P.F. Wickhem, a member of the local exemption board, assisted the Hanson County Red Cross chapter in giving each man a "well filled khaki comfort kit." Each kit included a towel, washcloth, soap, soapbox, shaving soap, khaki and white thread, khaki and white buttons, comb, toothpaste, toothbrush, and tobacco. The men then gathered with their families for a few minutes. When the train pulled in at the Alexandria depot, the soldiers who were already on board leaned out the windows, waving small flags and cheering.

The Hofer brothers and Jacob Wipf climbed aboard the train to meet Andrew Wurtz, another Hutterite, who was from the Old Elm Springs Colony, ten miles from Rockport. The train, carrying about 1,200 soldiers, left promptly at 4:30 p.m. The soldiers were part of the largest draft call of the war, 233,742 Americans who were to be mobilized between May 15 and 30 of 1918. All five Hutterites were assigned to share a sleeper compartment on the train, where they did their best to avoid attention. The men knew that they were targets for harassment; their clothing, beards, and accents gave them away as Hutterites. Resentment against the Hutterites and other German speakers had been mounting throughout the spring as the war effort intensified.

Stamping Out German

On May 25, the very day that the men left for Camp Lewis, the South Dakota Council of Defense banned the use of German, the "enemy language," in the state. The resolution meant that only English could be used in churches, schools, and other settings for public address. German speakers could continue to use that language in their homes. The Hutterites represented a clear target of the legislation since they both worshipped and taught school in German. The governor had appointed the council in April 1917 to coordinate war efforts across the state; it was one of many state and municipal organizations that sprang up to safeguard home communities.

Newspaper editors readily lent their support. The *Yankton Press and Dakotan* said: "We gain by the elimination of German, because language is fundamental. . . . Language is more powerful than race or nationality."[21] The *Alexandria Herald* expected that "pastors of German churches who have been accustomed to preaching in German will cheerfully and willingly obey the mandate."[22] One notable dissenter was the United States commissioner of education, Philander P. Claxton, who opposed any ban on the teaching of German: "the United States is at war with the Imperial Government of Germany and not with the German language or literature."[23] His was a lonely voice.

In some respects, the law was only playing catch-up with the expressed public will. Hatred against the German enemy, the so-called Huns, spilled out into anger and resentment against Hutterites and other members of South Dakota's largest ethnic group.[24] The South Dakota census of 1915 revealed that more than 22 percent of the state's population was of German ancestry. In some counties, it was much higher. In Hutchinson, home to several Hutterite colonies, German-Americans composed 77 percent of the population.

A grassroots campaign against German textbooks had quickly gained momentum across the state. High school students had burned German textbooks in Faulkton, in the presence of supportive board members. In Yankton, students took matters into their own hands after hours. They broke into the high school and hauled off German textbooks; then they drove to Observatory Hill, with fanfare worthy of a parade, and there they lit a giant bonfire. The local newspaper offered its blessing in the headline: "German Books Are Purified." In Groton, a group burned all the German books in the schools; in Lennox, the German textbooks simply disappeared. No arrests were reported in either case.

Efforts to eradicate German in all forms in South Dakota reflected a national hysteria. Near the town of Vermillion in South Dakota, Rhine Creek became Marne Creek. Germania Hall in Sioux Falls, which hosted state constitutional conventions, turned into Columbia Hall. The marches of Mendelssohn and Wagner disappeared from weddings. Pretzels disappeared from pantries. In San Francisco, where the Hutterites would in time be bound, members of a grand jury pledged to change the names of any streets suggesting ties to Germany: Berlin, Craut, Hamburg.

Hamburger stayed on menus by becoming victory steak. The sale of sauerkraut declined during the war, even though the dish was widely renamed liberty cabbage. C.C. Herreid, the food administrator for South Dakota, who didn't want to see anything wasted, including cabbage, tried to revive sauerkraut sales with limited success when he reminded citizens that the dish had originated in Holland.[25]

Neighbors Demand Allegiance

Apart from their German roots, the Hutterites presented a special target because of their well-known refusal to lend support to the war campaign. The federal government had settled on bonds as the preferred instrument for financing the war. The Liberty Loan bond campaigns were meant not only to collect money to pay for the war but also to test a citizen's loyalty to the nation. William G. McAdoo, the secretary of the United States Treasury, said that the Liberty campaigns "capitalized the profound impulse called patriotism. It is the quality of coherence that holds a nation together; it is one of the deepest and most powerful of human motives."[26]

The campaign to sell government securities went out as the "Liberty Bond" or the "Liberty Loan." The first drive ended on Flag Day 1917; there followed several other drives, including one in April 1918, a month before the four Hutterite men left for Camp Lewis. Hanson County had set purchase quotas that April for every precinct in the county, including the two Hutterite colonies, Rockport ($11,500) and Rosedale ($8,150). In an editorial, the *Fulton Advocate* noted that "this bunch of slackers or don't care's down at the colony" contributed "not one cent."[27] Every other precinct in the county had purchased bonds and did so above and beyond their allotment.

"Someday there will be a reckoning with that bunch of slackers down on the river," the paper said.

As the United States was drawn ever deeper into the war, that defiance was increasingly risky. In the grip of a patriotic fervor, prominent professionals and businessmen from nearby Yankton, including the mayor, put the Jamesville Colony on notice that it was time to help finance the war.[28] These community leaders, members of the Liberty Loan Committee of Yankton County, did some quick calculations and decided that a quota of $10,000 in bonds would be reasonable for the colony. When the colony refused to buy bonds, the committee, with the sheriff's backing, paid an unannounced visit. While the Hutterites watched, they rounded up a hundred steers and a thousand sheep. The colonists never once offered resistance but asked only that the men not take either workhorses or cows with calves.

The mob then drove the animals to Utica; from there, they shipped them to Yankton, where the cattle and sheep were sold for $16,000 at auction.[29] The Hutterites said that the animals were worth more than two times that amount, about $40,000. Members of both the federal War Loan Committee and the Red Cross knew about the strong-arm methods by which the money was raised and refused to accept it, so the loan committee members themselves bought Liberty bonds with the proceeds. Even though the men masquerading as patriots had clearly committed robbery, punishable by law, many newspapers in the state approved of the confiscation, including the *Sioux Falls Press*, which offered this endorsement:

> Irregular? Yes, by ordinary peace standards of conduct. But these infernal ideas that are cropping up here and there in this country that an American citizen claiming the benefits of this land can choose for himself whether or not he shall help the nation protect itself against destruction are somewhat irregular too. If the . . . [Hutterites] do not like the idea let them pack up what they can carry away and return to that part of Europe whence they came. We shall ask them to be so good as to leave behind the land this nation practically gave them.[30]

The Hutterites had grown accustomed, over the centuries, to facing the scorn and abuse of others. So this kind of harsh treatment from their neighbors during wartime would not have surprised the colonists of Jamesville or their sister communities. A letter sent by three Hutterite ministers to President Wilson soon after the United States joined the war a year earlier spoke to that troubled past: "Our history is written with blood and tears; it is largely a story of persecution and suffering. We have record of over two thousand persons of our faith who suffered martyrdom by fire, water, and the sword."[31]

Martyrdom's Roots in the Reformation

The Hutterite faith began during the religious upheaval known as the Protestant Reformation in the sixteenth century.[32] Until that time, it had been a Europe of many nation-states but of only one religion. While kings and princes managed the affairs of government in a crazy quilt array of fiefdoms, the Catholic Church had served as the officially sanctioned hand of God. The voice of God spoke in Latin, conveyed to the people by priests, who read and interpreted the Bible, sold indulgences and church positions, and dispensed forgiveness. Authority rested on high, and grace trickled down to the masses through churchly intermediaries. As so often happens when power is centralized, abuses ran rampant.

Martin Luther, a Catholic priest and theologian, emerged as a forceful challenger to the monopoly of the church (the Reformation is generally said to have begun in 1517, when he nailed his Ninety-five Theses to the door of the All Saints' Church in Wittenberg, Saxony, now part of Germany). Christian believers enjoy salvation as a free gift from God, he said, and should not be invited, let alone pressured, to make payments to the church to reduce punishment for their sins. In his view, lay Christians formed a holy priesthood, capable of discerning God's will on their own directly through the Scriptures. When Luther refused to retract his writings, Pope Leo X excommunicated him. Luther's legacy would include a powerful breakaway denomination, the Lutheran Church, giving shape to the emerging Protestant wing.

The religious challenge to the state church spread throughout Europe, in step with demands for political and economic reforms. In Zurich, Switzerland, a Catholic priest, Ulrich Zwingli, influenced the city council's decision to break ties with the Catholic Church by citing the Bible. Where was the biblical basis for clerical celibacy? Why was the Mass said in Latin?

But members of Zwingli's Bible study circle pressed for even more radical changes, dissatisfied that Luther and Zwingli continued to accept the Catholic practice of welcoming all babies into the church. These associates of Zwingli believed that faith in Christ required an internal conversion that would result in a changed life. This radical change, they were convinced, could happen only when believers reached an age of accountability and spiritual maturity as adults and could give public expression to their faith. So it was that in 1525, Conrad Grebel, Felix Manz, and Georg Blaurock confessed their faith in Christ and baptized one another as adults.

Others followed their lead, forming a loosely knit group. In practicing a second baptism—all of these believers had been christened by the Catholic Church as infants—they became known by the disparaging name of Anabaptists, or rebaptizers. One of the leaders of the movement was Menno Simons, a former Dutch priest who would lend his name to the Mennonite branch of Anabaptists, from which the Amish would later break away. In 1533, Jacob Hutter, an Austrian hatmaker by trade and a preacher by conviction, joined the group that would later take his name, the Hutterites. Three years later, the authorities in Innsbruck, Austria, tortured him by pouring brandy into fresh wounds and lighting these furrows in the flesh; then they burned him at the stake in the town square.

Catholic leaders recognized the threat to their authority in this emerging lay priesthood of believers. To their mind, if the church is composed of units of two or three or more people independently gathered together in prayer and Bible study as the earliest believers did, then what role is left for the archbishops, the priests, the hierarchical church structures? And how would the state maintain order if baptized babies were not automatically added to the tax rolls as new citizens? And so the state church responded with ferocity, tracking down suspected Anabaptists and ordering them to recant under threat of torture and death. The authorities had many methods of persuasion: imprisonment in dungeons, severing of limbs, removal of tongues, screws driven into thumbnails, flogging on a bare back. Thousands of Anabaptists died privately in prison or publicly through drowning in a river, beheading in a square, or burning at a stake.

But even so the leaders of the Catholic Church could not check the spread of these believers, who were passionate to share the Gospel at any cost. Accounts in the *Chronicle of the Hutterian Brethren,* a weighty history that describes the witness of more than two thousand martyrs—and in the parallel Mennonite tome on persecution, the *Martyrs Mirror,* which in one edition fills 1,290 pages with stories—testify to the readiness of these Christians to give up their lives for their faith.[33] Hans Schmidt, a Hutterite missionary, sang as he was led to his execution in 1558:

> For all who dare
> His cross to bear,
> A crown of joy Christ does prepare.
> Their grief shall be
> Turned to pure bliss and ecstasy
> By Jesus Christ eternally.

Schmidt was strangled with a rope, chained to a stake, and then burned.[34] Other believers met similar fates. Maeyken Wens could neither sing nor pray aloud as she was put to death; in her ashes a son found the tongue screw that the Dutch authorities had used to silence her in 1573. Dirk Willems escaped from a prison in the Netherlands and fled on foot but then turned around to help his pursuer, who had fallen into an icy pond; Willems was recaptured and executed in 1569.[35]

The Hofer brothers and Jacob Wipf had grown up with such tales of heroic martyrs. By preserving the stories of martyrs in their sermons and hymns, the Hutterites had engaged in what Elizabeth A. Castelli, the author of *Martyrdom and Memory,* refers to as the memory work that shapes and sustains a culture. For the Hutterites, as for many other believers, Christian identity was "indelibly marked by the collective memory of the religious suffering of others."[36] But more than social memory was at work. The accounts of Anabaptist martyrs contributed to a living narrative that the Hutterites knew any one of them might be asked to contribute to at an unexpected hour.

Though the Anabaptists shared many convictions, they formed distinct communities. The cluster of believers who would become known as the

Hutterites emerged in the Tyrol, a region tucked between the Swiss Confederacy and Austria, in the early 1530s. Soon thereafter, they were persecuted by Archduke Ferdinand I—a staunch defender of the Catholic Church and ancestor of the man whose assassination triggered the start of World War I. So, they migrated eastward to Moravia (now divided into Slovakia and the Czech Republic), a safe haven for Anabaptists.[37] The Hutterites' reading of the Bible made plain that adult baptism, nonresistance, and simple living were not enough. Alone among the Anabaptists, they sought to take the New Testament at its communal word, insisting on the full sharing of property and possessions, just as the early believers in the book of Acts were said to hold "all things common."[38] Christ commanded his disciples to give up their possessions to follow him. With Acts 2 and 4 as their guide, the Hutterites committed to do the same, to practice a complete community of goods.

In the centuries that followed, the Hutterites were a people without deep roots, the better to flee as their faith required. Through the good graces of the nobles in Moravia, who appreciated the Hutterites' rigorous private schools and industriousness in the trades (their workshops produced barrels, cutlery, porcelain, pottery, wagons), the group flourished. The second half of the sixteenth century became known as the Hutterite Golden Age.[39] It was short-lived. War, famine, and political chaos buffeted the region. With the Catholic Church ascendant, the surviving Hutterites were formally expelled in 1622 and sought refuge in Upper Hungary (now Slovakia) and neighboring countries.

For a century and a half, they wandered, often forced to flee for their lives. Their numbers dwindled to only a few dozen. In the late 1750s a group of Lutheran refugees joined with this remnant and helped to revive the Hutterian Brethren. The hybrid group migrated to the Ukraine, where Russian authorities extended freedom of religion and exemption from military service. The Hutterites settled near Mennonites, who likewise enjoyed religious independence in exchange for their proficiency with a plow.

At times dissension came from within, as some believers had misgivings about the Hutterian principle of "what is mine is thine." During one such period, from about 1819 to 1859, the Hutterites even gave up the practice of community of goods—in effect, the world was without fully vested

Hutterites for nearly half of the century.[40] When church members resumed
the practice, about half the group favored retaining private ownership, as
the Mennonites did. Then a powerful threat from outside struck the community in 1870 when Czar Alexander II decreed that only Russian would
be spoken in schools and, more significantly, that the country would begin
universal military training. The grandparents of the Hofer brothers and
Jacob Wipf were among the stream of Hutterite immigrants who soon left
to settle along the James River in South Dakota. The experience added to
the Hutterites' living memory of how quickly a state could turn militaristic
and prompt a people to flee.

Boarding the Military Train

As they entered the military train on May 25, 1918, the Hutterite men from
the Rockport Colony carried this Anabaptist religious mantle with them—
the teachings of Jesus Christ, the stories of the martyrs, a sense of the inevi-
tability of persecution, a view of the world as starkly divided between God
and Satan. They also climbed aboard fully aware that in the midst of World
War I, some Americans believed that they—the German-speaking Hutterites—should be counted among the enemy. When the fifteen-car train
started heading west, the men found themselves moved from one Pullman
coach to another. At first, a conductor lodged them in a compartment in the
rearmost coach, reserved for the Hanson County recruits. Tensions must
have flared with other recruits from home because that first evening he led
them through the train to a different coach. Here too, the recruits, many of
whom were from Canton, south of Sioux Falls, objected to having to share
their space with Hutterites. The conductor, who was worried about name
calling escalating into a physical confrontation, led them to a third car, saying, "I want to give you a place where you can be by yourselves; they're
supposed to behave."[41]

As a target on a train full of about five hundred young men getting
stoked for war, the Hutterites took a precautionary measure. With a two-
by-four piece of lumber, they barricaded the compartment door so that no
one could enter the room.[42] The five of them shared this safe space—the
three Hofer brothers, Jacob Wipf, and the Hutterite neighbor who had met

them at the station, Andrew Wurtz. All was quiet through the night and into Sunday morning, when the men managed to have a makeshift worship service. They were watchful of their neighbors, even as they kept their distance—there had been time enough to see the card playing and hear the cursing. Just as the other recruits had decided that the Hutterites needed to be put in line, so too the Hutterites withdrew in judgment of the men with whom they were forced to share this journey. As Michael Hofer said in his first letter home, "We were able on Sunday until noon to be edified a little in the fear of the Lord and in the word of God, which was a special grace of God from the heavenly father. For these poor people (the world) are to be pitied as they travel along the broad path to hell."[43]

For the Hutterite men, who were born and raised in South Dakota and likely had never before left the home farm region, there was a sense of childlike wonder in traveling across the country. They were especially taken by the mountains in Montana, a sign of a world well made. David Hofer wrote to Anna, his wife:

He is our wise Creator, when we see his handiwork, how everything is so wisely created. We've been in the mountains all day; that's a wonder to see. Mountains up to . . . [6,000 to 8,000] feet high, very dangerous to travel. Sometimes [the train] goes right through the mountain, into one side of the mountain and out on the other side. It's up to two miles through the mountain. Some places [we pass] under rocks; if they should come down, we'd all be buried, but our heavenly Father has protected us from encountering any accident so far.[44]

William Danforth, a thirty-year-old eager soldier from their hometown, Alexandria, was equally impressed.

To one who has never seen the mountains lifting their lofty peaks in the sky, some barren, and others covered with evergreens, with the fresh mountain streams running everywhere, with here and there a peak covered with snow, the sight is surely inspiring, and one not to be forgotten. At points the train ran high up on the mountain sides, and the distance down into the valleys was almost terrorizing.[45]

He described Tunnel No. 20 in Montana, two miles in length and whose archway was built of pure cement. Over the next eight miles they passed through seventeen more tunnels, he said, many of which were hewn out of solid rock. To offer a sense of the winding route, Danforth said he was told that a hypothetical train consisting of sixty-two coaches at one point in the trip would have its engine and rear coach on parallel tracks, with the engine in a tunnel in Idaho and the coach in a tunnel in Montana.

If the trip to military camps was an eye-opener for a well-educated law-yer like Danforth, it was that much more so for Hutterite and Mennonite farm boys from South Dakota. Michael Stahl, the Hutterite neighbor of the Hofers and Jacob Wipf, had left from the Parkston train station half a year earlier, on September 22, 1917. During the two days en route to Camp Funston in Kansas, whenever the train passed through large cities, he recalled, "there were always big bands playing and lots of singing going on."[46] In Lincoln, Nebraska, for example, the 1,500 men "came off the train like cattle" and entered a large hotel. There, they sat down to supper. The soldiers were treated to dancing and music on stage, "to put them in a good mood and give them some fun." Stahl only hints at the discomfort he felt as a Hutterite young man raised on martyr hymns.

J.B. Waltner, a Mennonite draftee, left from his home near Freeman, South Dakota, two weeks later, bound for Camp Cody in New Mexico. He describes the train picking up recruits along the way until the coaches were full, with just enough room to play cards and shoot craps. "There was much profanity and misconduct on the train in general," he said. "Taking the name of the Lord in vain, even blaspheming to an extent that I marveled at Divine forbearance."[47] At each stop, he said, Red Cross girls came to the station to sell cigarettes, postcards, and other items. "The yelling, singing of war songs and other tumult kept us all awake thru the night and did not completely subside until our train pulled into camp the next day at noon." Another Mennonite, E.E. Leisy, who traveled from Harvey County in Kansas to Camp Funston, remembered the "Comanche yells" and the "war-whoop of democracy" that recruits shouted while hanging outside the train windows.[48]

A Knock at the Door

When the train carrying the five Hutterite draftees arrived in Judith Basin, Montana, southeast of Great Falls, a band of fellow recruits marched to their compartment door around three in the afternoon. They knocked, but the Hutterites kept the door closed. They knocked again. The Hutterites knew two of the men, Danforth and James Albert Montgomery, a farmer; all of them had registered for the draft on the same day in Beulah.[49] Danforth said that he wanted to talk with them and asked them to open the door just a bit. Wurtz described their apprehension: "Out of fear, we did not respond nor open the door for a period of time. However, as we all knew him, and as he said that we should open the door only an inch, we did not anticipate trouble." They should have known better. "They stormed into our room," Wurtz continued, "and then we were placed in great peril."[50]

Danforth and the other men who burst into the room said they only wanted to talk. But David Hofer recalled the escalating conversation: "They began to talk about our faith and carrying [on about the] war. Then it was about our beards."[51] For Hutterites, the beard is an outward sign of obedience to God, which can be trimmed but never taken off. The rowdies on the train decided to enforce a different code of dress—all soldiers should be clean-shaven, they said. They grabbed Jacob Wipf and carried him into another car, where they shaved his beard and cut his hair. The men came back, this time for Joseph Hofer, and took off his hair and beard. Michael Hofer received the rough treatment next, followed by the third brother, David. Only Andrew Wurtz seemed to have escaped the unbidden barber (his hair and beard would be cut on arrival at Camp Lewis).

When it was over, the conductor moved them into a small room several cars ahead, their fourth place on the train, with a gentle admonition that they should not let anyone in, no matter what. As if to make amends, the supervisors of the train approached the Hutterite men at dinner time, inviting them to eat. At first the men refused, but then agreed to go, when, as Joseph said, the supervisors promised them that they could eat together. While it's not clear whether the supervisors joined them at the table, they apparently shared warm words, as Joseph noted: "The conductor asked us whether we spoke German. We said, 'Yes!' He said that he can too."[52]

In writing to his wife, Anna, David said the soldiers were on the wild side: "The plebs always scream when we come to a city, just like wolves in the cold winter."[53] But he assured her that the railroad crew was to be trusted. "The officials on the train are decent people. They realize that we are very different people." It's clear that the soldiers who did the barbering regarded it as little more than a prank. Danforth, in his letter about the trip, said that "some of the boys treated the Russians to a free barbering. Of course, the job was that of novices, and our friends looked somewhat worse for the wear." Danforth quickly moved on to talk about the free post cards to write home and the free dining car service on the train ("plenty of good things to eat and all we wanted at that").

With midnight approaching, Michael Hofer wanted his wife, Maria, to know that all was well. He began a letter:

> It's now 11:30 and time to go to sleep. We are going here so fast through the mountains and beside the mountains. If one thinks back how we have come here from our dear community, one could cry bitterly. Especially if one reflects on where we are being taken. It is deplorable. But God has promised us that he will stand and go before us if we only will trust in him.[54]

The train steadily moved on, crossing Idaho and into Washington. On Monday, they stopped in the town of Beverly, with Tacoma due west, across the Cascades. They traveled through the day and the next night, arriving at Camp Lewis with the midmorning sun.

Chapter Two

Forced Migrations

The worldly sword and the spiritual sword cannot dwell together in one
sheath; each has its own sheath.
—The Chronicle of the Hutterian Brethren

Camp Lewis Welcomes Recruits

The best way to picture the importance of Camp Lewis to the nation during World War I, according to a correspondent for *Collier's Weekly*, was to stand in the Texas Panhandle and face north, drawing an imaginary line through the middle of the country—through Oklahoma, then Kansas, and Nebraska and the Dakotas, right up to the Canadian border. If you looked east from that line, you would have seen fifteen national army training camps. If you looked west, you would have seen one: Camp Lewis, at American Lake, Washington. The nearest army neighbor, Camp Funston, was in Kansas, about 1,800 miles away.

The recruits from Alaska, California, Idaho, Montana, Nevada, Oregon, Utah, Washington, and Wyoming, and many more from Minnesota and the Dakotas, all headed to Camp Lewis, some traveling as far as 2,000 miles. The *Collier's* correspondent wrote: "There in that great cantonment, far on the yon side of the Rockies, beyond the desert wastes and the Cascade snows; there in the brilliant wet green of a Puget Sound prairie, the men of the entire West are learning war."[1]

Stretching across about 70,000 acres, Camp Lewis was the largest of the

army's cantonments, as the training camps were known in military par-
lance, both in capacity and in the number of states whose soldiers it housed.
As the nearest city, seventeen miles away, Tacoma was eager to lay claim to
the camp, but the land itself had been a gift to the federal government from
all of Pierce County, whose taxpayers approved a $2 million bond for the
purchase early in 1916, well before the United States declared war.

It was, in many respects, an ideal place in which to train for battle. The
average summer temperature climbed to a comfortable seventy-one degrees and dipped down to a refreshing fifty-two degrees at night. Few of
the other training sites could compete with the vista at Camp Lewis. The
barracks were arrayed in two curving arcs, which opened southeastward
toward Mount Rainier, the "Great Sentinel of the Camp."[2] The mountain
stood thirty-five miles away, its broad top covered by glaciers and snow
fields, a white canvas etched where rock came poking through. On clear
days (the camp did have the unfortunate distinction of recording more entirely clouded days than any other cantonment), soldiers could see not only
Mount Rainier and its fir-clad companions in the Cascades but also the
Olympics to the northwest. Directly west, over the forested hills and out of
sight, but close enough to be felt, lay the Puget Sound and then the Pacific.

A forty-one-year-old military captain, David C. Stone, a quiet officer with
graying hair at the temples, had supervised the construction of the camp on
a tight deadline and with a vast work crew of ten thousand. During the summer of 1917, the men constructed 1,757 buildings, put down fifty miles of
roads, and laid twenty-seven miles of sewers and thirty-seven miles of water
pipe. The *Tacoma Ledger* called it the "most stupendous construction project
ever attempted in the northwest—the building in a little more than two
months of a city for nearly fifty thousand men, modern in every respect."[3]

In keeping with the military proclivity for order, army officials and civilian experts developed standard specifications for sixteen soldier cities
throughout the country, which local overseers like Captain Stone followed
in their building. For example, while the grounds at each camp might require some variation in layout, the standard shape was to be a letter "U,"
with the division headquarters at the bend of the letter and barracks spread
along the letter's two branches, with the middle space reserved for parade
and drill grounds.[4] The national design prescribed two-story, boxlike bar-

*The Hutterites arrived at Camp Lewis, Washington, in May 1918, shown here
in 1926. Tacoma Public Library*

racks for the soldiers, about forty feet wide by 120 feet long, with a kitchen
tucked into a short extension at one end.

Washington's efforts at nationwide uniformity didn't eliminate all sense
of competition among the cantonments. The local commanders in Washington State were eager to note that the cost per capita of constructing Camp
Lewis was as little as $142, the lowest of any of the camps, even though it
was a more ambitious undertaking.[5] As *Collier's* put it, "It took more lumber,
nails, electric wiring, water pipe, energy, character, tar paper, oratory, window sashing, and printer's ink to construct it than went into the building
of any other cantonment." The folks in the West considered that with this
camp the nation's leaders in the other Washington had received a bargain.

At the entrance to Camp Lewis stood a massive stone gateway, with
log blockhouses perched atop the columns on either side, a tribute to pioneer architecture. A visitor traveling to the camp from Tacoma by taxi (six

dollars) or by jitney bus (fifty-five cents in civilian clothes or thirty-five cents
if you were in khaki) would cross through Liberty Gateway and immediately
see broad roadways organized in a grid of longitudinal avenues (named
after states) and latitudinal streets. Each of the avenues was "bordered by
endless rows of long, two-story barracks of unpainted pine, hundreds and
hundreds of them, which stretch away in a bewildering expanse of roofs
until they are lost in the encircling forest."[6]

The camp was bursting at the seams, with tens of thousands of men
shoehorned into the officially designated company barracks. To accommodate the overflow, hay sheds were turned into barracks for at least a thousand others. The Young Men's Christian Association, or YMCA, which in
partnership with the War Department provided recreational programs and
spiritual nourishment, set up more than 360 cots in a gymnasium. Hundreds more soldiers ended up sleeping in warehouses. Still the men kept
coming. The commanders even pitched tents along the crest of a hill, row
after row of tents, four men to a tent. The *Trench and Camp*, a newspaper
published by resident soldiers, reported that the ground in front of the hay
sheds had been cleared and smoothed and in one instance a flag installed to
lend a touch of dignity. The soldiers were making the best of the shed quarters, the paper said, although one young man from a wealthy section of Los
Angeles reported that "his new home didn't appeal to him very strongly."[7]

Meals were served at six in the morning, twelve noon, and six in the
evening each day in the mess hall on the lower floor of the barracks. At
the early meal, the cooks and their helpers, known as the "kitchen police,"
would pile metal plates with a hearty combination of steak, potatoes, and
rice and fill cups with coffee as the men filed by. The menu for lunch might
be stew, mashed potatoes, boiled onions, and peas with pie for dessert. For
supper, the soldiers could tuck into fried bacon, cold canned salmon, potato
salad, peas, and bread and butter. The army's daily ration was an impressive
4,761 calories. "The American soldier," according to *National Geographic*
magazine, "is the best fed soldier in the world."

The Hutterites Arrive

To handle the conveyance of troops and supplies, two railway lines, the Northern Pacific and the Chicago, Milwaukee & St. Paul, connected to the camp along spurs that followed the side branches of the letter "U"; the two main stations were just down the road from Liberty Gateway, near division headquarters. In May of 1918, the arrival of special trains turned Camp Lewis into the Grand Central Terminal of the West. At 9:40 p.m. on Monday, May 27, a train arrived with 68 men from Minnesota, 90 from North Dakota, and 349 from South Dakota. The 10:30 train added 489 more from the Dakotas. At 11:59, another South Dakota special brought 507 men.

Even more trains arrived on Tuesday, including the Chicago-Milwaukee car that carried the Hofer brothers and Jacob Wipf on the journey of about two thousand miles from South Dakota. They arrived at ten in the morning, part of the final surge of incoming troops. The camp began the week with 40,443 men; by the weekend, it would grow to more than 52,000, a city less than a year old that was already half the size of Tacoma (population, 96,965). With so many men pouring into camp, the officers struggled to keep everyone on a timely schedule. On the day they arrived the soldiers from Hanson County, assigned to the Twenty-ninth Company, Eighth Battalion, One-hundred-sixty-sixth Depot Brigade, waited until 3:30 p.m. for their first meal.

David A. Janzen, a twenty-three-year-old Mennonite draftee who like the Hutterites had family roots in Russia, had arrived at Camp Lewis a month earlier, having traveled by train from California. Whereas the Hutterites felt fearful and out of place during their trip, Janzen described a fine ride on the Southern Pacific line, as young men played cards and checkers and he had ample time to think about his new life in the military. He was ready, even eager, to put on a uniform, though not to take up arms; he expected to be comfortable in this military camp, as long as he could serve as a noncombatant.

Janzen described the camp on his arrival as a "mess of human avalanche."[8] The men were ordered out of the train coaches and marched by twos to the receiving tent where they underwent physical examinations. Then they were divided into companies. When each group reached two

hundred, they marched to the barracks. Then came bedding. "We were issued mattresses like sacks which we had to fill with straw," he said. "It had
an opening on one side to be tied together but not many city slickers knew
it and so our rooms became a mess, straw all over the place. It looked as if
a farmer had bedded his prize Jersey herd."

The following morning the men lined up according to height, each one
being given a number to count off by way of checking attendance. In the
days that followed, Janzen said, they learned to march and to respond to
commands. By the time the Hofer brothers and Jacob Wipf arrived, he said,
the men in his unit had been transformed: "After thirty days of such drilling
it was easily seen how a fat pouch began to slide off a roly-poly man or how
the spindly bank teller set his feet down firm and solid and a swing came to
the men as they marched to and from the drillground."

The sense of pride and excitement in Janzen's voice is nowhere to be
found in the letters the Hutterites sent home soon after their arrival. Writing to his wife, Maria, Michael Hofer assured her that they were in fine
health and trusting in God's care. But that hopefulness soon gave way to
deep worries:

> Dear spouse we have now come into a suffering that no one before has ever
> imagined. It is indescribable what is happening here in this world. And as
> our dear savior says in the New Testament that we also should come before
> kings and princes for my namesake, but we should not fear what we should
> say, for the Holy Spirit will speak through you. Dear spouse, they tell us
> whoever does nothing will be sent to the guardhouse. That is where we are
> now. They tell us that we will be in the guardhouse for a very long time. To-
> day, someone left who had been here for five years, and we cannot hope for
> anything otherwise.[9]

The length of that unnamed prisoner's stay could not have added up to five
years—at least at Camp Lewis—but it was long enough to have made a deep
impression. Perhaps the guards exaggerated the confinement to make a
point. At any rate, Michael's sense of foreboding was clear: "If we should no
longer see each other again, then may God grant us that we see each other
again in heaven." In closing, he reminded his wife that his letters would

pass through military censors: "I cannot seal this letter, since it will be read by others." Joseph, too, reached for heavenly images when he wrote to his wife, also named Maria, from the guardhouse on the second day: "God only knows if we will see each other again in this world; [if not], then it will be in the next world, with God's help. Don't make too much of this, for we have a strong God and a strong Rock."[10]

View from the Guardhouse

The Hutterite men landed in Guardhouse No. 54 almost immediately. On the day of their arrival all of the new recruits lined up alphabetically, with a typist at the end taking down names, occupations, and hometowns for the enlistment and assignment card. One of the sergeants approached Robert S. Shertzer, a second lieutenant, with a smile. "These men over here," he said, pointing to the Hutterites, "they just came along, and said, 'This is as far as we go.'"[11] The men were standing by the barrack service window where each of the recruits was to sign up for a blanket, a bed sack, and a toilet kit. Shertzer told the men they had to sign up to receive their personal supplies. "They said, 'We can't sign any papers. We don't believe in war. We won't do anything for the Army.'"

With Shertzer's encouragement, they eventually signed a supply form to receive blankets. He also met with the men privately to talk with them about their religious views and explain what was expected at the camp. But later that day Shertzer found the four men again standing off by themselves along the barracks while other recruits lined up in front of Sergeant R.B. Hilt. "What is the matter with those four men?" Shertzer asked. "They won't fall in," Hilt replied. Shertzer spoke to the Hutterites: "I explained to you men about this. This has nothing to do with fighting. . . . I read the orders to you, and you will have to obey orders or else you will have to go to the guardhouse."

The Hofer brothers and Jacob Wipf said they could not line up as soldiers. So on their first day at Camp Lewis, hours after their arrival, the men were locked up, soon joined by their neighbor from South Dakota, Andrew Wurtz, who likewise had refused to sign up to serve. Within days, they would be moved to a second guardhouse, joined there by a couple of

Mennonites. They numbered, as Michael Hofer put it, "five brothers and two Mennonites."

Meanwhile, the other Hanson County recruits were spread out among several barracks. They had received their blankets along with instructions on how to make up their cots. Early on they had access to a social hall operated by the Young Men's Christian Association, with entertainment provided. But as a fellow Alexandria resident, William Danforth, noted, "We have plenty of entertainment within our own camp, for there are men here from all walks of life." The Hutterites weren't the only Hanson County recruits in confinement. One of the men came down with the measles, which placed his entire barracks under quarantine. Still, Danforth said, it was an auspicious welcome: "I can only say that the boys who had an opportunity to come out here [and didn't] missed the chance of a lifetime."

When the Hutterite men went to the mess hall they were accompanied by guards in front and in back. While the early letters hint at the troubles the men were facing at Camp Lewis, they rarely describe their daily routines or detention hardships in detail, maybe in deference to the military censors or simply because they did not wish to complain. For example, David Hofer called on his wife, Anna, to use her imagination in picturing their situation. "Dearly beloved spouse," he wrote, "if you think about where we are, far from home and farm, from wife and children, then I can't describe the misery in which we find ourselves."[12]

Like his brother Michael, David reminded his wife that they must be circumspect in what they write: "I must close now with my simple writing and one has to be careful what we write, and we can't write very often, not as often as we would hope. . . . We are not permitted to seal our envelopes. We have to hand them over to an officer who looks them over." The men urged their wives to pray as Paul directed: without ceasing. Michael wrote: "Do not tire. Also, pray in your hearts for us. Even at work you should often pray in your hearts, more often than with the mouth, for now is when one needs every little verse that one learned in childhood."[13]

With an apocalyptic touch, Joseph reminded his wife, and perhaps himself as well, that they should not be ashamed to find themselves in the guardhouse:

We are not in prison because we have done bad things, but instead because of our conscience and faith, and because of the Word of God. And we hope that he will not permit too much sadness to come our way, for he has promised that he will be with us until the end of the world, which is not very far off. Christ said there will be wars and rumors of wars. And this is now fulfilled.[14]

The officers pressed the men in the days that followed to line up in formation and to fill out the enlistment and assignment cards, which would allow them to leave the guardhouse, but the men were steadfast in their refusal. The card required each recruit to list his hometown, age, and basic information. William V. Clarke, a second lieutenant, said that he ordered the men to complete the cards in the mustering office on June 2, several days after their arrival. He offered each one a pen and a card, but each had refused in turn. The men said they could not do so because of three words printed on the cards: "Declaration of Soldier." Jacob Wipf, the oldest of the men and often their de facto leader at the camp, said, "Boys, I can't do it," and the others followed his lead.[15]

Among the Hofer brothers, David, the eldest, was generally the more outspoken. On another occasion when they were ordered to sign the enlistment and assignment cards, David spoke up first to state their opposition. Just as they had done when meeting with the draft board in South Dakota, the men appealed for an exemption from any military service on the ground that they had wives and children and a farm to help support. But the camp officials, who apparently by this time were familiar with the Hutterites' communal farming, rejected that appeal. All three brothers mentioned that outcome, with a sense of resignation, in letters home.

During their days in confinement, through narrow fields of vision, the five Hutterite men watched the Ninety-first Division prepare for war. Michael Hofer described their glimpses of camp life: "We go from one window to another. There our sorrowful eyes see nothing more than how the world leads its life."[16] The view from outside the guardhouse was decidedly more upbeat. Virtually every press account portrays a camp full of recruits raring to confront the German army with green fir-tree insignias on their uniforms and bayonets in hand. "Every man is eager to go," the *Post-Intelli-gencer* said—or, as one major put it more colorfully, "if they chafe occasionally it is only for a chance to get within shooting-distance of the Hun."[17]

Most of the men assembled at Camp Lewis were being trained for offensive operations as foot soldiers in a large mobile unit bound for the trenches in Europe. Organizationally, they belonged to the Ninety-first Division, which included two infantry brigades that were subdivided into four infantry regiments. Complementary units in the division included a machine-gun battalion, a supply train, and an ammunition train.

The authorities at Camp Lewis had plenty of time to anticipate a case like the one presented by the Hutterites. Throughout the spring there were signs of rising tension between men who refused to contribute to the war effort and the commanders who saw no alternative. Mary Darling, whose son Kenneth was confined at Camp Lewis in the months before the Hutterites arrived, recalled an encounter with an officer there (afraid of retaliation, she referred to him only as "Captain X"). Darling had asked that her son, as a noncombatant, not be required to train with a gun. "[Captain X] told me later that he loathed and despised the C.O.'s and pacifists, telling me most violently that I should be ashamed of myself. He also said to me that all of them should be killed and he would like to do the killing."[18]

Darling also reported that on several occasions a group of soldiers known as "the Ku Klux Klan" was spiriting away objectors to a lake at night, and forcing them underwater until they agreed to put on uniforms. In February, a Quaker named Clyde Crobaugh told of his experience with other objectors: "The captain has had us up before him and made all kinds of threats. . . . None of the boys will drill. There is going to be serious trouble soon."[19] As of March, there were about twenty men who refused to drill, fifty who would drill but not bear arms, and many more who would bear arms but not shoot.

Training for the Western Front

The officer in charge of turning these citizen-soldiers from the Western states into a fighting force to be reckoned with was Major General Henry A. Greene, the "sixth of a generation of fighting men."[20] A West Point graduate, Class of 1879, Greene had commanded infantry in Cuba during the

Spanish-American War and had seen action in the Philippines. Just prior to taking command at Camp Lewis, he led the Army Service Schools at Fort Leavenworth for a couple of years. Greene had received a rousing welcome when he arrived at the newly constructed Camp Lewis in September, including a banquet in his honor hosted by the Tacoma Commercial Club.

The business leaders in attendance frequently interrupted the commander with rounds of applause as he described the work ahead. "The end of the war MUST be a victory and a success for our side—for the God of battles also is the God of Love and Justice," Greene said, basking in "a storm of enthusiastic shouts and applause."[21] The audience wanted to know when the Ninety-first Division, composed of more than 27,000 soldiers, might be summoned to Europe. The men would move according to orders from Washington, Greene responded. "We live on rumors and hopes," one lieutenant added.

In the meantime, the camp commanders tried to duplicate conditions on the Western Front as much as possible, including thirty-five miles of trenches dug out of the loose coastal soil. A reporter touring the camp in June found several hundred men standing on a step with their guns pointed across the parapet and over barbed wire entanglements. Their assignment was to watch, all night and through the day, for any sign of opposition forces. The men had already been on duty for three days, with one more to go. Each night, somewhere along the trench, a detachment from another company, designated as the enemy, would try to reach the trench unnoticed. In the trench, dugouts had been carved into the earth on either side, with wooden bunks where men who were off duty slept.

"Everywhere about the field," the *Post-Intelligencer* said, "are men engaged in war work."[22] There under some trees, the reporter said, he watched men learning how to handle manual arms, thrusting bayonets through bags. Across the way, others climbed ropes, hand over hand. On the parade ground, facing division headquarters between Montana and Oregon avenues, the drilling was constant. One could hear the sounds of the 1903 bolt-action Springfield rifles fired on a nearby range, and the pounding on the heavy ordnance ranges eight miles away. Detachments of soldiers might be woken in the middle of the night and, in a commander's idea of essential training sure to be met with groans, told to dress for immediate departure.

Several regiments hiked across the camp's rough terrain for four days, dependent on war rations as they would be out in the real battlefield. "Camp Lewis has everything of war," the paper said, "except bloodshed."

One of the Hanson County recruits, Eldo Thiese, said his days began at 5:45, except for Sunday, when the men could sleep in half an hour. He wrote home: "I got pretty tired the first few days I was out here, but I am getting used to it now and it is not so bad—just good exercise."[23] On the day of his writing, a Monday, he said they exercised for an hour after breakfast, and then returned to the barracks. At 9:30 they headed out to drill for an hour and a half. Then they returned for dinner, or mess, collected their mail, and rested till 1:30. They had more drills or exercise till 3:30. "So you see," he said, "we don't put in such long days."

Apart from what the Hutterite men might have seen through the windows of the guardhouse, Major E. Alexander Powell, who served as assistant to the chief of staff with the Ninety-first Division, vividly described what they might have heard: "The air is filled with sound: the clatter of hoofs, the throbbing of motors, the rumble of motor-lorries, the brisk commands of the drill-sergeants, the rat-a-tat-tat of hammers, the distant crackle of machine guns, and the *slump-slump-slump* on the soft earth of thousands of marching feet."[24]

At the end of the day, as the men from the "Wild West" Ninety-first (whose battle cry was "Powder River! Let 'er Buck!" in apparent tribute to a daunting cattle crossing over the river in Wyoming) fell into quiet bonding conversation, came accounts from the frontier. "Nightly, across the pine tables in mess-halls or around the big stoves in the bunk-rooms, one can hear tales of wild adventure which would provide scenarios for a hundred novels or motion-picture thrillers. Here can be found men who, in frail Indian canoes, have braved the rapids of Cataract Canyon, who have faced death in Death Valley, who have hunted big game on the banks of the Big Horn and in the fastnesses of the Kawich Range have sought for gold."

The camp projected the image of being a home to Western explorers and adventurers, men cut from the cloth of one of the originals, after whom the camp was named. In their expedition on behalf of President Thomas Jefferson, Captains Meriwether Lewis and William Clark followed a southerly route along the Columbia River to reach the Pacific in 1805, never actually stepping foot on the territory of Camp Lewis proper but, given how far they had traveled, certainly passing through what they would have regarded as the neighborhood.

The Singing Army

Though soldiers would have been hard-pressed to find any dance halls at night, military authorities did allow the construction of an amusement park, known as a "joy zone," with a Ferris wheel and other rides, near the entrance to the camp. Within the camp itself, a soldier with free time had plenty of activities to choose from. The Liberty Theater, with 3,500 seats, opened in February with a concert by the Orpheus Male Chorus of Tacoma and the Philharmonic Orchestra of Seattle. Men signed up for baseball and football teams, whose rosters included professional players. A former world lightweight champion, Willie Ritchie, served as the camp boxing instructor. A boxing tournament held the first week in June packed out an arena, with seating for twenty thousand, on six consecutive evenings.

A quieter evening could be found at the Liberty Library, which boasted a collection of fifty thousand volumes, a place where men would gather around a large fireplace in the reading room, surrounded by sword ferns and windows hung with yellow cotton crepe. Any time was a fine time for "sings," regarded as a secret weapon in the war, essential to building up morale.[25] Each camp appointed a song leader. Officials back in Washington wanted camp commanders to encourage singing on marches and during the most menial of tasks, like a work detail extirpating stumps. In YMCA social halls across the camp one could hear a stirring religious song like "The Battle Hymn of the Republic," as well as secular plaintive titles like "There's a Long, Long Trail" and "Keep the Home Fires Burning." In mid-June the camp set yet another West Coast record by having twelve thousand men join in song under the direction of Robert Lloyd, the camp singing instructor, during a review of a depot brigade.

If the camp authorities had their way, they would have added five more voices to that choir: those of Jacob Wipf, Andrew Wurtz, and the Hofer brothers. Even Commander Greene took an interest in their case and was no doubt frustrated that the men could not be persuaded to become citizen-soldiers. The Hutterite men said that they had been summoned several times before the camp commander to explain their unwillingness to work. "We have already been ordered frequently to appear before the commandant; but have testified without fear and with God's help to our faith," Michael Hofer told his wife. "They say that everything would go just fine for us, but what work would we be willing to do? But we tell them that we can do nothing."[26] David Hofer also emphasized that only through God did they find the words to speak:

> We are still in the guardhouse and have been to the headquarters because of our basis of belief. With the help of God we have explained the basis of our faith, and with a calm heart. We experience the generous help of God towards us, as he has promised: When you are led before lords and kings, you are not to worry about how or what you are to say, but I will give you a voice and wisdom, which shall not be resisted by your opponents.[27]

Dark Methods of Persuasion

While the five men were trying to be faithful to their religious beliefs as best as they could discern, by staying put in the guardhouse, Hutterites at other camps were also coming under fierce pressure to make accommodations with the military. Fifteen Hutterites from Freeman, South Dakota, arrived at Camp Funston in Kansas in the fall of 1917, "no less interesting than odd" to army officials (and to the reporter who came up with that phrase).[28]

At first all of them refused to work, according to a report in the *Sioux City Daily Tribune*. Then two of the fifteen agreed to take assignments at the camp. After a Mennonite minister counseled them to accept jobs, all but six went to work as garbage haulers in the sanitary division. The six who would not accept any work were placed on a big truck during the day, like laborers without labor, having permission to leave the springless truck bed only to eat and to sleep. No one was to talk with them. The "queer men," as the reporter described them, ended up sleeping in the truck by day and staying up at night to pray.

One of the holdouts on the truck was Michael Stahl, the Hutterite from the Freeman area who described his train ride to Camp Funston in September in such vivid detail. In a memoir published after the war, Stahl offered a sharply different version of how he and the other church members fared at Camp Funston. His account of the opening weeks fills in the details, darker details, suggesting that camp officers or their subordinates went well beyond the verbal persuasion that the authorities had thus far applied with the Hofer brothers and Jacob Wipf at Camp Lewis.

At Camp Funston, soldiers resorted to harsh physical measures. Stahl's account is oblique, but it suggests a scarring experience. Stahl describes a group of the men being led by a soldier into a house:

> We were made fun of, treated with contempt and mistreated in many ways. The soldiers had rifles, revolvers and sticks and used them in godless ways with us. For our supper we received dry hard bread and water. We had to sleep on the floor in the middle of the rooms. The guards watched us from morning until the evening, the whole night with pointed rifles.[29]

Stahl said that soldiers repeatedly forced the men to ride on trucks through the day, urging them to work, but they refused. The soldiers would remove several men at a time and beat them with fists, or dunk them under water, as if to drown them. One of the men, Joseph Waldner, was hospitalized after being beaten in the face so badly that he could not eat.

To Stahl's way of thinking, the soldiers acted "just as if the devil had advised them." The soldiers turned from tactic to tactic in an effort to persuade the men to work. They led one Hutterite, Peter Tschetter, to an attic and there gave him a broom with which to clean it. He refused. In anger, they gave him a pen and ordered him to write down his address. "We are going to shoot you and we want to know where to send your body," they said. He wrote down his address. Then they put a postal sack over his head and told him they would now shoot him. They took two pieces of wood and clapped them together, as if to simulate a rifle shot. And then they let him go.

At Camp Funston, as would become apparent at Camp Lewis, the officers were inclined to get angry at this apparent lack of cooperation, which they regarded as a threat to military discipline, and to grow frustrated by the lack of recourse. They wanted their authority respected; they wanted to see conscientious objectors making a contribution. They could not understand what to them appeared as extreme and uncompromising pacifism on the part of many Hutterites, Mennonites, and other objectors. To an officer's eye, the objectors were either cowards or shirkers of their patriotic duty.

The ethnic lineage of many of these men raised a third, more ominous, possibility: these men might be using their religion as a pretext for assisting the enemy. At Camp Funston, Major S.M. Williams, the camp executive officer, said that many relatives of the objectors, "nearly all of whom are of German descent," caused trouble by "spreading conscientious objector propaganda, which is nothing but German propaganda."[30] If the officers failed to keep order among the objectors, he reasoned, they could fail among the regular recruits. The problems in camps might be traced to flawed policies in Washington, D.C.—where officials had originally decided that conscientious objectors should be lodged alongside regular soldiers—but it now seemed left to camp commanders to find a solution.

Two Kingdoms Clash

The four Hutterites from Rockport, who refused any work assignments, posed a challenge even for some fellow believers. In dividing the world so sharply into good and evil, and refusing to compromise with people on the other side, they sometimes alienated natural allies. David A. Janzen, the Mennonite from California who arrived at Camp Lewis one month before the Hofer brothers and Jacob Wipf, had signed up as a noncombatant. He was assigned to supervise a unit of conscientious objectors who refused to work.

Fifty years later, when interviewed about the Camp Lewis experience, Janzen readily recalled the impatience that he felt over their unwillingness to make a contribution at the camp. "They wouldn't do anything," he said. "If you told them to make up the bed, they wouldn't do it. [They used] the urinals, and then they wouldn't carry them out. They were just so stubborn."[31]

It was that refusal to do any work, he believed, that led to their being mistreated. Many of the conscientious objectors, in their determination not to be co-opted by the military system, responded to officers in ways that appeared disrespectful, he said. "When an officer would appear they would just turn their backs and look the other way. No wonder they looked at me as different when I would call out 'attention' and stand up immediately and not slovenly like a bunch of cows in a pasture."

Janzen remembered debating with David Hofer whether a Christian could in good conscience serve in any capacity on the European front: "He would always say, 'Janzen, you are going to the Devil if you're going overseas; you're going to the Devil.'" A short time later, in October 1918, Janzen would be working with a medical unit in southern France; David Hofer would be in chains.

As was typical of Hutterites, the Hofer brothers and Jacob Wipf held an uncompromising view of power and authority in which two kingdoms, one of God and one of the world, stood in conflict. By this dualistic view, Americans had to declare their loyalty to one kingdom or to the other. This demarcation allowed the Hutterites to divide all people into the righteous and the unrighteous, those bound for heaven (where the communal utopia awaited) and those bound for hell (best not to dwell on the particulars). They could be unshakeable in their judgment of others, so sure were they of their own righteousness.

Jakob Waldner, a twenty-six-year-old Hutterite from the Spring Creek Colony in Lewistown, Montana, spent part of 1917 and most of 1918 as a conscientious objector at Camp Funston. His formal education reached the eighth grade. Like the Hofer brothers and Jacob Wipf, he was hard-pressed to make personal connections with soldiers across the kingdom divide: "he constantly referred to them as beasts and as moved by the devil; and he seemed almost unfeeling toward what the common soldier must have been feeling as he was torn from his home and people, to be faced with not only camp regimentation but shipment overseas and battle."[32] For example, when told he would need to join about five thousand recruits in attending religious services at the YMCA, Waldner felt deeply troubled: "It is . . . a real den of murderers, for there they have theater every night instead of prayer."[33]

A Nation Woos Hutterite Immigrants

In the views of Waldner and the other Hutterites, one can see traces of the sharp words of Paul Tschetter, a Hutterite leader who joined a delegation of Mennonites, all of them from Russia, during an exploratory visit of the United States in 1873. More than anyone else, Tschetter is responsible for the settling of Hutterites in the United States. While crossing the English Channel, the water turned rough, and the great divide between the kingdom of the world and the kingdom of God was on full display, much to Tschetter's disapproval: "The godless were little disturbed by the great storm. They continued dancing and were merry."[34] And a week later, Tschetter was in no better humor, even though the ship was approaching the New York harbor and a pastor on board read from the Psalms on that beautiful Sunday: "the sermon seemed much too mild for such godless rabble."[35]

But behind that quickness to judge lay a fierce historical commitment to follow Christ and a communal memory of what the cost might be. The decisions that Jacob Wipf and the Hofer brothers were making at Camp Lewis were consistent with the actions taken by church members when they resisted governmental authorities in earlier generations. After Russia announced that Hutterites and Mennonites would have to serve in the armed forces, a Mosaic delegation of ten Mennonites and two Hutterites (Paul Tschetter and his uncle, Lohrentz) visited the United States and Canada in 1873, in search of their own arable promised land, maybe in the Dakota Territory or in the neighboring states of Kansas and Nebraska or maybe across the Canadian border.

The delegation arrived in New York on May 22 with clear instructions from the churches in Russia that they should seek out not only reasonably priced land but also a promise of religious freedom and exemption from military service, as well as the right to live in closed communities and to use the German language.[36] The delegates enjoyed an enviable bargaining position, with the United States and Canada competing for their attention and with railroad companies seeking to lure the immigrants to settle along their respective corridors, which crossed hundreds of miles of empty prairie, just waiting for enterprising farmers.

The railroads were partial to Germans, regarding them as better suited to the task of homesteading than were other Europeans; the Chicago, Burlington, and Quincy line printed an advertising brochure in German, for example, but not in French or Italian.[37] The Germanic peoples of Russia were especially prized, both for their work ethic and their mastery of farming on the steppes. The railroads marketed the land as free, and for many farmers it was. The Homestead Act of 1862 allowed citizens or immigrants to secure a quarter section, or 160 acres, of unclaimed public land; after living on it and improving it for five years, the homesteader took legal possession.

Most of the land that was available for homesteading was well off the railroad lines; the railroad companies had received large sections of contiguous land from the government in exchange for laying their lines north and west, and the companies were eager to sell off their private parcels. With the tracks running through river valleys, the railroad property tended to be in the bottomlands and of a better quality than the homesteader plots. The Plains of North America reminded the Hutterites of their home in southern Russia, a windy and dry expanse of land, hundreds of miles wide and many hundreds long. The winter wheat cultivated in the black earth of the steppes back in Russia should prove equally at home in the fine loess soil on the American plains.

While scouting out land, the lead Hutterite delegate, Paul Tschetter, tolerated the mandatory stops in cities like Chicago and New York, where he bemoaned the debauchery and "so much noise and tumult that my head ached."[38] Tschetter, a minister who kept a detailed diary during the trip, was relieved to reach the Great Plains. He told of taking a four-horse mail coach from Moorhead, Minnesota, one morning, sitting up front with the driver, "which suited me very much for I could thereby get a much better view of the land."[39] That morning he saw "black soil and a fine stand of grass."

The next day, the group took two wagons out to look over the land: "The soil is black with a mixture of shiny sand slightly beneath the surface. Still further down there is a yellowish loam. The grass is not so thick, although the wheat along the roadside looked good and was just heading."[40] But the region as a whole did not appeal to him, with more water and bottomland than what they were used to in Russia; South Dakota, in the end, would trump Minnesota.

An Audience with President Grant

The most significant encounter in the four-month-long exploratory visit took place on Long Island, far from the prairie land they had come to survey, at the summer home of President Ulysses S. Grant. Before uprooting their families in Russia and moving thousands of miles away, the Hutterites wanted assurances that the United States would provide a good home for an insular, hard-working, German-speaking, pacifist people. If the president would give his word to that effect, the case for moving would be that much more persuasive.

Jay Cooke—a trustee with the Northern Pacific Railroad, and perhaps more important, a Republican Party fundraiser who had supported Grant's reelection in 1872—agreed to arrange the meeting. The Northern Pacific agent who had accompanied the delegation in their exploration across the Plains, Michael Hiller, served as the interpreter, since he also spoke German. The Tschetters were joined by another member of the scouting delegation, a Mennonite minister, Tobias Unruh.

On the evening of July 27, near the end of their trip, the three men arrived at Grant's home in Long Beach, an unlikely party of presidential guests. They came without political or financial clout, and without even a command of English. But, as Cooke had noted in a letter of introduction to the president, these Mennonites and Hutterites from Russia would make ideal settlers to build up farms in the Great Plains: "They do not believe in wars or fighting, are moral, sober, frugal and industrious people, and desirable as citizens of our country."[41] So it happened that interests converged to bring about a "surprising encounter between three men with little formal education, social status or material wealth" and a cigar-smoking Civil War hero who knew how to sling barnyard language.[42] The visitors would no doubt have made a pious appearance. A photo taken earlier in the trip shows Paul Tschetter unsmiling, with dark hair parted in the middle, nearly covering his ears; a full beard; a plain jacket; and a black vest buttoned up to his chin.[43]

Tschetter had prepared a handwritten petition in German, translated into English for the president. In the letter, the Hutterites asked for an exemption from military service and from jury duty; they asked to be free from having to pay substitute money in the event of a draft, as happened during the Civil War; and they sought the right to govern their own schools. The tone was beseeching: "We the undersigned deputies therefore most respectfully beg to ask of Your Excellency to allow to us and all our brethren exemption from military service for the next fifty years, without payment of money on our part for such exemption."[44]

Before getting to the petition, the president likely engaged the men in small talk, seeking common ground as he had done earlier in the summer when he met with two Mennonites who were promoting immigration from Russia.[45] In that meeting, Grant spoke of having grown up on a farm where he milked twenty cows each morning and evening; even now, as president, he said, "he could hitch up and drive a team of horses as well as ever."[46] Though Grant as a soldier stood apart from his visitors, they may have heard of his inaugural address earlier in the year, in which he suggested a longing for an end to war, with a communal image that would have been reassuring to the Hutterites: "Rather do I believe that our Great Maker is preparing the world in His own good time to become one nation, speaking one language and when armies and navies will no longer be required."[47] Tschetter described an amiable encounter: "The President received us in the most friendly manner and we presented our petition to him personally. After reading it very carefully the President replied that we must have patience to wait for an answer to our petition."[48]

Only after the Tschetters and other delegation members returned home to Russia did they hear the president's response: Grant said that states had jurisdiction over these matters and that it was beyond his power, even as president, to grant their request. In a note dated September 5, 1873, Hamilton Fish, speaking on behalf of the president as secretary of state, did offer this assurance: "It is true, however that for the next fifty years we will not be entangled in another war in which military service will be necessary."[49] Having said that, though, he added that if there were to be such a war, Congress would likely not see fit to free them from obligations that would be asked of other citizens. This represented a slight but significant change in tone. Earlier, Grant had told Fish that "it may be proper to state to these people that it is entirely improbable that they will ever be called upon to perform involuntary Military Service."[50] Grant or Fish, or both, apparently thought better of this more generous suggestion.

Though the Hutterites did not receive the blanket exemption from military service that they sought, they returned to Russia with a report of ample land on favorable terms and of religious freedom. That the president said the nation should not soon be engaged in any war was reassuring—if his math were borne out, that would put the nation on a smooth course at least through 1923. Had they heard Grant's annual message to Congress several months after the visit, the Hutterites and Mennonites in Russia would also have been heartened by his kind reference to an "industrious, intelligent, and wealthy people, desirous of enjoying civil and religious liberty; and the acquisition of so large an immigration of citizens of a superior class would without doubt be of substantial benefit to the country."[51] He urged consideration of concessions that would allow them to settle in a compact colony.

From Russia to South Dakota

Back in the Ukraine, Paul Tschetter's report on the United States was compelling. Nearly every Hutterite family, communal and noncommunal alike, chose to leave. Rather than see their young men drafted into the Russian army, they migrated to the United States, settling along the James or Missouri rivers of South Dakota (being near water ensured power for milling, a leading industry for the Hutterites). While the Hutterites considered several locations, including Canada and even South America, they were drawn to the United States, in part because of the reception they had received from President Grant.[52]

Meanwhile, the Russian immigrants hoped they could persuade Congress to allow them to purchase large enough contiguous sections of government land so that, especially in the case of the communal Hutterites, all members could live and farm as a single body.[53] The railroads owned alternate sections adjacent to the lines. If the Hutterites bought sections belonging to the railroad, someone else might buy some of the government sections, breaking up the intended village.[54]

Senators from Indiana and Pennsylvania, well familiar with Mennonite and Amish settlers, were among the strongest advocates for a bill that would ensure the transfer of large blocks of land. Senator John Scott of Pennsylvania said, "I can with truth say that for thrift, industry, economy, integrity, and good morals, they are not exceeded by any other class of the population in that or any other State of this Union."[55] Not to be outdone in lavishing praise, Senator Thomas Tipton of Nebraska lauded the historic pacifist denominations, including the Society of Friends, also known as the Quakers. "[I]f there is any portion of the world that can send us a few advocates of peace, in God's name let us bid them welcome. We want settlers of that kind."

Despite several efforts, the advocates could not bring the bill to a vote. Senators from New England opposed immigration favors that would privilege the West. Some senators were uncomfortable with granting large blocks of land to a group, rather than selling smaller parcels to individual families; the refusal to bear arms also gave several senators pause, and a half century later it would give almost the entire nation pause.

Between 1874 and 1879, more than 1,200 Hutterites immigrated to the southeastern corner of the Dakota Territory.[56] One third of the arrivals, or about 425, practiced community of goods, in keeping with historical Hutterite practice; the remaining two-thirds settled on private farms, while seeking to hold fast to traditional cultural and religious Hutterite practices; these noncommunal Hutterites often affiliated with Mennonite churches. Paul Tschetter, who arrived in the Dakota Territory in 1875, led the noncommunal branch, which became known as the Prairieleut, or Prairie People, because they settled on farms on the rolling high ground instead of along the James or Missouri rivers or their tributaries.

The communal Hutterites favored the low-lying land along rivers. Three colonies that held fast to the principle of communal property were established, reflective of three Hutterite branches that continue to this day.[57] The Hutterites would not take advantage of the Homestead Act, opting instead to pay the going rate for large communal tracts. As one early historian put it, to find the Hutterites in South Dakota one only needs a map of the James River Valley.[58] Formed in 1874 about eighteen miles west of Yankton along the Missouri River, the first colony, Bon Homme, was led by a blacksmith, and this branch became known as the Schmiedeleut, or the smith's people.

The colony bought 2,500 acres for $25,000, $17,000 of it in cash. They built houses and a flour mill out of cream-colored chalk rock from the banks of the Missouri.

That same year, a second group from Russia, led by Darius Walter, arrived in the territory; they spent the first winter in sod houses on government prairie land at Silver Lake; in 1875, they moved about ten miles west of Freeman, at the confluence of the James River and Wolf Creek, and there established the Wolf Creek Colony on 5,400 acres. They became known as Dariusleut, or Darius's people.

In 1877 a third group, led by a teacher and elder named Jacob Wipf, formed the Old Elm Springs Colony near Parkston, about thirty-five miles southeast of Mitchell on the James River. Their descendants are the Lehrerleut, or the teacher's people.[59] The Rockport Colony, where the Hofer brothers and Jacob Wipf lived, was a daughter colony of Old Elm Springs; Jacob, who was called to service in the war, was a grandson of the teacher and elder whose name he shared.

The Hutterites' arrival in the Dakota Territory coincided with the forced removal of the Lakota people and other tribes. Under the Appropriations Act of 1871, the federal government in effect established reservations and opened the tribal land for settlement. The cordoning off of the Native Americans would take time. Lakota Indians continued to live in teepees throughout the region and pursued buffalo herds wherever they wandered. In the early 1870s, Peter Jansen, one of the Mennonites who had met with President Grant to talk about immigration from Russia, visited the territory, describing a place where "wild game abounded," including herds of antelope and flocks of chicken and ducks.[60]

All around them, the Hutterite pioneers saw a "vast expanse of ever waving wind-driven prairie grasses."[61] The surveyor general for the Dakota Territory, William Beadle, reported that Sioux Falls was little more than a military barracks and a small store in the 1870s. When traveling by wagon southwest from Sioux Falls, in the direction of the Hutterite colonies, he had to "stop and cut the gumbo, mud and grass from the wheels."[62] The first years were trying, with severe winters, grasshoppers, prairie fires, and drought. In 1883, a constitutional convention set the boundary (forty-sixth

parallel) between what would, in 1889, become North Dakota and South
Dakota. The land was filling up. In 1880, the territory had 81,781 people; five
years later, there were 248,569.[63]

In 1880, the population at the three colonies and a sister offshoot numbered 443, with the majority having one of five surnames: Hofer, Stahl,
Waldner, Walter, and Wipf.[64] The colonies multiplied rapidly.[65] As with the
biblical mandate on sharing goods, the Hutterites took God at his word
when he commanded, "Be ye fruitful and multiply." At the time of the First
World War, Hutterite women gave birth, on average, to nearly eleven children.[66] When a mother colony reached 125 to 150 people, stretching the
bounds of a viable organizational unit, it would divide in two, with half the
population remaining and the other half moving to a new location. By the
time the United States entered the war, the colonies numbered seventeen,
with a combined population of about two thousand.[67]

The Hutterites arrived in South Dakota as skillful tillers of the soil and
with an eye for good land. They plowed deep, cleared stones methodically,
and rotated crops. A visitor to the Bon Homme Colony in 1877 commented
on their agricultural prowess: "They get the most out of the soil, utilizing
every square foot under cultivation and introducing many profitable spe-
cialties which an American would never bother his head about." The three
original colonies, and those that would follow, were farming communities,
growing primarily wheat and flax. Like many of the smaller, neighboring
private farms, each colony had sheep, cattle, and hogs.[68]

But the Hutterites took advantage of efficiencies of scale. They trained
young men to be specialists: in raising cattle, grain farming, blacksmithing,
woodworking. Each colony sought to be as self-sufficient as possible. By the
time the nation entered the war, the colonies had "become quite prosperous" and "generally isolated from the rest of society," in the words of John
Unruh, a historian from South Dakota.[69]

The Hutterites appeared to have chosen their new national home well.
Their farms had flourished, they had maintained their German language
and culture, and they had avoided military service. The nonresistant alarms
at the colonies rang lightly only once in the years after they had settled in
South Dakota. When the United States declared war on Spain in 1898, some

Hutterites feared that a draft would follow. In anticipation of that encroach-
ment, they launched a colony in Manitoba, only about ten miles across the
border, a kind of safe haven, just in case. The Wolf Creek and Jamesville
colonies both contributed settlers. But the war proved brief and the settlers
missed the close company of the mother colonies; by 1905, the members of
the Canadian offshoot had all returned.[70] In a different century, they would
now confront a different kind of war.

Chapter Three

A Nation Rises Up

*Rather than knowingly wrong a man to the value of a penny, we would
let ourselves be robbed of a hundred gulden. Rather than strike our worst
enemy with our hand—to say nothing of spears, swords, and halberds
such as the world uses—we would let our own lives be taken.*
—Jakob Hutter

Nation Shows Patriotic Colors

Flags across the nation flew as if on full alert in 1918. Tacoma felt more than the stirring breeze that visited many towns; this was a community of powerful gusts, where patriotism billowed up as Patriotism. The publisher of the *Daily News* launched a campaign to plant the largest American flag in the world on the grounds of Camp Lewis. As donations from readers poured in to the paper's offices at the Perkins Building, the publisher contracted with the American Flag Company of New York to build a champion banner, measuring sixty feet by ninety feet and weighing in at 257 pounds. Each of the thirteen stripes, made of the finest grade bunting, was nearly five feet wide. The paper announced the flag's arrival in a photo headlined with a folksy touch of pride: "Here Is the Big Camp Lewis Flag. Is 'Six Stories' Long. If It Were Hung from the Topmost Cornice of the Perkins Building It Would Drag on the A Street Pavement. Some Flag, Eh?"[1]

In the winter of 1918, the newspaper had foresters searching the woods of western Washington, looking for a suitable pole on which to mount the flag. The pole could then be placed at Camp Lewis and rise at least 314 feet, well above the reigning record holder in England, at 215 feet. (Tacoma was not the only city to measure its patriotism by the yardstick. *National Geographic* magazine published a photo in late 1917 of a 200-pound flag manufactured in Manchester, New Hampshire. Measuring 50 feet by 95 feet, the Manchester challenger came within 650 square feet and 57 pounds of the Tacoma contender). The Tacoma flag was to be dedicated in May, but the commissioners of the flag had not fully anticipated the challenge of finding and securing a pole that would be able to support a flag of those dimensions. Memorial Day came and went that year without the flag on display.[2]

Even absent the banner, Camp Lewis found suitable ways to contribute to the national outpouring on a day devoted to the memory of soldiers who had died in service. A band of more than a hundred soldier musicians, billed as the largest group ever to make music on the Pacific Coast, furnished the entertainment, complemented by a twenty-one-gun salute at noon. In New York City, a woman named Rosie Rosenberg, who may have set her own record by having six sons simultaneously fighting for the nation, joined more than twenty thousand other marchers in a parade across Manhattan. Neighboring Philadelphia halted all business for two minutes at eleven o'clock on that day.

Down in Washington, D.C., President Woodrow Wilson called on Americans to pay homage to past defenders and to devote themselves to a day of prayer on behalf of the soldiers. Solemnity was in the air. The *New York Times* reported that there were "probably fewer sporting and athletic events than in other years, but greater attendance at churches and larger crowds at the cemeteries."[3] The president himself attended Central Presbyterian Church in the morning and then went to Arlington National Cemetery in the afternoon. In the valleys of the Ohio, the Mississippi, and the Missouri, the paper said, a "more martial spirit and a greater reverence" were apparent.

A Wary Onlooker at the Outset of War

The evidence in every town and city of unbridled support for the war on that Memorial Day would have been inconceivable only a year or two earlier. Many Americans had been hard-pressed both to grasp the underlying causes of the war and to offer convincing reasons why the nation on this side of the Atlantic should become involved; the territorial and economic rivalries among the great foreign powers ran deep. That the assassination of Archduke Franz Ferdinand of Austria, the heir to the throne of Austria-Hungary, on June 28, 1914, served as a flashpoint was common enough knowledge, as was the subsequent decision by Austria-Hungary to declare war on Serbia, the homeland of the assassin, escalating the conflict. By prior and emerging pacts, other countries took sides, with arrows of attack and counterattack and potential attack forming a complex map of uneven stitches: the Allies included England, France, Russia, Serbia, and Belgium, aligned against the Central Powers of Germany, Austria-Hungary, Turkey, and Bulgaria.

Apart from the geographic distance that suggested a conflict best left to others to resolve, the execution of the war itself gave Americans further reason for pause. The war of many monikers (the Great War, the War of Wars, the War to End All Wars) was also the War with a Fixed Address: deep in the trenchworks carved through France and Belgium. The central combatants along this ravaged seam—where the German forces arrayed against the French and the British—settled into a remarkably stationary battle.

From 1914, when the war began, until 1917, when the four Hutterites from Rockport were drafted, the battle lines here shifted ever so slightly, often by only a stone's throw. For years the progress most noticeable in this war of attrition came tragically in the counting of the dead. In the opening month of fighting, more than a hundred thousand soldiers died; by the end of 1914, some six hundred thousand had died; by 1917, the fighting had killed five million. With that record, it was no wonder that trench warfare would come to be called the "physical expression of stubbornness in the face of reason."[4]

President Wilson, with widespread support, appeared intent on keeping the United States out of the killing trenches. Political observers agreed that Wilson narrowly won reelection in 1916 only because he ran under the Democratic Party slogan, "He Kept Us Out of War." Wilson knew that the nation was deeply divided over the war. German-Americans and Irish-Americans, in particular, resisted any alliance with the British against Germany; and labor unions and socialists charged that American involvement in the war, if it came, would only benefit big business and the political elite, at the expense of the workers who would be called on to shoulder the bayonets.

Other ethnic groups, however, especially from eastern and southern Europe, associated the war with independence. For American Czechs, Slovaks, Poles, and Jews, the war provided an opportunity to help their homelands gain freedom from the German, Austro-Hungarian, and Turkish empires.[5] Politically, for the United States, it appeared expedient to avoid direct engagement, even if bankers and other segments of the national economy had a growing vested interest in supporting the Allies (J.P. Morgan served as the Allies' purchasing agent).[6] But the U.S. policy of professed neutrality began to shift after Germany sank the British ocean liner *Lusitania* in 1915, with 128 Americans aboard and then announced in 1917 that it would pursue unrestricted submarine warfare along the British Isles and off the coast of Europe, including targeting American ships (some of which were provocatively delivering munitions to Britain). The American decision to enter the war was effectively sealed with the discovery of a German telegram that promised to help Mexico reclaim the southwestern territory of Arizona, New Mexico, and Texas should the United States enter the war and Mexico become Germany's ally.

Making the World "Safe for Democracy"

When Wilson finally decided that the United States should confront Germany militarily, he had had ample time to consider the implications, beyond pitting American prowar and antiwar groups against each other with heightened intensity. Though he favored an army leavened by the spirit of volunteering, he knew that the war campaign would require heavy taxation and a national draft to field a force capable of making a difference on the ground. Beyond that, war would demand a singular loyalty.

On the night before he asked Congress to declare war, Wilson anticipated with prescience the national hysteria that would take root: "Once lead this people into war," he said, "and they'll forget there ever was such a thing as tolerance. To fight you must be brutal and ruthless, and the spirit of ruthless brutality will enter into the very fibre of our national life, infecting Congress, the courts, the policeman on the beat, the man in the street."[7] Conformity would rule the day.

Wilson's prowess as a speaker was on full display when he appeared before a joint session of the House and Senate on April 2, 1917, where flags in hands and on lapels created a sheen of patriotism. When the rousing ovation that greeted him subsided, he asked for a declaration of war. "The world must be made safe for democracy," the president said, putting the mission on the noblest of footing. In closing, he enumerated all that was at stake:

> It is a fearful thing to lead this great, peaceful people into war, into the most terrible and disastrous of all wars, civilization itself seeming to be in the balance. But the right is more precious than peace, and we shall fight for the things which we have always carried nearest our hearts—for democracy, for the right of those who submit to authority to have a voice in their own Governments, for the rights and liberties of small nations, for a universal dominion of right by such a concert of free peoples as shall bring peace and safety to all nations and make the world itself at last free.[8]

News reports the next day suggested how quickly public sentiment was coalescing—the "belligerent pacifists, truculent in manner" who encamped around the Capitol in opposition to the president's decision during the day were hauled off; by nightfall, it would have been "easier for a camel to go through the eye of a needle than for a disturber to get within pistol shot of the Capitol." The Senate passed a war resolution by a vote of 82 to 6 on April 4, and the House followed suit, 373 to 50, on April 6. A decision made, the nation turned to war in lockstep.

Just as the country only reluctantly came to a point where it was ready to declare war, so too was it slow to embrace the call for a universal draft in place of the traditional army of volunteers. Americans had hoped that even if war were declared, a small armed force would suffice, and that the "chief task of the nation would be to provide materials, not men."[9] At the start of the war in Europe, the United States had about eighty thousand officers and men in its regular army, all volunteers.

When the United States declared war, it did so with an army of about 133,000 men, supplemented by about 70,000 in the National Guard, with most of the soldiers stationed on the Mexican border; despite the declaration of war and the patriotic outpouring for the cause, men were slow to step forward to join the ranks. Even so, the chairman of the House Committee on Military Affairs, Stanley H. Dent Jr. of Alabama, voiced the sentiments of many Americans in saying that a volunteer system should be given time to test its merits.

But the Allies pressed for a rapid and ambitious American engagement. General Joseph Joffre of France, who as the supreme military commander had had a soberingly close view of the fighting on the Western Front, said that Americans should not be fooled by the "sunny propaganda which portrayed the German lines breaking and Allied morale high."[10] American troops were needed, he said, and President Wilson, who had resisted any appeals for obligatory military service only a year earlier, became adamant in his call for conscription.

"Pacifist" Leads the Army

With the United States poised to play a more robust military role than a volunteer army would allow, President Wilson turned to his secretary of war, a former student of his at the Johns Hopkins University, to assemble that force. Newton Diehl Baker was, in many respects, an odd choice to lead the armed forces. A lawyer by training and a Democratic mayor of Cleveland by experience, he himself had never served in the military (poor eyesight kept him out of the Spanish-American War). In early 1916, his mayoral term just ended, he opened a law practice, Baker, Hostetler and Sidlo, in the city he had governed; two months later, he was appointed secretary of war.

Baker left the law firm in the care of his two partners, one of whom, Joseph C. Hostetler, had Amish roots and would have been able to provide the war secretary with an insider's view of the historic peace churches who were certain to press for an exemption from military service.[11] A month after the United States entered the war Hostetler mentioned to Baker that President Wilson "should have me or somebody like me who knows the low German peculiarities" send a letter to make the case for a contribution to the nation.

By this time, Hostetler had left pacifist roots far behind. He told Baker that at times he thought that "every German, Austrian and Turk, unnaturalized, might as well be shot, but I appreciate that there are a great many citizens of our country in Germany, and that we must think of retaliation."[12]

Baker went to Washington at forty-four as the "mildest, most peaceful, most intellectual and shortest man to exert managerial authority over the armies of the United States."[13] His early views on the war were well known; he had been a member of the American Union Against Militarism, a prominent antiwar group and a forerunner of the National Civil Liberties Bureau, which was itself a forerunner of the American Civil Liberties Union. Professional soldiers were inclined to agree with Theodore Roosevelt, the former president, who himself wanted to lead a division of volunteers against the Germans, in suspecting that Baker was, at heart, an amiable pacifist—and in no way did Roosevelt mean that to be taken as a compliment.

Baker accepted the label but always with a significant twist. "I'm so much of a pacifist that I'm willing to fight for it," he once said in a rejoinder. And in a speech to the national convention of the Reserve Officers Association, he said, "I am a pacifist. I am a pacifist in my prayers. I am a pacifist in my belief that God made man for better things than that civilization should always be under the deadly blight of the increasingly deadly destructions that war brings us. I am a pacifist in believing that the real contribution to that sentiment lies in adequate, sane preparedness on the part of any free people to defend its liberties. Peace will not come by merely wishing it. We must work for it. We must fight for it."[14] On the day that he assumed command of the army, he would again seek to burnish his credentials while clarifying his peace stance: "I believe in peace and in the proper enforcement of the laws of peace—by force if necessary."[15]

Unlike Roosevelt—a hero to those Americans who had been pressing for a standing national army even while European bodies piled up in the trenches—Baker did not swagger as if spoiling for a fight. He was studious by nature; given free time, he was more apt to curl up with a book and a pipe than to seek out exercise. As a boy he read the entire *Encyclopaedia Britannica* and was a regular visitor at the hometown Martinsburg Library in West Virginia. At school, German, as it happens, was his best foreign language, and public speaking his best means of communication (Wilson had likewise studied German). Baker was an excellent extemporaneous speaker, which would serve him well as army secretary, just as it had in the court-room and in the mayor's office. He could frame the clearest of arguments, speaking without notes for hours at a time and appearing to do so without preparation, as he once did before the United States Supreme Court.

Though his mother was an ardent Episcopalian, Baker was less comfort-able in going to church and discussing religion. He recalled a year teaching Sunday school as one of his most impressive failures, but during the war he would be called upon to consider the finest of religious distinctions in trying to assemble troops representative of the nation while fielding appeals from the smallest of sects intent on securing exemptions. As it happens, like his law partner Joseph Hostetler, Baker had family ties to the historic peace churches: his wife's grandfather, Jonus Leopold, was a member of the Coventry Church of the Brethren in Pennsylvania.[16]

One for All, All for One

Baker set about to raise the largest army the nation had ever seen—at least one million men in 1918 and three million to follow—and an army as di-verse as it was expansive. Though Wilson only formally announced his in-tent to institute a draft in April, at the time when he called for war, he had been planning for just such a step. On February 3, the United States ended diplomatic relations with Germany. The president paid an unannounced visit to Baker's office on February 22 and asked that a proposal for raising an emergency army be prepared within twenty-four hours. Baker, in turn, assigned the task of drafting that document to his judge advocate general, Enoch H. Crowder, who had trained at West Point and the University of Missouri Law School. While serving as a young cavalry officer at a fron-tier army post years earlier, Crowder had conducted a thorough study of the Civil War draft—with an eye toward learning from past imperfections, which had led to widespread rioting and antidraft violence during the war between states.

Now on deadline, Crowder set down the key principles that would shape the draft. Hiring substitutes should be prohibited. Service should be for the duration of the war. All male citizens who fall within the prescribed age cohort should be registered. The draft proposal that Baker presented to Congress on April 7, a day after the lawmakers officially declared war, reflected in large measure the work overseen in a single day by Crowder, Baker's point man in the army, who became administrator of the draft agency, the Selective Service System.

The mass conscript army should be, in the first place, an effective fighting force, Baker knew. But he also saw an opportunity to strengthen the national fabric at home through a shared mission. In this regard, he and Wilson were of one mind: The army could serve the crusade for Americanization, unifying the different classes and ethnic groups into a homogenous middle class and tightly knit nation.[17] The surge in immigration at the turn of the twentieth century had stretched the ties that traditionally bound Americans. The nation was going to war with one-third of Americans having been born overseas or being the child of an immigrant and with one of every five soldiers having been born overseas. Some of these so-called hyphenated Americans, whether German-Americans or Asian-Americans, appeared determined to retain dual national identities, which Wilson and Baker saw as an unacceptable threat to the national interest.

The debate preceding the war had also underscored a widening class divide between Americans of wealth and the mass of workers, a struggle that some regarded as a second Civil War—an analogy that seemed especially true whenever blood was drawn on picket lines. The success of the Industrial Workers of the World in workplace organizing and of Socialist candidates at the polls (in municipal elections in 1917, voters favored the party in scores of races) suggested that many Americans felt the system was unfair. They did not believe the rhetoric out of Washington or see evidence of the equality promised in the second sentence of the Declaration of Independence. In response to this fracturing, Baker pledged a national army that would be a measure of all Americans, bar none:

> Now, it strikes me as rather an interesting reflection that while we are in this war to make the world safe for democracy, democracy is making itself manifest here among us; for that is democracy—the cooperation, without distinction of fortune or opportunity, of all the men of the nation for the common good. . . .

For when, on some moonlight night, on the fields of France, some American boy's face is upturned, some boy who has made the grand and final sacrifice in this cause, no passerby nor no imagination that reaches him will be able to discern whether he came from a blacksmith's forge or a merchant's counter or a banker's counting room. He will simply be an American, and our affection for him, our adoption of him, our pride in him, will be as undiscriminating.[18]

In service to the nation, Baker said, the army could take men of "every variety of religious belief and political opinion" and weld them "into a homogenous group."[19] To achieve this broad representation, and to assemble a force of sufficient size, the administration set out to register all young men between the ages of twenty-one and thirty.

A Place for Religious Scruples

Despite the administration's commitment to fielding a unified and representative army, the proposed draft measure did allow men of fighting age to be exempt from regular service on several grounds. Men who had dependents or who were critical to an essential farming or industrial enterprise might be excused. There was also a provision for conscientious objectors. Members of pacifist religious sects—like the Hutterites, Mennonites, Quakers, and Brethren—could be released from regular service. Their exemption, though, came with an important caveat:

Nothing in this act contained shall be construed to require or compel any person to serve in any of the forces herein provided for who is found to be a member of any well recognized religious sect or organization at present organized and existing and whose existing creed or principles forbid its members to participate in war in any form and whose religious convictions are against war or participation therein in accordance with the creed or principles of said religious organizations, but no person so exempted shall be exempted from service in any capacity that the President shall declare to be noncombatant.[20]

In that tangle of legalese, the Wilson administration opened the door for conscientious objectors from established churches to avoid combat duty but did so in a way that raised immediate concerns.

The invitation, for starters, was limited; it would not be extended to other potential objectors like a young man who felt morally opposed to the war but had no membership in a historic peace church. The leaders of the pacifist denominations, who might have been expected to feel reassured that their young men were in line for an exemption, also had misgivings. They focused their attention on the last phrase in the provision. Even though the bona fide conscientious objectors would not be required to bear arms, they would still need to perform "noncombatant" service—and the meaning of that term stood out as a critical blank to be filled in by Wilson and Baker at a later date.

If conscientious objectors had to perform noncombatant service, then what kind of service was expected and under whose watch? The wording of the draft provision could mean that all religious objectors would have to perform noncombatant *military* service. If that were so, then commanders at each army camp might have broad discretion to set the terms for such service. The commanders might reason that drilling in uniform would be fine training for these men even if their formal work assignment was kitchen duty or road construction.

Some objectors, those with "more tender consciences," in the words of the Mennonite historian C. Henry Smith, would never accept that degree of immersion in the military system.[21] For these absolutists, enabling those who would fight—whether by preparing their meals or nursing them to health—was no different than joining them with gun in hand.

Then again, the objectors might be invited to do noncombatant service for a relief agency outside of the military's purview, and all would be well. The phrasing was ambiguous, but the stakes were high. What was clear was that service of some kind would be compulsory and that the administration intended to have each man, regardless of creed or country of origin, do his part for the duration of the war.

That represented a different military expectation on the part of the government. The principle of equivalency—that you paid a fine, or hired a substitute to take your place in the army, or performed alternative service—pre-vailed in the earliest days of the colonies. But apart from occasional com-pulsory militia training and temporary drafts, the nation kept to a volunteer military tradition.

In the most recent conflict, the Spanish-American War of 1898, consci-entious objectors did not have to contend with national conscription, and the fighting was over within weeks. In the Civil War, in contrast, nearly one in every five men of military age in the South and one in sixteen in the North died during four years of conflict. But members of pacifist churches in the North could buy an exemption for $300; in the South, they could pay $500 or hire a substitute to fill the ranks of soldiers.[22]

Peace church members with a keen sense of history recalled alternatives to service earlier in the nineteenth century, when men could pay small fines to be excused from having to train with a state militia. And now here the pacifists were facing the prospect of having their young men shipped off to military training camps—with no apparent recourse—for a noncombatant role that was yet to be defined.

Petitioning Washington in the Eleventh Hour

In the month between the release of the draft proposal and a vote on the measure in Congress, representatives of the historic pacifist denominations and other lobbyists for conscientious objection descended on Washington with urgency. One group after another, with independent but overlapping concerns, appealed to Wilson, Baker, and members of Congress to make changes in the planned draft. April 12 was a particularly busy day. Three Mennonites with unusual qualifications for a people known as the "quiet in the land" traveled to Washington. Peter Jansen of Nebraska had served in the state legislature; Maxwell Kratz of Philadelphia was a successful at-torney; and Peter H. Richert was a church leader from Kansas. As ambassa-dors on behalf of a more liberal branch of the church, they pressed lawmak-ers to allow church members who were drafted to do their service outside of the military.[23]

Meanwhile, three prominent members of the American Union Against Militarism garnered an audience that day with a former colleague from the antiwar organization, Secretary Baker himself. The delegation of this secular wing of antiwar advocates consisted of Jane Addams, the founder of Hull House in Chicago and a leader of the settlement movement; Norman Thomas, a Presbyterian minister who would soon become publisher of the *World Tomorrow* magazine and who after the war would go on to run for president six times as the head of the Socialist ticket—and who, as we will see in chapter 8, had a brother jailed for his refusal to serve in the war; and Lillian Wald, a nurse and president of the organization. They too appealed for an alternative to noncombatant service within the military—and, just as important, they argued that any exemption should be based on an individual's moral conscience rather than membership in a certain denomination.[24] The opportunity for alternative service, they insisted, should be more broadly available.

The well-connected delegation could point to John Nevin Sayre as an example of someone who had scruples against war but no standing within a denomination. Sayre was a leader of the Fellowship of Reconciliation, a mainstream Protestant pacifist group; but he was also a young minister within the Episcopal Church of America, which supported the war effort. As it happened, he enjoyed an inside track in appealing to the president to base exemptions on individual beliefs rather than on church memberships: his brother, Francis, had married Wilson's daughter, Jessie. They were all family. In 1915, John Sayre and Woodrow Wilson stood together in a small chapel of St. John's Episcopal Church in Williamstown, Massachusetts, selected as godfathers of the couple's son. The two men also shared Princeton University. Sayre had graduated in 1907, when Wilson served as president of the university.

So Sayre took his case directly to Wilson: "To put the matter concretely, Quakers might be excused from going to the front, but individual Jews, socialists, or Episcopalians like myself . . . might be drafted into it . . . . Conscience is always an individual and personal thing . . . and . . . the creed or principles of a religious organization cannot be substituted for it."[25] Relationships aside, the president disagreed. He worried that men, if allowed to stand individually, would conveniently calibrate their beliefs to escape their civic duty.

Historical Precedents for Pacifism

As lawmakers considered the draft measure, advocates for conscientious objectors continued to pay visits to Washington and write letters—always as the petitioner. Military exemption in the United States was and remains a political privilege, rather than a constitutional right. If James Madison had had his way, though, the Second Amendment to the Constitution, which in many quarters has come to signify an ironclad guarantor of the right to bear arms, the National Rifle Association's own amendment as it were, might have been just as closely associated with the refusal to bear arms. When the members of Congress were crafting the Bill of Rights, Madison proposed that conscientious objection be protected by the Constitution:

> The right of the people to keep and bear arms shall not be infringed; a well-armed and well-regulated militia being the best security of a free country; but no person religiously scrupulous of bearing arms shall be compelled to render military service in person.[26]

The representatives were divided. Congressman Egbert Benson of New York, for one, argued that such an exemption should be left to the "humanity" or discretion of the legislature, in a given historical moment, and not elevated to a constitutional right—adding, "I have no reason to believe but the Legislature will always possess humanity enough to indulge this class of citizens in a matter they are so desirous of."[27] The House of Representatives approved the amendment by a small margin, but the Senate did not follow suit. As a result, the conscientious objector clause in the second amendment, which would have guided the nation's treatment of objectors in this war and every other conflict, was lost.

With that right having eluded them, representatives of the historic peace groups were at the mercy of lawmakers at the outset of each new war. Along with the Mennonites, the other two main pillars among peace groups were the Society of Friends, also known as Quakers, and the Church of the Brethren, also known as the Dunkards. Though separated by their time and place of origin, the Mennonites (the sixteenth century in Germany, Switzerland, and the Netherlands), the Quakers (the seventeenth century in England),

and the Brethren (Germany in the eighteenth century) all shared the conviction that human life is sacred and that the biblical principle of peace trumps
any justification for war.

Not all of the church bodies were equally gifted in lobbying for this
conviction. As the nation made ready for the Great War, the Mennonites,
Amish, and Hutterites in particular struggled with how to present a co-
herent and persuasive best case to officials in Washington.[28] These groups
traditionally rejected charismatic leadership or any effort to unduly lift up
one member of the community over others. They also were slow to embrace higher education, which left the workings of Washington that much
more of a mystery. Given this foundation, church leaders were generally
ill-prepared to serve as church spokesmen to the world, and the young men
drafted as soldiers even less so.

In contrast, the Quakers, America's best-known pacifists, were much
more comfortable in the corridors of power. The sect, who had been present on the major battlefronts since the Battle of the Boyne in Ireland in
1690, had ably filled the "role of a healer of the wounds of war."[29] Early in
World War I, they had formed an ambulance unit, drawing on English and
Irish volunteers. As soon as the United States declared war, the Society of
Friends met in Philadelphia and swiftly formed the American Friends Service Committee, which would represent exemption interests of the broader
organization.

The committee had a promising contact in Grayson Murphy, the chief
of the American Red Cross in France. He had attended a Quaker college,
Haverford, and was friends with Rufus Jones, the chairman of the American
Friends Service Committee. Operating under the slogan "A Service of Love
in Wartime," the committee was hopeful that it would have a reconstruction
program in place in France, perhaps in partnership with the American Red
Cross, that would allow conscientious objectors to perform service outside
the direct command of the military.[30]

On May 18, 1917, a month after the nation declared war, and after a flurry
of hearings and debates, Wilson signed legislation to assemble an army:
"An Act to Authorize the President to Increase Temporarily the Military Es-
tablishment of the United States." The noncombatant provision remained,
as it was first proposed, an ambiguous obligation to perform service in

some manner. And there was no provision for nonreligious objectors to secure an exemption as noncombatants. Politicians and military officials from the president on down were worried that allowing individual appeals would encourage a latent minority of slackers and draft dodgers. Wilson said it would be "impossible . . . because it would open the door to so much that was unconscientious on the part of persons who wished to escape service."[31] Lawmakers had agreed: when Senator Robert LaFollette and Representative Edward Keating proposed an amendment to the draft bill that would recognize individual political objectors, only a few colleagues voted with them. With the terms of the draft set, the next step was registering young men across the nation in a single day, on June 5.

Registration by the Millions

Even though they had deep misgivings about the noncombatant obligation, peace church leaders generally directed the young men in their flocks to register as required by the government. For example, shortly before registration day, a delegation of Hutterite leaders went to Pierre, South Dakota, to discuss military service with Governor Peter Norbeck. It was, in effect, a courtesy call among neighbors, since Norbeck was not in a position to alter the terms of the draft. The Hutterite leaders said they were willing to allow their young men to register but not to be drafted for any service related to the war. Farming, for example, they could do.

The leaders agreed on a plan that blended cooperation and resistance. Hutterite men would register and report for their physicals, reasoning that the "mere act of registering" would not infringe on pacifist doctrine.[32] It was like showing up for a census, some said. But, should the Hutterites be drafted and required to report at military camps, that cooperation would end at the camps; the men should refuse to wear a uniform or to advance the war effort through their work.[33] That was the directive that the Hofer brothers and Jacob Wipf took with them to Camp Lewis.

Registration day went smoothly, with more than 9.5 million signing up at several thousand Selective Service sites, whose local boards were made up of business and civic leaders. By having registration take place at local polling places across the country—rather than at police stations, for example—the federal government encouraged the view that the draft was not a conscription of the unwilling but rather a selection of volunteers, community by community.[34] For Wilson, it was a "great day of patriotic devotion and obligation."[35]

A lottery then determined which of the men would be among the 687,000 needed for immediate service. On July 20, in a ceremony at the Senate Office Building, a blindfolded secretary of war dipped his hand into a glass bowl with 10,500 numbered slips inside capsules, reflecting the largest number of men that had been registered at any of the 4,647 local draft boards.[36] Secretary Baker drew the first number: 258. Every No. 258 at each of the local draft boards was to be summoned for medical exams, and, if he passed, was ordered to report for induction into the army. The drawing went on until 2 a.m.

In the course of the war, only 12 percent of the men who registered—and their number would reach twenty-four million—were ever inducted. Draftees made up 77 percent of the four million American soldiers. The administration suspected that thousands of young men of military age failed to register on that day, and many others would follow suit in subsequent registration days. The number of Americans who dodged registration may have reached three million, the majority of them poorer men from isolated regions (and not, as a rule, conscientious objectors).[37]

The summer introduced an awkward dance of negotiation. The peace advocates continued to make their views known while waiting for a ruling on noncombative service, hopeful that the definition would exclude their young men from having to serve in the military. They faced the challenge of explaining their appeal for an exemption without appearing to be unpatriotic. Members of the historic peace churches, especially the Mennonites, Amish, Brethren, and Hutterites, faced the added complication of making their appeal on behalf of a heavily German-American constituency during a war against Germany.

They knew that many church members would fail at least one test of loyalty—they spoke in German and listened to sermons and read religious publications in that language as well. In framing their arguments, these sects reminded officials that they had often suffered because of their commitment to Christian nonresistance and had come to the United States to escape such persecution and to find religious tolerance. Even while making their case, they expressed their gratitude for government favors in the past and conveyed their present loyalty.

In a petition presented to President Wilson on behalf of the Hutterian Brethren Church, three ministers (David Hofer, Elias Walker, and Joseph Kleinsasser) introduced themselves as "men of lowly station and unversed in the ways of the world" and described community of goods and other principles of the church.[38] In a direct voice, they conveyed their central point: "Our young men could not become a part of the army or military organizations, even for noncombatant service, without violating our principles." Before closing, they assured the president of their good intentions: "We would further say that we love our country and are profoundly thankful to God and to our authorities for the liberty of conscience which we have hitherto enjoyed." Given such a conversation, neither Wilson nor Baker could later say that he was caught off guard by the refusal of conscientious objectors like the Hofer brothers and Jacob Wipf to work in the army camps.

Wilson and Baker, meanwhile, cloaked their intentions. They wanted to limit the number of conscientious objectors and bring as many men as possible into the military service, certain that, once on board, even men with scruples could be persuaded to do their part and be transformed into fighters.[39] In the summer of 1917, Wilson and Baker applied a soft touch to achieve rapport and direct church members toward compliance. In meeting with the pacifist delegates, they sought to appear sympathetic and hide the condescension that would sometimes be apparent when they spoke about pacifists among themselves or with their staff members.

The secretary was strikingly accessible to visitors. Rufus Jones, a lead negotiator for the Society of Friends, said he often went as part of a small delegation to meet with Baker that summer: "His ante-room was crowded usually to its utmost capacity."[40] As the summer wound down, Jones said, it was becoming apparent that an exemption from combatant duty would not mean an exemption from the military. They urged Baker to recognize the seriousness of the situation: "We are opposed not only to the taking of human life but we are further prevented by our religious principles *from participation in any military system or military service.*"[41]

A ruling on August 8 removed any doubt that that was just what was expected of the men: all draftees would be in the "military service of the United States from the time specified for reporting to the Local Board for military service." When men traveled to military camps, they would travel as soldiers, a distinction that may well have been lost on the Hutterites, coming as it did so late in the process. Three days later the government announced that conscientious objectors would be placed in army camps as part of the draft quota.

Baker Expects Objectors to March in Step

President Wilson asked Baker in August whether he had adopted a noncombatant policy with regard to the conscientious objectors. In his reply, Baker, who enjoyed a close relationship with Wilson and had a private telephone wire running to the White House, said he thought the conscientious objectors should be segregated in the camps and have "suitable work evolved for them."[42] Baker felt confident that by segregating conscientious objectors from other soldiers, many could come around and agree to serve—leaving perhaps only a small core of Mennonites, Amish, Hutterites, Quakers, and Brethren. If the country were to allow objectors to do service outside of the military, such as with a Quaker reconstruction unit in France, he reasoned, it would only encourage more defections from the military.

In some ways it's understandable that Wilson and Baker seemed to be responding to conscientious objectors without apparent forethought. Harlan Stone—the dean of Columbia University Law School and a member of the Board of Inquiry that would evaluate the sincerity of objectors—suggested that before the war such resisters were not on the minds of legal scholars either. He characterized the term "conscientious objector" as one of many "new expressions" that were "coined as a by-product of the war."[43] Before the war, the term referred to someone who refused compulsory vaccinations. As further evidence of its recent emergence at the time, the term often appeared in quotation marks during the war.[44]

The lack of coordination on the part of the historic peace churches and even on the part of an individual sect—in the case of the Mennonites— played into the hands of government negotiators. The most comprehensive statement made by Mennonites came at Yellow Creek Mennonite Church in Indiana on August 29, 1917, signed by nearly two hundred church leaders and delegates. The statement was unequivocal: "We hold that Christian people should have no part in carnal warfare of any kind or for any cause."[45] If summoned, young men in the church should "meekly inform" the authorities that they could not agree to combatant or noncombatant roles within the military. But communication would not always be so clear. At one point Aaron Loucks, a Mennonite representative, led a delegation in meeting with Baker and afterward reported, in error, that the government promised service that would not fall under military authority; a delegation of Quakers and Church of the Brethren soon corrected the record.

Meanwhile, in the fall of 1917, a delegation of Hutterites visited with Baker. He advised them to let the draftees report for duty, as they were inclined to do, and then at the camps request noncombatant assignments. Baker assured the Hutterites that their men would not be asked to do anything that would violate their consciences. Baker had made similar personal pledges to other delegates. In meeting with Loucks and two other members of the Mennonite War Problems Committee, D.D. Miller and Sanford G. Shetler, Baker had put his hand on Miller's knee and said, "Don't worry. We'll take care of your boys."[46]

When the first draftees began to arrive at camps in September, a poll showed that objectors were a small minority, putting Baker even more at ease. Baker visited Camp Meade in Maryland that fall, spending time with the twenty-seven objectors, many of them Amish, Mennonites, and Quakers, in a cantonment of 18,000 men—the pacifists represented a miniscule fraction of a percent of the local military force. (The War Department counted only 276,843 adult men in all of the historic pacifist denominations and other antiwar sects combined.)

Baker made a point of noting that one of the resisters on the sidelines watched the recruits play football and baseball for a couple of days and decided to join the company. Afterward, Baker told Wilson that "they seem well-disposed, simple-minded young people who have been imprisoned in a narrow environment and really have no comprehension of the world outside of their own rural and peculiar community. Only two of those with whom I talked seemed quite normal mentally."[47] He was sure that they would "come gradually to understand." He wrote again to the president: "It does not seem from this first survey as though our problem is going to be unmanageably large, or so large that a very generous and considerate mode of treatment would be out of the question."[48]

Part of the problem, Baker thought, was that conscientious objectors saw themselves in too grandiose a light: "The fact about the conscientious objectors is that they acquired quite unwarranted importance in their own eyes. To each of them he and his cause became the pivotal and central thing in the world while, of course, as the case then stood, they were, frankly, relatively unimportant."[49] With hundreds of thousands of men to train and move to the front lines, and tons of materiel to transport with them, Baker wanted to keep the several hundred conscientious objectors in perspective.

In less than two years, nearly three million American men would enter the Army and receive training. Only about twenty thousand men arrived at camps with conscientious objector certificates and an even smaller number—less than four thousand—would stand firm as objectors (and of that number, about 1,300 would agree to noncombatant military service).[50] He assumed that military personnel would have Mennonites, Hutterites, and others serving in uniform even without having defined noncombatant service. When H.P. Krehbiel, a Mennonite leader from Kansas, told Baker that young Mennonite men might be forced to leave the country to ensure their religious liberty, as "they have done in former years," Baker quickly sought to assure him that such measures would not be necessary. "That," Baker said, "would be a sad, sad affair and it shall never happen."[51]

Baker even managed a touch of humor in referring to the many American religious groups at his door, with their confusing array of beliefs. Each group, some of which before the war he never knew had even existed, sought special exemption. "I am beginning to feel that nothing short of a comprehensive knowledge of Professor James's book on 'Varieties of Religious Experience' will ever qualify a man to be a helpful Secretary of War," he said.[52]

Along with varieties of Mennonites, Brethren, Amish, and Hutterites he heard from Seventh-day Adventists; Russellites, later known as Jehovah's Witnesses; Molokans, members of a small Russian Christian pacifist sect living in the Southwest; and others. At one point Baker joked with the president, the son of a Presbyterian minister, about a religious group that felt compelled to read to him the seventeenth and eighteenth chapters of the book of Revelation while making its case. Wilson, a Bible reader with his own sense of humor, replied that when *he* met with the group, there was no reading from Revelation—they figured that the president knew the passage by heart, he intimated, unlike his wayward secretary of war.[53]

Commanders Face Resistance on the Home Front

But conditions on the ground at the training camps soon challenged Baker's sanguine view. In fact, Washington's strategy for dealing with conscientious objectors led to conflicts as soon as men began reporting to camps. Reflecting differences of opinion within the pacifist denominations about how cooperative their draftees should be, and the lingering uncertainty about the provisions of noncombatant service, the burden of best response fell on the shoulders of the recruits—and they were not of one mind. Confronted with orders from their superiors when they stepped down from trains, recruits who arrived as conscientious objectors had to think quickly even as they took stock of their new surroundings. Some men accepted their place as regular soldiers. Some put on a khaki uniform and carried a rifle to a target field but insisted that all work assignments be noncombatant. Others refused to convey any sign of being part of the military system, including saluting officers. Some accepted work assignments but then had misgivings and withdrew to their bunks.

Conservative Mennonites, Hutterites, and Amish were among those most inclined to direct their young men to resist any participation. The Brethren and Friends allowed their young men more freedom to follow their conscience once they arrived. Regardless of exactly where the participation line was drawn, anxiety filled homes and churches: "The boys wrote many frantic appeals to the home ministers for guidance. And they received different kinds of advice from the ministers."[54]

Meanwhile, the camp officers were duty bound to shape raw recruits into a cohesive fighting force as quickly as possible. Confronted with what many officers regarded as disloyal insubordination, they responded forcefully with the measures of persuasion at their disposal: a kind word and polite request at the outset gave way to ridicule, bullying, intimidation, haz-

ing, isolation, violence. A favorite punishment involved having the uncooperative recruits shovel and carry loads of sand and dirt for no apparent
purpose other than to exhaust them and compel them into service. Mail
would be stopped, and personal belongings taken away. With fists or hoses,
guards would beat them. Objectors were scrubbed down with brushes in
cold showers. They were put in guardhouses on a diet of bread and water.
Through newspaper reports, letters home, and visits from ministers, word
began to leak out about the mistreatment of objectors at camps across the
country.[55]

Beginning in September, officials in Washington issued a series of orders meant to address the mounting problems with conscientious objectors and to bring some consistency to their treatment. In September, Baker
said that Mennonite (which no doubt in his mind included Hutterite and
Amish) objectors should not be forced to wear uniforms, since, as he put it,
"the question of raiment is one of the tenets of the faith." That rule, in time,
would be extended to most other objectors. In October, Baker directed that
the objectors be separated from regular military personnel and treated with
"tact and consideration."

Finally, in December, he said that all men with "personal scruples against
war" could qualify as conscientious objectors. Washington was ready to officially recognize the rights of resisters who arrived in camp without certificates of membership from the traditional pacifist denominations.

Of course, the results of these directives still depended largely on the
willingness of local commanders to carry them out. One commander might
decide that locking up uncooperative recruits in a guardhouse on a bread-
and-water diet constituted "segregation"; another commander might place
all the objectors together in a more comfortable bunkhouse. And the meaning of "tact and consideration" was wide open to interpretation. Throughout
the war, some camp officials simply ignored these directives from Washington. Though the Hutterites arrived at Camp Lewis months after Baker
had decreed that no one should be forced to wear a uniform, they spoke of
having to resist orders to do just that throughout their time in the military
system.

Camp Funston in Kansas was among the most punishing. Major General Leonard Wood, who served as army chief of staff from 1910 to 1914

and afterward as Roosevelt's chief ally in campaigning for a mass conscript reserve army (Wood was known as the "prophet of preparedness"), commanded the camp with the sternest of hands. In an irony that would not have been lost on the religious objectors, Woods's supporters portrayed him as the sacrificial lamb, a "martyr engaged in a long and largely thankless struggle to ensure a powerful America."[56] In any camp, the commander enjoyed power and latitude. Given his national stature, Wood arrived at Camp Funston as a commander's commander. Having lobbied for a large standing army for years, Wood did not welcome resistance from inside the ranks now that the nation was finally getting its house in order. He regarded objectors as dangerous scoundrels and traitors; they would not be coddled under his watch. In fact, were it up to him, he once said, they would have been placed in labor battalions and shipped off to France, if not executed at home by a firing squad.[57]

Without those options, Wood was determined at least to force objectors to do their part on the home front. Peter Tschetter, who had suffered the mock shooting at Camp Funston that fall, and Joseph Waldner, who had been beaten so severely that he was hospitalized, could have confirmed that Wood, and certainly some of his subordinates, meant business. Of the fifty-six Hutterites who reported to military camps during the war, many, like Tschetter and Waldner, ended up at Camp Funston, where they grew desperate to secure a way home.

In the spring of 1918, just weeks before the Hofer brothers and Jacob Wipf left for Camp Lewis, federal authorities charged three Hutterite leaders from South Dakota with attempting to bribe army officers at Camp Funston. The district attorney for Kansas said that John J. Wipf, Jacob's father and the leader of Rockport Colony, had offered Lieutenant W. Paul Jones $1,000 if he arranged for the release of the men. Jacob Hofer of the Rosedale Colony was charged with paying $120 to Lieutenant C.C. Ray as a bribe. The third Hutterite leader, J.P. Entz of New Elm Spring, was accused of having knowledge of both bribes.[58] The three Hutterites posted bail and returned home, with a trial scheduled for the fall. By then Washington was ready to acknowledge that objectors had been mistreated at Camp Funston.

But using a fist or other blunt instruments were not necessarily the most effective means in winning over recruits. With gentler appeals to loyalty, for example, Major General J. Franklin Bell, who presided over Camp Upton in New York State, persuaded a majority of conscientious objectors there to serve in the army.[59] Camp Meade in Maryland also proved to be a reasonably good home for objectors. As early as September 1917, conscientious objectors were segregated from other recruits. Many men did basic housekeeping, work with which they felt comfortable. They went on hikes to stay in shape. When the opportunity for furloughs came in the summer of 1918, most of the objectors at Camp Meade made the cut. Isaac Baer, a resister, described the camp in almost idyllic terms as an "island of peace in a sea of war."[60] A visit to Camp Meade in the fall of 1917 likely gave Baker a false impression of how well the army's incorporation of conscientious objectors across the country was going.

A Way Opens for Farm Furloughs

It was clear to the historic pacifist denominations that the situation at the military camps would not improve as long as their young men were being treated as soldiers. The Society of Friends continued to press for the means to perform noncombatant service independent of the military, whether by working for the Red Cross or on private farms or gardens. Speaking for other peace groups, the Friends said that they should not be required to do any service, even noncombatant, as soldiers in the military.

Samuel T. Ansell, who became the acting judge advocate general and Baker's chief legal adviser when Crowder took charge of Selective Service, sent a memo to Baker on September 18, 1917, in which he addressed their concerns: "They contend they cannot be directed to mobilize, and insist that they are subject to no military order. In a word, they contend that under this act they cannot be drafted into the Army of the United States."[61] Ansell said that the president could not compel men to serve once they were outside of the military, and so conscientious objectors would have to do noncombatant service within the military—however the president defined noncombatant service.

The army remained wary of offering a farm furlough option, not wanting to appear to favor conscientious objectors. Henry P. McCain, the adjutant general and chief administrative officer, stated the reservations plainly: "It would subject the Department to criticism on the ground that it was not giving equal treatment to all drafted men, but was favoring a class of men whose attitude makes them the least deserving of favor and whose services are of the least value because of their being in effect permitted to choose how and where they will serve."[62]

Still, in January, Baker signaled his readiness to grant furloughs to soldiers during the harvest and planting seasons, but without stating outright which soldiers might be furloughed. The bill that he presented to Congress allowed the War Department to furlough soldiers into civilian work in agriculture or reconstruction as needed. Theoretically, soldiers of any standing might be furloughed, but conscientious objectors were the natural candidates. Peace church officials had been pressing for just such a furlough, and objectors who refused to serve were continuing to pose challenges to the operations at training camps. Congress passed the Furlough Act on March 16, 1918.

Four days later, nearly a year after the draft had been authorized, Wilson and Baker finally defined what they meant by appropriate noncombatant work. From this day forward, conscientious objectors would be expected to serve as healers (in the Medical Corps) or suppliers (in the Quartermaster Corps) or builders (in the Corps of Engineers) within the Army of the United States. If they refused to accept such work, they would be subject to punishment. The March 20 order reflected no apparent sympathy for the conscientious objector. Neither Wilson nor Baker could be accused of giving these men special privileges, which would have created a tempest in towns across the country.

The Furlough Act, however, which had been approved earlier, gave the military a discreet way of funneling objectors to farm fields. Any men who were furloughed were technically still soldiers, but that was little more than a formality. They would be assigned to work on private farms and even paid wages (anything above $30 a month, the pay of a private soldier, would be directed to the Red Cross).

Worst Possible Timing

The Hofer brothers and Jacob Wipf would likely have taken an assignment on a farm anywhere in the United States and worked from dawn until dusk. That would have put them at arm's length from the military, working in the role of farmers, not soldiers. But for reasons that remain unclear, they never received that opportunity. The commanders at Camp Lewis could have chosen, at the moment when the four Hutterites refused to line up in formation or complete their paperwork, to simply put them in a segregated unit and wait for further word from Washington. There was reason to exercise some patience; after so many months, the policies regarding conscientious objectors finally appeared to be ready. Only a few details remained to be worked out. Baker still needed some means of deciding which objectors were sincere and deserving of furloughs.

The process of sifting the "sincere" from the "insincere" began in earnest several months after the furlough program was approved, just as the Hofer brothers and Jacob Wipf were settling in. On June 1—four days after the Hutterites had arrived at Camp Lewis and immediately been placed in the guardhouse on charges of disobeying orders—Baker announced the appointment of a three-member Board of Inquiry, consisting of some of the country's finest military and civilian legal minds. He directed the board to judiciously evaluate the 2,100 or so men who claimed to be opposed to military service and had been segregated at the various army camps. The objectors who were found to be sincere could look forward to a farm furlough, or, in a few cases, an industrial job. For men who had already been court-martialed or, in the case of the Hofer brothers and Jacob Wipf, were awaiting trial, the Board of Inquiry arrived too late.

Throughout the fall of 1917 and winter of 1918, officials at camps across the country were reluctant to use the powerful disciplinary measure at their disposal: the court-martial. They were not even sure they could bring up conscientious objectors on charges like refusal to obey a military order.[63] Through April, no Hutterites, Mennonites, or other objectors were court-martialed (about forty other men were court-martialed between September 1917 and April 1918, in trials lasting as little as eighteen minutes). In late April, however, Washington made clear that commanders were authorized to take conscientious objectors to trial when warranted. The most common concerns were refusal to obey orders, to wear a uniform, or to drill.

But commanders could not simply bring up on charges any man who refused to work. If such men were *defiant* or *insincere* in refusing to follow orders, then the commanders could proceed with charges; otherwise, men who refused to serve would await the Board of Inquiry. In a setting where discipline was next to godliness, the courts-martial cases began piling up. In two months' time, during May and June, trials were held for more than half of the Mennonites, Hutterites, and Amish who would ever be court-martialed during the war. The Hofer brothers and Jacob Wipf had the misfortune of arriving at Camp Lewis just after commanders across the country appeared intent on using trials to send a message to conscientious objectors and just before the Board of Inquiry opened the way for farm furloughs. As we shall see, that timing proved calamitous.

Chapter Four

Standing Trial

*We dare not disobey God for the sake of man's command, though it cost
our life. We must obey God rather than men.*
—Jakob Hutter

Worrisome Signs for the Defense

In the summer of 1918, the Hofer brothers and Jacob Wipf awaited their
trial for refusing to follow even the most basic of orders that they saw as
military service. They had no access to independent legal counsel, putting
their trust in a higher power. The military code had permitted the men to
hire an outside lawyer of their choosing, if one were available, and to assemble, as they were able, the most robust of defenses.[1] But they chose instead to accept as a defense lawyer whomever the army would appoint from
within its own ranks; their deference was not all that surprising, given the
Hutterite community's long-standing reluctance to file suit or use other
levers of legal power for personal advantage.[2]

Just as Hutterites in the home colony practiced *Gelassenheit*, bending
themselves in submission to the will of God and to the rules of the community, so too these men appeared resigned to the government's findings.
In their letters, the men offer no indication that even among themselves
they carried out any research or prepared formal statements in advance of
the trial. The letters do suggest an absolute trust that God would give them

words as needed to testify, if not with the eloquence of a lawyer, at least in keeping with their convictions.

Apart from the absence of independent legal counsel and of personal preparation, the men approached the trial with yet one more handicap. They had limited formal schooling, reaching no higher than the eighth grade. The education they did receive prized rote learning and conformity to church doctrine. In a trial, they would be called on to answer a challenging set of questions intended to uncover inconsistencies or faulty reasoning with no script to follow. Like most of the Mennonites and Amish, the Hutterites arrived in court without having had many opportunities to make public and personal faith statements; in the best of circumstances, they were understandably not always articulate in expressing their religious convictions.

To make matters worse, court-martial defendants generally entered a hostile courtroom with mediocre assistance at their side. Defense counsels might not even try to secure a fair trial; they were often, in fact, antagonistic toward the very men they were defending. As a special War Department Board on Courts-martial noted immediately after the war, amid calls to reform a system of military regulation that was in many ways unchanged since 1775, "courts-martial have always been agencies for creating and maintaining the discipline of armies" rather than engaging in the "nice exemplification of technical rules of law."[3] H.E. Foster, a lawyer from Seattle who represented objectors at Camp Lewis, put it more bluntly: "A court-martial trial is a trial where the party sitting in judgment is more or less prejudiced and the matter prejudged before hearing."[4] In the World War I courtroom, transparency was not a high priority; the members of the court used a secret vote to determine questions of law and to reach a verdict.

Moreover, most counsels for the defense lacked formal legal training during World War I. Court-martial procedures and the Articles of War were well established in the American military, but only in 1919, after the war, did the special board urge inducements for young officers to study law and only in 1948 did the government require counselors to be attorneys. In this respect, though, the Hutterites were fortunate. Merton A. Albee, a thirty-year-old attorney and second lieutenant, served as their defense counsel. He had studied at the University of California at Berkeley and also spoke German.

While an undergraduate at Berkeley, Albee had served as vice president of Die Plaudertasche, one of five German clubs on campus.

As the trial approached, the Hutterites had one more reason for worry, if they had known about recent cases at camps across the country and the legal directives coming out of Washington. Roger Baldwin—the director of the National Civil Liberties Bureau in New York, a leading advocate for conscientious objectors—protested the severity of the courts-martial sentences that spring. Baldwin told officials in Washington that sentences of twenty-five years were becoming the norm and that objectors were being convicted on unfair grounds—like refusing to pick up a rake. In April, the secretary of war, Newton Baker, had said that objectors could be court-martialed if they refused to work and, moreover, showed signs of being insincere or defiant.[5]

Now, Baldwin argued, military courts were finding sullenness or insincerity in every case. How can the military fairly judge whether someone is sincere? How would one go about identifying sullenness in a young man whose noncooperation is driven by a religious or moral stance against warfare? But the challenges from the civil liberties bureau touched a nerve in Washington. In a letter on May 19, Frederick P. Keppel, a former Columbia University dean who served as the assistant secretary of war responsible for conscientious objectors, told Baldwin that the government had had enough—the bureau was aiding slackers and encouraging conscientious objectors; the Army would no longer cooperate with requests for information from the National Civil Liberties Bureau. An ally of the objectors may have been sidelined, but not silenced, as the government would learn in the coming months.

Accused of Violating Two Articles of War

The Hofer brothers and Jacob Wipf were tried jointly on June 10, with six military men—two lieutenants, two sergeants, a corporal, and a private—called up as witnesses at the court-martial. Harol D. Coburn, a lieutenant colonel, served as president of the court-martial. Henry Harmeling, a second lieutenant, served as the judge advocate, or the chief prosecutor; James D. Fletcher, a second lieutenant, was on hand as the assistant judge advocate.

Looking across the courtroom at Camp Lewis, the Hutterites counted, in addition to Lieutenant Colonel Coburn, thirteen officers who would sit in judgment (a mix of majors and captains, seated according to rank). A verdict in this case required only a simple majority (and the commanding general, who reviewed decisions, could even then reject the verdict).

The most common charges against pacifists thus far in the war were two related violations of the Articles of War, disobeying a superior officer (No. 64) and disobeying a noncommissioned officer (No. 65). The four Hutterites stood accused of doing both. The men were charged with violating the Sixty-fourth Article of War on two separate occasions by failing to follow the orders of superior officers. Only a few hours after they arrived at Camp Lewis, on May 28, and before their uniforms had been issued, Robert S. Shertzer, a second lieutenant, commanded them to fall in with their platoon, a formation known as retreat, the first step in organizing the company. They refused. Then a few days later, on June 2, William V. Clarke, also a second lieutenant, ordered the men to sign enlistment and assignment cards, and this too, they would not do. The men were also charged with disobeying an order from Reynolds B. Hilt, a sergeant, who, like Lieutenant Shertzer, had commanded the men to fall in with their platoon on May 28. In disregarding this order from a noncommissioned officer, the military authorities said, the men had violated the Sixty-fifth Article of War. The Hutterites pleaded not guilty to both charges.

"Soldiers" Refuse to Sign "Statement of Soldier"

In the opening testimony, Lieutenant Clarke described overseeing the preparation of the enlistment and assignment cards—the "E. and A." cards, as he called them—in the mustering office on that first Sunday in June, a few days after the men had arrived. Clarke said that he explained to the Hutterite men that they had to sign the cards, that every incoming recruit had to do so. The men were to fill in the name of the town and state where they were born, their age, and their occupation—nothing more than basic biographical information. He told them that if they refused to do so, they could be subject to prison terms of two to twenty-five years. They replied that they couldn't sign the forms, he said, because the heading read "Statement of

Soldier."[6] Clarke continued: "I explained to them that by being drafted into the army, that they were already soldiers."

Joseph S. Gibson, a corporal, was there in the mustering office that day, and he testified next. In confirming Lieutenant Clarke's account, Corporal Gibson noted that the lieutenant had offered each of the men a pen with which to sign the cards. One of the Hofer brothers seemed poised to sign the card, Gibson said, but then Jacob Wipf said "something in a foreign language." Corporal Gibson said he heard the word "nicht" ("no") and thought the men were speaking in German, but he couldn't understand what was said. After that, none of the men signed the cards. Steward J. Dean, a private who was sworn in as the third witness, confirmed these accounts.

Lieutenant Shertzer, who was next on the witness stand, recalled that he met the Hutterite men at the barracks on the day of their arrival at Camp Lewis. All of the men in the Twenty-ninth Company were lined up alphabetically; Shertzer was at the receiving end of the line with the typist, who was taking down names and other information from each recruit. The four Hutterites suddenly stepped out of the line—the Hofer brothers at their place toward the front of the line and Jacob Wipf toward the back—and asked to be put together. A sergeant came up to Shertzer, with a smile, and said, "These men over here, they just came along, and said, 'This is as far as we go.'" The sergeant asked Shertzer what he should do. Shertzer said he would talk to the men in a little while. Meanwhile, the Hutterites went to stand next to the barracks window where clerks issued each man blankets, a bed sack, and a toilet kit. Shertzer said he approached the men a short time later and recalled the conversation.

Shertzer: What is the matter?
Hutterites: We won't sign anything.
Shertzer: You must sign up for blankets if you want any, if you want to sleep here.
Hutterites: We can't sign any papers. We don't believe in war. We won't do anything for the army.
Shertzer: You will have to do that, if you want to sleep here.

Shertzer left the men at that point, and when he returned, they had indeed signed up to receive blankets but remained standing outside the barracks. He invited them to join him in an office inside to talk about what was still troubling them. They pulled out a paper addressed to Mennonites by Secretary Baker and endorsed by President Wilson. Shertzer did not recall or note many of the particulars, but the paper indicated that conscientious objectors would not have to serve in the army. Shertzer responded, "I will show you the orders that bind me," and he withdrew a paper that spelled out the duties of conscientious objectors, including that they take sanitary care of themselves and their sleeping quarters.

The Hutterites then showed the lieutenant their certificates of membership in the church. Either David Hofer or Jacob Wipf spoke up, Shertzer said, saying, "Well, boys, we can't do it. We can't do anything in the army. Our religion is against it." Shertzer responded: "I explained to them that until their case was decided, they would have to do what the rest of them there did. We didn't have uniforms for the men, anyway. I intended to treat them very fairly." He had the clerk take down their names for exemption claims.

Men Who "Won't Fall In"

At five o'clock that afternoon, Shertzer said, the company was divided into two squads, with Shertzer taking charge of one group and Sergeant Hilt the other. The Hutterites were assigned to Hilt's section. When Shertzer checked on Hilt's group, he found the Hutterites standing up against the barracks.

Shertzer: What is the matter with those four men?

Hilt: They won't fall in.

Shertzer: They will fall in.

To the Hutterites, Shertzer said: Here, you men fall in that last squad there.

Hutterites: We can't do anything like that.

Shertzer: I explained to you men about this. This has nothing to do with fighting. I read the orders to you, and you will have to obey orders or else you will have to go to the guardhouse.

Hutterites: We can't.

Shertzer: Sergeant, take them over to the office. We will have to put
   them in the guardhouse.

Prosecutor Harmeling then asked Shertzer whether the men appeared
to be defiant or sullen, a crucial point in determining their possible guilt.
Shertzer's response suggested that military officers themselves were not of
a single mind as to what qualified as defiant and sullen.

Shertzer: No, sir; it wasn't exactly that, unless you say defiant and sul-
   len means that they came here with the intention of disobeying,
   and not doing anything that was required in the military line. . . .
   They intended not to obey anything. But, they were meek about it.
   But they were not defiant in the sense that you usually think of the
   word defiant.
Prosecutor: Did they offer any explanation?
Shertzer: Yes, sir; they were always explaining.

Sergeant Hilt, who testified next, suggested that, like Lieutenant Shertzer,
he tried to be fair to the Hutterites when asking them to line up for retreat,
for parade rest, that first afternoon. He even made a special allowance so
that they could stand together.

Hilt: "I told them to fall in with the rest of the men, and showed them
where to line up. I had a place for them—all four in the same place." The
men shook their heads, he said, and said they couldn't line up with the
others.

The prosecution rested its case. Before the Hutterite defendants were
called to the stand, the presiding officer at the court-martial, Lieutenant
Colonel Coburn, wanted to be sure that they understood their rights, including the right to testify in court and to submit a separate written statement. He offered a rapid-fire summary in a legal language that nonlawyers
in the room would have been hard-pressed to follow.

President: You may also make an unsworn verbal or written statement of the case, which may consist of a brief summary or version of the evidence, with such explanation or allegation of motive,
   excuse, matter of extenuation, etc., as you may desire to offer, or it
   may embrace with the facts, a presentation also of the law of the

case and an argument both upon the fact and the law. . . . Do you fully understand all that I have said to you?

Michael Hofer: Not quite all of it.

Jacob Wipf Takes the Stand

The defense attorney, Lieutenant Albee, took over, trying his best to translate the legal terms into plain English. Jacob Wipf then approached the bench as the first defendant to be examined. To the close observer, the clash of worldviews was immediately apparent. In keeping with American legal custom, the judge waited for Wipf *to swear* to tell the truth. But for generations, Hutterites and other Anabaptists had declined to offer such an oath.

Since Jesus told his disciples in Matthew 5 not to offer oaths—"Do not swear at all: either by heaven, for it is God's throne; or by the earth, for it is his footstool"—they would answer simply and honestly, letting their yes be yes, and their no be no. An oath implies that some guarantee is needed to ensure that the truth will be told. The four men on trial would have said that Christians should always tell the truth, under oath or not. When in court, Anabaptists reached for an alternative to swearing, which judges generally accepted—and as Lieutenant Colonel Coburn did on this day. So the trial continued, with Wipf *affirming* to tell the truth.

The early line of questioning pursued the Hutterites' possible links to the enemy, Germany:

Q: Now, what are the principles of your religious organization as they have existed from the beginning? That is, with regard to participation in war?

A: I don't understand that, quite.

Q: Are the members of your church permitted by your church principles to engage in war?

A: They are strictly against war. That is why we left Russia.

Q: Are you forbidden to be a soldier?

A: Yes.

Q: Are you loyal to Germany?

A: What does that mean?

Q: Are you in favor of Germany?

A: No; no.

Q: Why do you use the German language and the German printing in your work?

A: Well, they started there in Germany, and they just kept going as a colony and always kept talking like this. But my father can speak the Russian language. But, we have never gotten out in the world, and just kept that language because they started in Germany.

Q: You have no particular liking then, for the ideals or citizenship of Germany?

A: We have nothing for Germany.

The prosecutor wanted to know exactly why the men would not serve in the armed forces in any capacity.

Q: Are you willing to take part in any noncombatant branch of the service of the army?

A: No; we can't.

Q: What are your reasons?

A: Well, it is all for war. The only thing we can do is work on a farm for the poor and needy ones of the United States.

Q: What do you mean by poor and needy ones?

A: Well those that can't help themselves.

Q: Would you include soldiers who are crippled for life?

A: Yes. They are poor and needy ones. . . .

Q: If you were in the service, such as the Medical Corps, where you would attend the wounded soldiers, would your conscience and the teachings of the church permit that?

A: We can't do that, because a soldier, he will go and fight, and that is helping the war, and we can't do that.

Q: And if there were wounded soldiers about, you couldn't help them? You couldn't help them because you would be afraid they might recover and go back to the war; is that it?

A: Well, it would be helping the war.

Q: Would you be willing to be placed on a farm by the government
and grow wheat for soldiers?

A: No.

The prosecutor then wanted to know if the commitment to nonviolence
extended to the home.

Q: Does your religion believe in fighting of any kind?

A: No.

Q: You would not fight with your fists?

A: Well, we ain't no angels. Little boys will scrap sometimes, and we
are punished; but our religion don't allow it.

Q: To put the case like this: If a man was attacking or assaulting your
sister, would you fight?

A: No.

Q: Would you kill him?

A: No.

Q: What would you do?

A: Well, in a way, if I could get her away, I might hold him. If I was
man enough, I would do that. If I couldn't, I would have to let go.
We can't kill. That is strictly against our religion.

As exhibit A the prosecutor offered a note that had been prepared by
John W. Kliewer, the president of Bethel College and a Mennonite Church
leader from Kansas, and Peter H. Unruh, a Mennonite who had been active in representing the church's interests in Washington. Their note, dated
April 10, offered counsel for "Mennonites in Training Camps." The note
described the work options open to noncombatants in the Medical Corps,
the Quartermaster Corps, and the Engineering Service. The draftees, they
said, could do the prescribed work or refuse and receive detention. They
wrote: "The conscience of each must decide what he will choose." These
two Mennonite Church leaders were comfortable in having men accept
noncombatant assignments; what the prosecutor did not say and perhaps
did not know was that other Mennonite Church leaders were unwilling to
make such a compromise.

The prosecutor forged ahead, suggesting that this memo gave the Hutterites the church's blessing to accept work at the camp. Wipf responded that if he worked in the Medical Corps or the Quartermaster Corps, if he did any work linked to the army, he would be thrown out of *his* church, the Hutterite community. As often happened during the war, when outsiders conflated the Hutterites and Mennonites, they sowed confusion. Later questioning would establish that the four Hutterite men were not familiar with the specific teachings of the Mennonites and regarded them as having a separate religion, even if they shared European Anabaptist roots. At the colonies in South Dakota, Hutterite leaders had been quite clear in stating their opposition to work in the military camps.

The Hofer Brothers Testify

The prosecution then called David Hofer to testify, anticipating that the four men who held so much in common would not offer much variance on the witness stand. Hofer met with only one-fifth as many questions as had been put to Wipf.

Q: Have you any sympathies,—I mean, do you favor the cause of Germany as against the United States in any way?

A: Well I ain't got nothing for Germany. I wouldn't talk one word for Germany, because they done our old folks.

Q: They persecuted you?

A: Yes; killed just thousands of our old folks four hundred years ago.

Q: Would you be willing to grow wheat for the poor and needy ones?

A: If it would go for the poor and needy ones. . . .

Q: Do you pay taxes?

A: Yes, sir.

Q: Do you vote?

A: No; never voted. None of our members never voted. We don't take any part in this world; not a bit. If we are persecuted there, we go to another one, just like Christ said. If the government wants us to go out, we leave our property right there and go out.

Michael Hofer followed, facing even fewer questions and offering the tersest of answers.

Q: Do you believe that you cannot do anything to help the war in any
way in behalf of the United States?
A: I can't do anything for war.

The final defendant on the stand, Joseph, ended with a testimonial, reminding the court of the religious imperative behind all the words and
actions of these brothers from the Rockport Colony.

Q: Do you personally believe that you could not take part in war in
any form?
A: I do believe that we can't take any part in the war.
Q: Why do you believe that?
A: Why do I believe that? Well, Christ says that you shall not kill. We
confessed that this is right, and my conscience tells me that.

When Joseph Hofer finished testifying, Lieutenant Albee, the defense
counselor, said, "It is recognized that this case does not come within the
ordinary conscientious objector class where the objector is asking noncombatant service, and it is a delicate case to handle on that account." The testimony of the men had made clear the beliefs of the church, he said. But he
wanted to add for the record, "for my own satisfaction," that he had read an
article written by Peter Riedemann, the early Hutterite leader.

The article offers a "very straight statement that no Christian can take
part in war, or draw the sword in any manner." "Therefore, a Christian
should neither carry on war nor bear any worldly sword, as also St. Paul
warns us and says (Romans 12), 'Do not revenge yourselves dear brothers, but give way to anger'—that is, let anger pass by—'for the Lord says,
revenge is mine; I will repay.' And it goes on, in the words of the author,
thereafter, to state that no man shall draw the sword." With that final appeal
to a biblical mandate, the defense rested its case. The prosecutor made no
closing statement. The court adjourned at 4:20 p.m., less than three hours
after the proceedings had begun.

To readers of the court-martial transcript nearly a century later, the Hutterites appear to be at pains to answer their interlocutors honestly and politely. On multiple occasions, they confess to being confused about a point.
While they were clear in stating that they could not personally take any

actions that would, to them, signify support for the war, their justification was often limited to saying that they were duty bound to obey the church; they did not speak ill of other draftees who chose to participate in the military or question whether the United States was justified in declaring war against Germany. They also were reticent witnesses. They did not elaborate on the church's teachings on peace or present a personal appeal or convey their keen interest in the farm furlough program. Preparing in advance for the trial might not have altered the outcome, but it would have given the men a more forceful defense and, in the church's interest, more compelling testimony.

A More Robust Defense

The Hutterites' limited trial preparation stood in contrast to that of Amos Showalter, a Mennonite college graduate who came from a long line of ministers in Virginia. In the same month that the Hutterites stood trial, Showalter graduated from Goshen College in Indiana with a bachelor's degree in biology and left almost immediately for Camp Funston in Kansas. He arrived ready to contribute as a noncombatant soldier. At the outset, he agreed to scrub floors at a base hospital but apparently changed his mind after one day. At his court-martial on October 23, 1918, he presented an unusually eloquent defense of his position, one that the Hutterites would likely have embraced. His fluency was possible in part because he had prepared a written statement to be shared in court:

> But I cannot take part in any enterprise which involves that destruction of human life, no matter how depraved or degraded that life may be or how worthy the ultimate purpose of that enterprise. I cannot perform duties in any branch of the military establishment because in so doing I feel that I would be instrumental in the taking of human life and therefore guilty of murder. Since my early childhood I have been taught the religious principle of non-resistance which Jesus expressed when he said "Love your enemies; do good to them which hate and pray for them to suffer injury, abuse or insult rather than to recompense injury, abuse or insult for their like," and this teaching has been the mould in which my character was cast.[7]

Even in cross-examination, Showalter conveyed thoughtful composure in responding to the prosecutor, Second Lieutenant George Imbrie:

> Q: Private Showalter, do you believe in the American institutions?
> A: Will you explain that question please?
> Q: Do you believe in the American government?
> A: I do.
> Q: Do you believe in supporting it?
> A: I do in so far as I can.
> Q: What do you mean by "in so far as I can"?
> A: So long as it does not conflict with my belief and my duties towards God.[8]

Despite Showalter's measured responses, Imbrie was not impressed, branding noncombatants "cowards" who hid behind the "skirts of their women" and "from the bayonets of the Huns in Europe." Showalter was sentenced to life imprisonment, which was subsequently reduced to twenty-five years, to be served at Fort Leavenworth.[9]

Thoughts Turn to Home

The Hofer brothers and Jacob Wipf believed they had acquitted themselves reasonably well in the courtroom, especially given the high stakes and the newness of all that unfolded. David Hofer wrote to share his thoughts with his wife, Anna:

> That was a difficult test. Dear spouse, that is something our dear brothers, fathers and patriarchs never had to do, what we young brothers in faith had to do. We had to defend our beliefs in front of the twelve sworn-in ones. But God stood at our side, and gave us voice and wisdom and a calm heart. I had no more fear than I would have if I were at home. Then they asked us if we could work on a farm raising wheat for a soldier. We said no, but if you would send us to the farm of poor suffering people, we could work there. Maybe we said too much, but it seems to us that we could work in such a situation, because our brothers had said that if the government would put us on a farm by ourselves, there we could work. There our preachers could visit us, perhaps

also our families. Dear spouse, if only our heavenly father could lead us out of this misery, no matter where, even if into dire poverty.[10]

For his part, Michael wanted his wife, Maria, to know that "God our Heavenly Father still cares for us":

[The military officials] also don't know what they should do with us. They have told us that everything must go to the president. He will decide what will be done with us. God the Lord will take care of his own. He also will not forsake us if we only continue to trust in him. The prophet said, Lord, when there is affliction, then men search for you. When you discipline them, then they call out to you in fear. My dear spouse, we paid too little attention to the wonderful time of grace. For now one is able to see what he is missing when the community is taken away—namely, when evening descends and we could all gather nicely for prayer. We, however, must accept it with patience, and say with the poet: when the just person is in pain, God wants to make him joyful, and those with broken hearts should laugh again. While a Christian is here [on earth] he must walk through streets of sadness, but I will stand by him, the highest trust and help in the midst of everything.[11]

Joseph, too, wrote to his wife, Maria, a day after the court-martial, with a sense of resignation:

Now my dear spouse, we are still imprisoned in the guardhouse. But we were not at home—that is, in the guardhouse—when your letter arrived. We were before the court being court-martialed. We do not know, however, how things will turn out. Our case will come before Newton Diehl Baker, the Secretary of War in Washington. Whatever they make of it we will have to accept. There is someone here who has been in prison for five years. But this does not alarm us. God is with us. And if God is with us, who can be against us?[12]

Eldo Thiese, one of the "Hanson County boys" who had traveled to Camp Lewis by train with the Hutterites, also wrote home after the trial. He told his parents that all of their officers were present at the court martial. The charges against the four men made him feel personally vindicated for participating in the beard assault on the train: "We surely get credit now for trimming them up on the way out. I will bet the next bunch will do what they are told."[13]

Sentence Announced: Twenty Years of Hard Labor

Though the four Hutterites may have heard the news earlier, Lieutenant Colonel George V. Strong, the judge advocate for the division at Camp Lewis, formally issued the verdict five days later, in a memo to the judge advocate general of the army. Less than three weeks after their arrival at Camp Lewis, all four men were found guilty of all charges. Each was to be dishonorably discharged, to give up all pay, and to be sentenced to twenty years of hard labor, "at such place as the reviewing authority may direct." Strong noted that a psychiatric examination of the men prior to the trial showed that each of the men was mentally normal and fully aware of what he was doing in disobeying the orders—indeed, they had determined to take that step before arriving at camp.

The reasoning applied by the military tribunal seemed to be that anyone of sound mind who refused the military's offer of noncombatant service, an offer reasonably and generously made, must be insincere. The tribunal also regarded these men as soldiers. In refusing to obey orders, the men were disobedient soldiers. By that assumption and logic, the Hutterites stood no chance in securing a different outcome. They saw themselves as Christians, not soldiers; and as Christians their refusal to obey military orders was a sure sign of sincerity. The Hutterites and military officials were talking to one another across kingdom walls.

The Hofer brothers and Jacob Wipf were among 504 conscientious objectors who were court-martialed during the war, resulting in 503 convictions and a single acquittal (John J. Entz, a Hutterite from Hutchinson County, South Dakota, was acquitted in February 1919 on a technicality).[14] Of the men who were court-martialed, about 142 were believed to be Mennonite, Amish, or Hutterite, which gave these closely linked sects the largest share of imprisoned believers.[15] Of the 142, eight were Hutterite. The inconsistency in the punishment meted out to convicted conscientious objectors is striking. The first Mennonite to be court-martialed was Elmer Hershberger, who was brought up on charges a month before the four Hutterites, on May 5, 1918. He was convicted after failing to rake leaves and perform other work. A majority of the courts-martial of Mennonites took place in two months, May (34) and June (48) of 1918.[16] Some camps relied more heavily than others on the court-martial enforcement. Camp Travis, Texas, led all cantonments by putting thirty-three men on trial; next was Camp Funston, Kansas, with thirty-one; Camp Zachary Taylor, Kentucky, twenty-eight; and Camp Cody, New Mexico, fifteen.

Of the Mennonites court-martialed, one received a sentence of three months, the most lenient punishment; one person, a sentence of two years; and another person, three years. Six men received five years; thirty-three men, ten years; eighteen men, fifteen years; nine men, twenty years; and sixty-one men, twenty-five years. One person each received thirty years, thirty-five years, and forty years.[17] Given the spread of sentences, the Hofer brothers and Jacob Wipf fell in the median, receiving an average sentence for objectors. Roger Baldwin of the National Civil Liberties Bureau would have told the men that the long sentences were given "for moral effect," and they should be released soon after the war ended.[18] Their letters reveal that they fully expected to serve out their full terms—if they lived long enough to do so.

Perhaps most striking is the severity of the sentencing for men who reported to training camps and then refused to serve compared with those who were drafted and fled or those who failed to report for duty. David B. Hostetler, a Mennonite draftee from Reedsville, Pennsylvania, never reported for duty at Camp Meade, Maryland, in April 1918. Hostetler (who happened to be a distant relative of Joseph C. Hostetler, Secretary Baker's law partner) was arrested on April 30 and court-martialed eight days after the Hutterites, on June 18, and sentenced to only five years. One would think that a draftee who traveled to camp and then refused to perform service would be seen in a more favorable light than someone who refused even the initial order to report to camp. Another Mennonite, Oscar Ervin Hartman of Fulks Run, Virginia, went into hiding instead of reporting to Camp Lee, Virginia. During the war he actually held down jobs at local lumber mills and slept in the woods at night. Finally, on June 1, 1920, he turned himself in at Camp Humphreys, Virginia. A court-martial followed the next month. Found guilty, Hartman received three months of hard labor.

The first draft defiers to be sentenced in the West were Albert Bloss Jr., a teacher of manual training, and Walfred Marker, a dairyman, both from Seattle. They refused to report to training camp, citing their opposition to the war. Because they did not belong to a peace church, they were denied the exemption available to conscientious objectors. Still, they were sentenced to ten years at Alcatraz, half as long as the Hutterites, who did report to camp and did belong to a peace church. Even draftees who fled the country were sentenced to fewer years. John B. and David G. Goertzen of Henderson, Nebraska, escaped to Canada and returned after the war. They were court-martialed in May 1920. They were sentenced to two and three years, respectively, relatively light sentences, perhaps because the war was recent history. In the case of the Goertzens, though, as deserters they also lost their citizenship (which would not be restored until ten years later).

By war's end, the army reported that 337,000 men failed to show up for service when called, but as many as three million evaded the draft by failing to register as required in the first place (numerically, at least, evaders posed much more of a threat to the war effort than did objectors).[19] The majority of these men suffered no penalty for their actions. In any event, failing to register for the draft was regarded as a civil offense, subject to relatively mild penalties in federal court.[20] As the Hutterites learned, military justice was less forgiving.

In the weeks that followed, the Hutterite men at Camp Lewis remained confined in the guardhouse. During the day they were able to read their Bibles and hold their own worship services, though they could not sing aloud. ("But one can also praise our great God in stillness," Michael wrote.[21]) Like Michael, David said that he too went from window to window, never seeing anyone that he knew. In this place, he said, he often thought of his small children at home—and why God would have these four fathers go through this experience. "Sometimes I think so much about it that I would like to scream, but that is of no use," he wrote. "One has to have patience until it seems to God that it is time to lead us out of this misery."[22]

For Joseph, one of the greatest challenges was the tedium that came with being locked in a guardhouse:

> We are now very well treated, ever since we were court-martialed. We have not had any temptations. But the "sitting around" is not for a person who is used to working. But we must wait with patience to see what our loving heavenly father allows to happen to us, and must accept it. Who knows to what end? Certainly not for any harm, but rather for the benefit of our poor souls.[23]

Andrew Wurtz Undergoes His Own Trial

On Friday, June 14, just before bedtime, the authorities came and took away Andrew Wurtz, the Hutterite who arrived with the Hofers and Jacob Wipf, and a Mennonite detainee. Wurtz returned on Sunday morning, only to be removed again on Monday afternoon, this time to the base hospital. On July 1, Michael Hofer reported that they had no news of the whereabouts of "Brother Andreas." Andrew Wurtz would later detail the efforts to which military officials went to compel him, when he was isolated from the others, to work. Once a sergeant ordered him to polish the soft wood floor of a barracks. Wurtz refused, saying that to do so would advance the war effort:

> [The] sergeant ordered ropes brought which were used to bind each leg and while I had the polisher handle, they pulled one leg at a time. Suddenly, they pulled both ropes, causing me to fall backwards, hurting my back and head and rendering me unconscious. They pulled me along the floor, up and down the hallway over the door ledges. I uttered an outcry—the slivers from the floor had penetrated my entire body. (I had only a light T-shirt and pyjamas on.)
>
> Yet, that was not enough; next, they took me into my room, filled the bathtub with cold water, told me to remove my clothes (which I did) and forced me under the water. I tried to hold my breath but could not; the four men could not hold me under the water. They tried again; I saw that I was becoming unsuccessful in my attempt to hold my breath. I said, "In Jesus name,

I have to give up my life; I hold my promise that I promised on my knees."
They held me under the water till they thought that by this time I should be
expired. They lifted me out of the water and all I heard them say was that
they would be back later to do it again. Around twelve o'clock they took my
pulse and I heard them say that I was still living.[24]

Behind the scenes, through private correspondence, Joseph Kleinsasser,
a Hutterite minister from the Milltown Colony in South Dakota, took up the
cause of the five men, as he had for other Hutterite conscientious objectors.
Earlier that spring he had written to Frederick Keppel, the assistant secretary of war responsible for conscientious objectors, asking that Hutterite
men be allowed to do farm work. He argued that there was "no wisdom in
taking Hutterite men away from their families and farms" only to lock them
up in military camps. "Ain't the U.S. in need of many farms?" he asked.
"Have they no use for grain or meat?"[25]

Now he wrote to Keppel, urgently asking him to intervene so that the men
at Camp Lewis would be treated less harshly. He was especially concerned
about the lengths to which camp officials had gone to persuade Wurtz to
work. Kleinsasser did not mince words: "They tortured him and [came]
pretty near [to] killing him. For 2 weeks they put him in water every day,
and held him there until he was stiff and could not move a limb anymore.
. . . Now dear friend Keppel, is there no reasonable way to find out a person's
convictions, or stand, or religion? Is it necessary to torture people to find
out his religion?" Kleinsasser was among the first peace church leaders to
characterize the treatment of the objectors, at least in this case, as torture.

Two weeks into their confinement, the Hofer brothers and Jacob Wipf
said that they had not yet heard from their wives and family members at
home. Joseph seemed surprised that he had not received more letters and
that he and the others had not had any visitors from home:

We are still in good health, both in body and soul. But you can imagine, dear
spouse, how one might be disposed when you are gone from home for three
weeks and have received only three letters from home and also have not seen
anyone, so that it appears as if everyone is afraid to come here. What should
we do here all alone?[26]

While nearly all of the surviving prison letters are those sent by the men to their wives, several of the letters that carried news from home began to arrive in mid-June, just after the court-martial. It's clear that some of the letters posted from South Dakota never reached the men because when Anna Hofer wrote to her husband, David, on June 14, she assured him that she had already written five letters, two of which were returned. She said she kept track of the passing time by counting the Sabbaths. "Yesterday was the sixth Sunday already and God knows how many more Sundays it will be until we see each other with our mortal eyes, perhaps never more in this world, but we hope to see each other in glory."[27] In a second letter, she added, "Dear David, it appears that I will have to spend my life with my children by myself."[28]

Susanna Hofer, mother of the three brothers, urged her boys to hold fast:

May he continue to be with you and comfort you in your misery, as he has promised that he will be with us until the end of the world. Let us only trust him. My dearly beloved children, what dangerous days are coming upon us, and it is probably as our Savior has said, that faith will be no more and love will lose its warmth and injustice will take over. Let's not give up in the tribulation that has come upon us.[29]

In writing to the imprisoned men, Joseph J. Wipf, a minister at Rockport and Jacob's uncle, was more frank than immediate family members in his account of how they were faring at home. He noted that three other young men from Rockport had shipped out to a military camp; during the war, Rockport would send ten men to army camps, more than any other colony.[30] He also reported that Jacob Wipf's father was among a group of men who had traveled to Canada to purchase land for new colonies, "because the way it seems we cannot stay here, for we are not safe on any roads and highways." Wipf recounted a story that must have given the four men a flashback to their time on the train: "Today they attacked our brothers and wanted to shear them; they were twenty-five and six of ours, but the way it seems, God did not permit them to do this, for the clippers didn't cut, and they returned home unscathed."[31]

On Saturday, June 22, the Hofer brothers and Jacob Wipf learned that they would be sent to Alcatraz in the coming weeks. Michael Hofer wrote home as one whose faith was being sorely tested, but had stayed strong:

> We are completely yielded to the Lord. Whatever burdens he gives, he also provides a way out that we can endure it. . . . For God will also be with us there (that is, Alcatraz). He has promised to his own, that when they pass through the fire, he will stand beside them so that the flames do not burn them. "And if you go through the water, I will protect you so that you do not drown in the torrent."[32]

Beyond having faith in the Lord's protection during whatever trials might befall him on earth, Michael also kept his eye on the promise of an eternal reward. In the last letter that he sent from Camp Lewis, he focused on better days to come: "For nothing else is promised to us except that we must enter the kingdom of God through the cross and suffering."[33]

The day after finding out that they were bound for Alcatraz, Joseph wrote one of his longest letters home, equivalent to more than two typewritten pages. Clearly, the weight of the twenty-year term hung heavy about him as he wrote to Maria, "my dear and never-to-be-forgotten spouse." He saw only suffering ahead, and then a reward:

> We, however, must hold firmly to God and plead to him with prayers for the strength of his Holy Spirit, so that we might win the battle and remain firm unto the end, and fight for truth as so many of our forefathers did who came out of the fight with bloodied heads. And now they are yonder and have received their reward. And, dear spouse, if we want to go there where they are now, then we must also follow in their footsteps and give heed to their faith. For the children of God are called to nothing else than to affliction, cross, tribulation, persecution, and hatred from the world.[34]

The weeks that followed continued to test their spirits. He described the two high fences that surrounded the guardhouse in which they were locked up, "as if we were the worst scoundrels imaginable."[35] Increasingly, there are references to a reunion in heaven: "And if it should be that we do not see each other again in this sorrowful world, then it will hopefully happen yonder where no one can separate us again; where there will be no pain, no sorrow, no suffering, and instead there will be found there pure joy and happiness."

Meanwhile, the abusive treatment meted out to Andrew Wurtz had the desired effect. Wurtz agreed to work in the camp garden—but only alone, not in the company of men in uniform. He was able to visit with the Hofer brothers and Jacob Wipf on the night before they were transferred to Alcatraz. Wurtz would later be moved to a dairy farm where he carried manure compost for three months, until his release. The other four Hutterites, meanwhile, apparently suffered no immediate physical mistreatment over their refusal to work at Camp Lewis; in time, they would have their own horror stories to share.

While the Hofer brothers and Jacob Wipf prepared to head south to Alcatraz, most of the men at Camp Lewis traveled east, bound for the war. The Ninety-first Division, consisting of 27,000 men, shipped out between June 21 and 24 and then sailed for Europe in July. When the Ninety-first left, the Thirteenth moved in (the new men were still training in trench warfare at the camp when the armistice was signed). The first combat for the Ninety-first Division would come in September, at the Meuse-Argonne offensive.

Secretary Baker, who had been under pressure to supply the Allies with a timely and sufficient contingent of American troops, was pleased to report to the president on June 5 that the United States had more than met its commitment. The nation had supplied three hundred thousand troops in April and May instead of the one hundred twenty thousand pledged. By June 23, the nation had an army of nine hundred thousand men in Europe, about five months ahead of schedule. Four o'clock on that afternoon was "zero hour" for the 362nd Infantry from the Ninety-first Division at Camp Lewis: at that hour, the men started on their 7,000-mile trip to the trenches.

Objections Raised a Century Later

The treatment of the four Hutterite men appeared to fly in the face of the military's own expressed counsel in handling these cases. Through yet another instance of unfortunate timing for the men, this counsel arrived two weeks after their trial. The War Department issued a statement on June 25 calling for a sensible compromise with objectors who would not work—a compromise that would allow the men to avoid imprisonment. The reasonable alternative lay with farm furloughs, which had been available on the books for several months and would finally be put to use. The furloughs would allow men who would not lift a hand while in uniform to still make a valuable contribution:

> In short, every effort is being made to respect the sincere scruples of a small minority of our people, at the same time that their power to contribute to the nation's efficiency is turned to good account. There is unquestionably strong sentiment in many quarters against the granting of immunity from military service to any group in our population, however small. But many objectors are not without the courage of their convictions. They would resist compulsion to the end. We might imprison or shoot them. Prussian practices such as these would hardly appeal in a Democracy. On the other hand, a method which conserves the man-power of the nation, and accords to furloughed objectors a lot that is endurable and serviceable, but in no sense pampered, will, it is believed, commend itself to the common sense and practicability of the American people.[36]

The War Department's readiness to grant furloughs came as a relief to conscientious objectors across the country. But for those objectors whose cases had been expedited, the generous tone of the department's statement would bear little connection to the reality of life behind bars.

Deciding who would qualify for farm furloughs fell to the three legal experts who composed the Board of Inquiry. Early in the summer of 1918, the board members began to interview conscientious objectors and, by gauging their sincerity, place them in combatant or noncombatant service in the military, or, in cases where the men were judged sincere in their pacifist convictions and wanted to be as distant as possible from the military, on a farm selected by the government; in exceptional cases, the board could also recommend that an objector be assigned to reconstruction work in Europe under direction of the Society of Friends.

The board was made up of Major Richard C. Stoddard, chairman of the Judge Advocate's Office in the Army; Judge Julian W. Mack of the federal court, who had a reputation as being the most favorably inclined toward conscientious objectors among board members; and Dean Harlan F. Stone of Columbia University Law School, who would later become a chief justice of the U.S. Supreme Court. In August, Stoddard was sent overseas, replaced by Major Walter G. Kellogg, who also worked in the Judge Advocate's Office. In civil life, both Kellogg and Stoddard were lawyers. As of May 24, the Army had recorded 627 men (and counting) who had refused to work at camps across the country. These men were not to be forced to wear a uniform or bear arms if that went against their conscience. The board journeyed across the country to meet with the objectors, beginning at Camp Gordon along the coast in Georgia, and then visiting all camps east of the Mississippi, before heading west.

Members of the Board of Inquiry visited Camp Lewis on July 9 to interview the conscientious objectors there. They held three sessions that day, starting at 9 a.m. and finishing at 9:15 p.m. Objectors generally appeared before the board singly or in small groups. The three members of the board—Stoddard, Mack, and Stone—examined each man, judging whether he was sincere and deserving of noncombatant service or a furlough. Even while the panel members interviewed men at the camp, the Hofer brothers and Jacob Wipf were locked away in the nearby guardhouse, holding similar religious and moral convictions to those men being interviewed but having been convicted one month earlier. Norman Thomas, the publisher, socialist, and civil liberties leader, argued that no conscientious objector should be tried until he had been interviewed by the board. As it was, the Hutterites were among about two hundred men who were court-martialed before they had a chance to see the board.[37]

The board acknowledged the presence of the four Hutterites but classified them apart from the other objectors. The board report notes that the Hofer brothers and Jacob Wipf had already been court-martialed: "Therefore no opinion now expressed."[38] The board did not have authority to reconsider such court-martial cases. While board members may have informally visited with the four men that day, the Hutterites had already been judged and it was not theirs to conduct, in effect, an appeal. The Hutterites had been found guilty of failing to fall in and to sign the enlistment and assignment cards. These were regarded as orders that the men were bound to obey, even as conscientious objectors. They were not alone in refusing such orders, but they had the misfortune of receiving a timely trial, an example to be set for Andrew Wurtz and others.

If the four Hutterites had been kept in the guardhouse but not yet brought up on charges or tried by court-martial, it's highly likely that they would have had a chance to appear before the Board of Inquiry and would have been successful in their appeal for a furlough. The odds were favorable. The majority of recruits from the peace churches who refused noncombatant service were indeed found to be sincere and transferred to farms or to reconstruction work in Europe. Harlan Stone, the Columbia dean who sat on the board, said that in the large majority of cases the "task proved to be much simpler than had been anticipated."[39]

Of the twenty or so religious groups represented, the majority of men were Quakers, Mennonites, Hutterites, or members of other established sects (the less well-known included the Christadelphians and the Molokans or Holy Jumpers). In June and through the rest of the year, the board examined about 2,100 men, with only 122 being found insincere. The board recommended 1,500 for farm or industrial furlough; 88 for the Friends' Reconstruction Unit; 390 for noncombatant service; and 122 (those found insincere) for general military service.[40] Seventy-six percent of the men interviewed qualified for an assignment effectively outside of the military, either in the form of a farm furlough or reconstruction work overseas.

Kellogg said that, if an objector belonged to a well-recognized sect like the Hutterites, the board wanted to find out when he became a member and whether he had a certificate from the church. "If his answers were satisfactory and if he was in appearance and bearing an honest man," Kellogg said, "the Board was likely to find him sincere."[41] Men who were opposed to war but did not have church membership were more difficult to evaluate. In any case, however, he said, "The difficulty of determining the sincerity with which a conviction is held must be apparent to all."[42] If the high-powered legal minds on the Board of Inquiry deemed it so, one imagines how must more challenging it must have been for the officers in the Hutterite case to take a measure of their sincerity and render a fair decision.

Two other Hutterites from the Rockport Colony, Joseph Kleinsasser and Michael D. Hofer, point to the easier path that the Hofer brothers and

Jacob Wipf came so close to being able to take. Kleinsasser and Hofer, a first cousin to the Hofer brothers, left the colony for an army training camp one month later, on June 28. When they arrived at Camp Funston, they likewise refused to do any kind of service. But instead of being placed in a guardhouse and brought up on charges, they had an opportunity to appear before the Board of Inquiry, where they were found to be sincere in their stance. By September, both men were working on farms through the furlough program, while the Hofer brothers and Jacob Wipf languished in the steely, dark bowels of Alcatraz. Joseph Kleinsasser and the other Michael Hofer would be home in time for Christmas.

Chapter Five

The Dungeons of Alcatraz

They would let neither fire, water, sword, nor executioner terrify or persuade them. . . . They would accept neither glory nor kingdom, nor all the world's pleasures and goods in exchange for their faith in Christ, in whom they had their foundation and assurance.
—The Chronicle of the Hutterian Brethren

Traveling by Armed Guard

During the two months that the Hofer brothers and Jacob Wipf spent at Camp Lewis, records show, they never threatened an officer or attempted to escape. On the contrary, they appeared to be the most cooperative of prisoners, inclined to obey their superiors in every way that they in good conscience could (except, of course, by serving as soldiers). But when it came time to leave the camp on July 25, two months to the day after their induction into the army, they looked the part of hardened criminals. The men were chained together in pairs and placed in the escort of four armed lieutenants, who accompanied them by train to Alcatraz.[1]

The army's *Manual for Courts-Martial* made clear that prisoners should not be placed in irons "except in the extraordinary case" of a prisoner deemed a "desperate or dangerous character" at risk of escape.[2] This was, the 1918 manual promised, the time of a "more enlightened spirit of penology." Nevertheless, even though the guards removed the chains from the Hutterites' feet during the day, they kept their hands manacled at all times.

At night, the men lay on their backs, chained by hand and foot, a Hofer and a Hofer, a Hofer and a Wipf. They scarcely slept.

They arrived at San Francisco, tired and in shackles, on July 27, about to become intimate with a twenty-two-acre island home associated with some of the nation's worst miscreants. The island was formally designated the United States Disciplinary Barracks, Pacific Branch, but it was better known as Alcatraz, or simply "the Rock." Alcatraz served as one of three detention centers for military prisoners, the closest destination for convicts from Camp Lewis up the coast. The Atlantic Branch was at Fort Jay, New York. The Disciplinary Barracks at Fort Leavenworth, Kansas, served as the nation's chief military prison.

The ride to Alcatraz on a prison launch took roughly twenty minutes, charting a course due north across the San Francisco Bay, with Treasure Island and Yerba Buena visible off to the east and the wind blowing in from the west through the strait known as the Golden Gate, the passageway to the Pacific (construction of the bridge would not begin until 1933). The temperature was in the mid-sixties but felt colder, as it always did out on the bay. The men were chained together in the cabin of the launch, and the door between the cabin and the engine room was locked on the engine room side as a security precaution.

When the men arrived at Alcatraz, they disembarked at the island's only safe boat landing, the wharf where nearly a century later ferries deliver tourists every thirty minutes. Today visitors pay thirty dollars to take a ferry to the rockbound volcanic island. They walk by the empty cages in the cellhouse at the top of the island, listening on headsets to an audio tour and imagining what it would have been like to be hauled in chains to this forbidding place. The National Park Service, as it happened, inherited the bay's second treasure island after the federal government closed the prison in 1963. The many proposals for the site included opening a gambling casino or a hotel and convention center. But simply allowing visitors to walk where criminals once walked, including four conscientious objectors from South Dakota, turns out to have been an inspired choice. More than 1.3 million tourists visit Alcatraz each year.

From the dock the Hofer brothers and Jacob Wipf climbed a path, passing the military guard barracks (built in 1906, closed in 1933), with the bay

The U.S. Disciplinary Barracks, Pacific Branch, was better known as Alcatraz, or "the Rock."
Golden Gate National Recreation Area, Park Archives, Interpretation Negative Collection (GOGA–2316)

off to their right. Gnarled trees marked the way, bending and twisting in the wind, the trunks always leaning out into the sun, where branches ended in wispy curls. The men walked under an arch of the guardhouse and through the entryway known as a sally port (1857–1901), within yards of a trapdoor through which soldiers gone bad were lowered into a dungeon in the 1800s. At the far end of the sally port they could see rifle slats in the brick walls, a reminder of when Alcatraz served as a defensive outpost (both Great Britain and the Confederate forces drew concern in the early years). Looking left, they might have had their first glimpse of the cellhouse on the hilltop, shaded by trees, its windows barred. Off to the right, just as the path curved sharply left in the first switchback, stood the Military Post Exchange (1910–1933), which served as a general store, cafeteria, barbershop, and post office.

Continuing up the hill, rock walls now blocked their view of the cellhouse, and the eye naturally turned out to the bay, glimpsing San Francisco, a mile and a quarter away. They passed one of the prison commandant's

The Hutterites would have had to climb a series of switchbacks to reach the cellhouse on top of the hill.
Golden Gate National Recreation Area, Park Archives, Barbara E. Corff Collection
(GOGA–36639)

favorite buildings, the schoolhouse (1918–1933), built to turn lives around. After several more switchbacks, the men reached the eighty-four-foot lighthouse, rebuilt in 1909 and visible for nineteen miles out to sea, an impressive sentinel for four farm boys from landlocked South Dakota. With a few steps they reached the massive barracks known as the cellhouse. A quotation from Alexander Pope, spread across the entrance in large letters, greeted them: "Hope Springs Eternal in the Human Breast."

Descending into the "Hole"

Each prisoner was to receive fatigue trousers, a belt, a fatigue blouse, two flannel shirts, two pair of shoes and socks, a woolen overcoat, a half bar of soap, a comb and hair brush, a toothbrush, a tooth powder can, and three blankets. The house rules ensured a standard welcome for all of the arrivals:[3]

*Atop the cellhouse entrance a quotation from Alexander Pope greeted
newcomers: "Hope springs eternal in the human breast."*
Golden Gate National Recreation Area, Park Archives, Office of Resource
Management Photo Collection (GOGA–18346.229)

- On admission each convict was searched and deprived of all possessions except clothing.
- He then took a bath and was issued prison dress. His hair was cut short, and he had to shave off any beard or mustache; however, during his last month of confinement he was allowed to grow a beard again, if he wished.
- Prisoners received a wholesome and sufficient ration (unless they were in solitary confinement, in which case they received 18 ounces of bread a day and as much water as they desired).

The orientation for the Hutterites came to a standstill after the bath. In keeping with regulations, the guards ordered them to put on their prison uniforms; when the men refused, the guards walked them down the first-floor corridor in Block A, alongside rows of stacked cells, to a locked door. The door opened to a flight of fourteen stairs leading down into darkness. In single file, they descended to the basement of the prison, a place of solitary confinement known as "the hole." In this dungeon, each man entered a cell under a sloping brick arch, six feet high at the uppermost point; the cell itself measured six and a half feet wide by eight feet deep. Guards left a uniform on the floor for each man. Before they left, a guard warned, "If you don't conform, you'll stay here 'till you give up the ghost like the four we carried out yesterday."[4]

Cold Currents Deter Escape

The setting of the prison contributed to its grimness and utility. Even if a prisoner managed to escape from a cell or otherwise break free on the island, the bay offered an effective natural deterrent. The waters surrounding the island average a frigid fifty-eight degrees, with strong currents running six to eight miles per hour, and the mainland at best more than a mile away. In 1926, Colonel G. Maury Cralle, who was then serving as the military commandant, was reported to have said, "Go ahead, swim!" in response to rumors of a planned mass escape.[5] Shortly before the Hutterites arrived, two convicts on a scavenger gang managed to elude a sentinel on the island during a heavy fog. They tried to reach a nearby rock outcropping known as Little Alcatraz, each man swimming with his own log, lashed by the currents. One man made it to the island, where he was in effect stranded, left crying out for help; the other one drowned.

Two other prisoners (one sentenced for stealing thirty-one dollars at Camp Lewis, and the other for stealing seventy-five dollars) tried to take advantage of the influenza epidemic that was sweeping through San Francisco in 1918. After stealing uniforms and donning flu masks, they made off in an army launch. Several days later, they were caught. In one scheme noteworthy for its desperation, four prisoners put to sea in a butter vat stolen from the post bakery. When wind and tide turned against them, they went ashore back on Alcatraz and hid in an old powder magazine on the west side of the island. They were caught and soon back in irons. A dough-kneading trough proved to be no better a getaway vehicle later that year for three men who were quickly caught.

Daunting as the choppy waters may have been, escape was possible. In 1878, two prisoners commandeered a boat in a successful escape; and in 1884, two prisoners reached the mainland safely after they stole a boat. Four men whose stay overlapped with the Hutterites escaped from the island on a raft of pine boards during a storm that swept the bay the day after Thanksgiving in 1918; the authorities found the wreckage of the raft several days later and assumed that the men had drowned. But in February 1919 the police captured one of the men and from him learned that all four had safely escaped (for a time they were anxiously headed out toward the Pacific until a competing current sent them to shore) and then separated once on land; the other three remained at large.

During an inspection of Alcatraz the next month, Secretary Newton Baker commented on the forlornness of the setting, saying it was no wonder that men would try to escape. Most often, though, fleeing prisoners were caught or presumed drowned. The best odds for escape lay in a dash for freedom while assigned to a work party on the mainland.[6] At least nine men successfully fled from their work crews at Point San Jose in 1877.

Alcatraz's reputation as a fearsome prison came in large measure courtesy of the high-profile offenders sent to the island well after the Great War —Al Capone, George "Machine Gun" Kelly, Alvin Karpis, and other members of the criminal elite. A small, rocky island serving as a high-security federal prison had powerful associations. There was France's infamous Devil's Island, in the penal colony of French Guiana. An American author, Blair Niles, wrote a novel called *Condemned to Devil's Island* in 1928, a tale of starvation, dysentery, malaria, and solitary confinement, which was subsequently made into a movie, *Condemned*.

Alcatraz became, in the public mind, a foreboding prison shrouded in secrecy. In the movies that it inspired, conditions were inhumane, guards sadistic, and inmates ever resourceful. In *Escape from Alcatraz* Clint Eastwood played Frank Morris, who organized an actual 1962 escape; Sean Connery, in *The Rock*, starred as an imaginary inmate who saved San Francisco from a missile attack by right-wing fanatics.

Heralding the Science of Penology

The Hofer brothers and Jacob Wipf arrived at Alcatraz at a time when the prison administration took a very modern approach to rehabilitation, in keeping with the emerging science of penology. The title change in 1915 was one indicator: the Pacific Branch, Military Prison became the Pacific Branch, United States Disciplinary Barracks. Simple confinement and punishment would no longer suffice. Soldier-prisoners were on a redemptive path, even if they didn't know it when they arrived. They were assigned to one of several disciplinary companies and referred to as "disciples." Most were immediately appointed to the rank of first class. Men could wear a variation of a regular army uniform rather than the old inmate uniforms, which were stamped with the letter "P" for prisoner. Hard labor might be served while learning skills like blacksmithing and masonry. If all went well, the men would be returned to regular service.

The commandant at the prison was Colonel Joseph Garrard, who was assigned to Alcatraz in 1917 and spoke of the barracks as a reform school, a place for turning around lives. Garrard had graduated from West Point in 1873 and took part in a series of "campaigns" and "expeditions" against the Sioux and other Indians, as the Alcatraz newsletter, *The Rock*, politely phrased it. A retired colonel in the cavalry, he came from a long line of military and political royalty, including a great-grandfather, James Garrard, who was governor of Kentucky (1796–1804). By the time he took over at Alcatraz, Garrard had served nearly half a century in the U.S. Army.

An editorial published in *The Rock* six months before the Hutterites arrived noted that all prisoners, regardless of their previous conduct, had, in January 1918, been issued the highest conduct grade and "accorded all the privileges of first-class prisoners."[7] The editorial went on:

> It was the determination of the Commandant that no man here should enter upon the new year with a handicap upon his life if such a handicap could be removed. By the introduction of this new feature the men were assured of the kindly interest in their welfare on the part of those who had been placed in authority over them. They were given to understand that it is not the policy here to mete out punishment in a harsh, cruel manner for offenses

committed in days gone by, but rather, in the spirit of the broadest charity, to benefit them physically, intellectually, socially, and morally, so that at the end of their detention they may reenter society stronger and better men than they had ever been before.[8]

Indeed, *The Rock* itself, which was first published in 1915, was further evidence of the new disciplinary approach. The newsletter intended to "portray the reasonableness of justice and the beauty of compassion and tenderness." Mottos were stenciled on the white walls around the cellhouse, there to provide additional moral uplift: "The Stone Rejected by the Builder Has Become the Top of the Arch," "Hope Springs Eternal," and "The Objective of Life Is to Achieve Perfect Character."[9]

To become the better men that Alcatraz envisioned, prisoner-soldiers needed to abide by the rules, of which there were many. Whenever "The Star-Spangled Banner" was played or sung, all officers, enlisted men, and prisoners within hearing were expected to halt, face toward the flag, and, upon the last note, salute. Since "the discipline of a command may be correctly gauged by the state of its uniform," the men were expected to keep theirs "clean and spotless," and when out of doors, buttoned. Even personal belongings had their own proper place. They were to be put in a prescribed order on a shelf, with clothing and a towel at one end, and shoe polish, Bible, and regulations book at the other.

Regulations governed relations between prisoners and officers. When an officer passed by, prisoners were to halt, turn to the officer, and properly salute; if the officer was standing, passing prisoners were to salute while marching. In all conversations with an officer, the word "Sir" needed to precede all questions and end all replies. The word itself had to be spoken distinctly and with a rising inflection. Prisoners were to inspect the bulletin board each day after 5 p.m. to be familiar with regulations, both new orders and standing orders.

"Alcatrazians" Sample Culture and Classes

The commander, Colonel Garrard, took great pride in the educational and cultural offerings presented for the benefit of Alcatrazians, as residents of

the island, guards and prisoners alike, were known. After extensive reno-
vations, the assembly hall reopened on a celebrative note in January 1918,
bringing together inmates as well as several officers of the garrison and
their wives. An article in *The Rock* described the new look: "The hall presented an unusually attractive appearance. The ceilings had been painted a
pure white, while the walls were finished in a pea green and leaf green."[10]
To mark the occasion, a full band, directed by Claude Goldsbury, led the
inmates in songs like "Long Boy" and "Where Do We Go from Here." There
followed several moving pictures, including the five-reel comedy *Gift of
Gab*. The renovation included sprucing up the library and reading room,
where the shelves held 4,600 books and, among the recent contributions,
an unusual selection for a prison full of men: a complete set of the *Ladies
Home Journal* for 1917.

Visiting artists were the norm on the island. In the summer of 1917 the
newsletter noted that "Mr. Hother Wismer, one of the leading violinists of
San Francisco, whose name has become familiar to the men of this Institution because of the many pleasing concerts which he has given here, rendered another excellent program last Friday evening."[11] As at Camp Lewis,
the officers at Alcatraz encouraged men to become singing warriors. Chaplain James Ossewaarde led singing instruction on Thursday evenings, followed by an informal song service on Sunday evenings.

Essential to the rehabilitation was a prison school with departments for
educational, vocational, and military training. In the educational branch,
known as the graded school, inmates could study subjects like grammar,
reading, writing, and arithmetic. Once they progressed through this graded
school, they might qualify for a correspondence course with the University
of California in mechanics, freehand drawing, French, salesmanship, or
penmanship. The vocational branch offered training in masonry, carpentry,
printing, gardening, and other trades. Those inmates who were convicted
of strictly military offenses might enroll in the third branch, which covered subjects like drill ground tactics, bayonet combat, small arms firing,
castrametation (the art or science of laying out a camp), and patriotism. At
the beginning of 1918, about two hundred men were enrolled in the graded
school, 466 in vocational training, and 82 in military training.

In one class, "Instruction in Patriotism," Chaplain Ossewaarde, who was also the editor of *The Rock* newsletter, introduced the subject with the fire of a biblical prophet:

> The call "Wake Up America" was like a voice crying in the wilderness. Now, however, the awakening has come. We have been brought face to face with the fact that disloyalty is rampant within our national borders. Secret plottings against life and property have been brought to light. Attempts to paralyze the very life of our nation have been disclosed. We now know that in nearly all departments of our varied activities there are those whom we have regarded as loyal but who are conspirators and traitors. We have begun to realize that vast multitudes, especially among the foreign born population, are Americans in name but aliens at heart. Many enjoy the benefits which this country affords, grow fat on its richness, but they criticize it, condemn it, and despise its authority. In place of due appreciation expressed in unqualified allegiance we find that ingratitude which even bites the hand that is extended in loving ministration.[12]

Such rhetoric suggested that however well meaning the efforts at reform, these four Hutterite convicts, who hailed from the enemy nation of the Huns and still spoke German, arrived as marked men in the minds of prison officials like Ossewaarde.

The news from Europe no doubt inflamed Ossewaarde even more, when he compared the contrasting trajectories of fighting soldiers from Camp Lewis and the Hutterites he regarded as yellow-bellied cowards. The infantrymen, for their part, joined in the Allied offensive at the battle of Argonne in September, facing "days and nights of ceaseless shelling with shrapnel and high explosive and gas. They were bombed from the air and raked with machine guns of aviators and they never faltered. They came out tried and trusted veterans."[13]

In one measure of their success, the soldiers from the Ninety-first Division rolled back the German lines more than seven miles during the week of fighting. The conditions were arduous: "For days they lay, in rain and the bitter cold of night, without blankets, many without blouses even, chilled, hungry, exhausted, with eyes never closed in sleep for more than a brief nap, under heavy shelling until the line could be straightened and prepared for the next attack."

Conscientious Objectors as a "Pain in the Neck"

The military sent scores of conscientious objectors to Alcatraz between 1917 and 1920. By some accounts a hundred objectors in total were sent to Alcatraz, the majority actually arriving after the war had ended; many were transferred from Fort Leavenworth in 1919 after a series of uprisings there.[14] Most of the conscientious objectors, like the Hutterites, refused to drill or wear uniforms or comply in any way with the military authorities. They were of a different breed from, say, Private Charles Gruett, an infantryman who was convicted of stealing a nine-dollar overcoat at Camp Lewis and sentenced to Alcatraz for one year. As John A. Martini, a historian and former National Park Ranger assigned to Alcatraz, put it, "They were, in short, a pain in the neck to the island's commanding officer."[15]

While Colonel Garrard may have been predisposed to look on men like Gruett as candidates for reform, the conscientious objectors were counted an exception. Because they refused to cooperate, they became part of the "numbered prisoners" class of convicts, "men who had disgraced the army and were referred to only by registry number, never by name."[16] The officers set out to punish these men, not to reform them. If the men received work, it was breaking rock in the island's quarry, not learning how to launder shirts. The "numbers" men received all-black uniforms to set them apart from the convicts who were "disciples," and they lived in a separate part of the cellhouse—or in the dungeons below the cellhouse.

They were the lowest category of prisoner, relinquishing even their personal identity. The "numbers" couldn't converse with the first-class prisoners; they often couldn't even talk with each other. The only status lower than a regular "numbers" inmate was a "numbers" man who was undergoing solitary confinement in the barred alcoves in the dungeons, or, as the staff preferred to call the residence, lower solitary.[17] There were no lights in the dungeon. Prisoners were chained standing for eight or nine hours at a stretch. Meals were bread and water, or only water.

The island prison grew more tense when the military began adding conscientious objectors to the traditional mix of old-style deserters and chronic insubordinates. The army held no special animosity toward the old brand of prisoner, like Guy H. Broughton, a laboratory assistant in chemistry at the University of California who said he would rather go to prison than serve in the army. After less than two weeks in a cell at Alcatraz in late 1917, he asked to be shipped by train to the waters of American Lake at Camp Lewis. He was, in the mind of the authorities, a reasonable prisoner. Other men had a similar change of heart when the barred barracks of Alcatraz were looming. As one captain said: "We haven't tried a deserter here yet. All our prisoners have decided to go to American Lake willingly."[18]

But, as one Alcatraz author put it, "suddenly The Rock was swarming with military convicts who believed either in Social world revolution or an equally disconcerting brand of pure Christianity that actually wanted to turn the other cheek to the Kaiser. What's more these men were frequently willing to be torn to shreds for their beliefs, kept on preaching and spreading them, and, when 'reasoned with,' used arguments that reduced both officers and chaplains to a state of apoplexy."[19]

Alcatraz Addresses "Slacker Problem"

The island newsletter, *The Rock*, published what it called the official U.S. Army position on conscientious objectors in an article, entitled "The Slacker Problem," shortly before the Hofer brothers and Jacob Wipf arrived. The army claimed that, almost to a person, men who reported to military camps as objectors soon saw the error of their ways:

> They come here charged with the serious offense of desertion in time of war. Such an offense . . . is punishable even by death. These men are not immediately tried and given a sentence of ten or more years as could be done. The fact is taken into consideration that the offense might have been committed because of a misunderstanding or through thoughtlessness and inexperience, or while under the pernicious influence of unpatriotic persons. They are therefore carefully instructed . . . . They are given ample time to reflect upon their actions and to come to an intelligent decision.

As a result, misunderstandings are usually cleared up. Objections are removed and . . . they voluntarily and cheerfully decide to enter the service. . . . Of the fifty men sent here as slackers within the past two months, not one has been tried and condemned. A practical solution in each case was found and, with the few exceptions of those who were found to be mentally incapacitated, all are now on duty with the colors.[20]

At least two conscientious objectors who refused work assignments at Alcatraz underwent what prison officials called a conversion experience after reading Romans 13 during their daily devotions: "Let every soul be subject unto the higher powers. For there is no power but of God; the powers that be are ordained of God. Whosoever therefore resisteth the power, resisteth the ordinance of God."[21] After a prayer, the men announced their readiness to work.

Chained in Darkness While Rats Ran Wild

The Hutterites must have put Colonel Garrard and Chaplain Ossewaarde at wit's end. Here were military authorities, inviting men to turn their lives around in service to God and country, and these Hutterites refused to be helped. A little time in the dungeon, the prison officials figured, would make them reasonable. But the men were as unwilling to wear a uniform or accept a work assignment at Alcatraz as they were at Camp Lewis; they remained in their underwear in the damp and musty cells. For the first four and a half days they received half a glass of water each day but no food. Rats ran wild in the dark of their cells.

At night the men slept without blankets on the cement floor wet from water that oozed through the walls—there were no beds in the dungeons. There were also no toilet facilities beyond a pail assigned to each man. On the floor beside them were soldiers' uniforms, promising some warmth if they gave up their resistance. Wipf would later recall: "But, we had decided, to wear the uniform was not what God would have us do. It was a question of doing our religious duty, not one of living or dying—and we never wore the uniform."[22]

The dungeon was constructed with brick: on the walls, the ceiling, the

floor. There were two sets of alcoves, facing each other on opposite ends
of the basement, with four cells on each side. The eight cell rooms were
originally designed for basement storage when soldiers lived in the Citadel
barracks above. Each cell was fronted with a set of bars with a grill door in
the middle, fastened with a chain and padlock. Inside there was no lamp,
no toilet, no running water, no mattress, no chair, no furnishing. The only
light came from a dim bulb in the hallway in front of each set of alcoves,
turned on when guards arrived with food or on other business. For years,
including during World War I, inmates in solitary received only bread and
water; by 1936, federal regulations mandated a meal every third day but gave
guards some discretion. No reading materials were allowed in the dungeon,
though given the darkness, that regulation seemed pointless.

A Place of Dead Silence and Midnight Black

In recent years, Jim Nelson, a history interpreter for Golden Gate National
Parks Conservancy, broke away from the official tour route to lead a visitor on a walk through the basement.[23] With hardhats on and flashlights
in hand, they reached the basement by climbing down fourteen concrete
steps, bending low to keep from hitting their heads, and reaching out to
the white brick walls for balance. Once at the bottom, they walked along a
narrow corridor, lit now by several bulbs, to reach the first set of four cells,
all whitewashed and shorn of their bars. While it would be impossible for
two people locked up in adjoining cells to see or touch each other, voices
do carry well enough to allow conversations. One imagines the Hutterites
joining in hymns in the darkness or calling out to God in a loud prayer for
mercy.

After the iron cell bars were ripped out in 1940 and the dungeons closed,
few historical traces remained but the scratched name of a soldier or a
prisoner's registry number carved deep in the brick wall. Sometimes a date
follows, maybe the time served or the time still to go, like "11557 5yrs 2mos."
In one cell, we saw the number 11461 etched on the wall, a number that
belonged to Philip Grosser, a conscientious objector who followed in the
footsteps of the Hutterites. We also saw a carved memorial from another inmate, "Albert Herring July 1887." The military destroyed the official records

The Hutterites had to descend fourteen steps to the dungeon.

Alcatraz visitors now find the solitary confinement cells, which measure six feet high by six and a half feet wide by eight feet deep, whitewashed and shorn of their iron bars.

of the prisoners who served time in the Disciplinary Barracks. In effect, said John Martini, the historian, "only their graffiti marks these men's stay on the Rock."[24]

Nelson led the way down the central hallway that connected the two alcoves of cells. Hundreds of tourists were milling about upstairs in the prison cellhouse, taking in what the National Park Service calls "an award-winning audio tour" with interviews of former guards and inmates, but when Nelson and the visitor stopped talking in the basement there was dead silence. When they turned off the string of hall lights, it was midnight black, as it had been for the Hutterites. The hole is aging. Sections of the basement were sealed off by yellow tape, a response to scattered piles of mortar that had fallen from the ceiling. In places, with Nelson in the lead, they slip by wooden reinforcement beams jacked in place to secure the ceiling.

Prisoners spoke of cells that dripped water, conjuring up images of the

Pacific leaking in, as if by design, to heighten the punishment. But the dungeons were located 140 feet above the bay, so it was not seawater that came leaching through. The section of cells on the southeast side was located next to an underground cistern, and the water seeping through brick walls into the cells that the Hofer brothers and Jacob Wipf spoke of was from that adjacent cistern. Legends have long surrounded the Rock, with writers also describing nonexistent tunnels.[25] Regardless of the source of the water, the men made clear that the basement was miserably cold and wet.

Arms Crossed and Chained

The prison officials were determined to break the resistance of the Hofer brothers and Jacob Wipf, if not their spirit, during their first week in the dungeon. During the last 36-hour period underground, each man's hands were crossed one over the other and chained to bars in the door. The chains were drawn up so that only their toes touched the floor, a technique known as "high cuffing." David Hofer said that he tried to move the toilet pail closer so that he could stand on it to relieve the strain in his arms. Strung up like sides of beef, their blood draining down, the men received periodic visits from the guards. At least once they reportedly came with knotted lashes and hit the men on the arms and back; Michael Hofer passed out after one of the beatings.[26] Though they were too far apart to carry on a quiet conversation, if they raised their voices, they could communicate with one another. David Hofer heard Jacob Wipf cry out, "O, Almighty God!"

When guards led the men up the narrow steps and into the outside yard after nearly five days underground, other prisoners gathered around them in a show of sympathy. With tears in his eyes, one of the inmates said, "It is a shame to treat human beings that way."[27] The four men tried without success to put on their jackets that day in the yard; their arms were too swollen. They were apparently found to have contracted scurvy, their skin spotted from the disease presumably brought on by a lack of citrus fruit or other foods with vitamin C.[28] Though it's not known how much medical treatment the men received, a sizeable staff was in place. The Disciplinary Barracks had twenty-three officers and enlisted men on the staff in 1918, ready to offer services in medicine, dentistry, physical therapy, and psychi-

A lone prisoner walks near the lighthouse and commandant's house in the 1920s. When the Hutterites emerged into an outside yard after spending several days strung up by chains in the dungeon, they struggled to put on their jackets.
Golden Gate National Recreation Area, Park Archives (GOGA–34882)

atric care. Should it be needed, the hospital facilities included an operating room and an X-ray lab.

Letters Put All in the Hands of God

In their letters home, the Hofer brothers (or, as they were known now, Nos. 15238, 15239, and 15240) and Jacob Wipf (No. 15237) shared few details of their traumatic introduction to life at Alcatraz. Either they chose to self-censor their accounts or prison officials sanitized their words for them. There is no mention of sleeping on wet concrete in their underwear, of standing for hours in chains, or of being beaten by guards. The men also faced new limits on how often they could write home. At Camp Lewis, they were able to write several times a week; here at Alcatraz, prisoners could write no more than twice a month, and strictly in English. From the letters that arrived back at the colony in South Dakota, the families of the Hofer brothers and Jacob Wipf would not have known that the men were locked up in their cells day and night; or that only on Sundays were they allowed out into the courtyard, and then only for one hour, and always under the watch of guards.

The letters, in a perfunctory way, continue to convey assurance that the men are in reasonably good health and that God will see them through this trial. Michael Hofer wrote:

I and the brothers are healthy in body and soul and we wish the same health to you and to the whole community. If only I could see our little daughter! But everything is in the hands of God, our heavenly Father. We cannot thank him enough for the support that he has shown to us. He only wants to see what his children will do.[29]

Even so, one finds a greater measure of despair in his first letter home, written about two weeks after they had left Camp Lewis:

My dear wife, I want to write you a few lines regarding my health and my faith. I was sick for two days, but now I am better. I am also still strong in my faith in God and in the hope that my letter will reach you in the same spirit. We arrived in Alcatraz on July 27. We are now in the military prison of Alcatraz behind iron and locks. We don't know what will become of us. Our twenty-year sentence is not yet firmly established. We wish that God would come and bring an end to the world, for there is indeed nothing good left in the world. . . .

My dear spouse, if we no longer see each other in this world, then it is my hope in God that it will happen in the next world where no one will be able to separate us—where we will remain forever in joy.[30]

The absence of any detail in their letters home from Alcatraz, and the brevity of the letters in comparison with those from Camp Lewis, is striking. More than a month into their stay, Michael Hofer only alluded to the hardships they were facing. "First," he wrote, "a heartful greeting from me in chains. . . . I wish that I could see you with my eyes. The prospects of that do not seem to be good, but nonetheless I remain in hope that it will still happen, even if not very soon."[31]

Joseph, also, says nothing of the conditions at Alcatraz but much about how fleeting time is on earth: "We are here today, and tomorrow we are no more. It is as Paul says: like the grass that grows today but tomorrow is thrown into the oven."[32] He reminds Maria that for the full accounting of their early time as prisoners, the family can hear directly from the Hofer brothers' father, who apparently had arrived at Camp Lewis to see them shortly before they were transferred to Alcatraz.[33]

David Hofer also spared his family any description of life behind bars in Alcatraz:

My dear spouse and children, I'm sure you'll be anxious to hear how things are going during these dark days. We're all quite well, temporally and spiritually, and wish you the same. . . . It seems that we're supposed to stay here in this misery. But we have to pray to God that he will lead us on the right path. We all do not expect to see each other in this world anymore, the way it seems now, but we should not despair, with God's strength we hope to overcome, as we have promised God, we trust in him. He's the only one who can help us, as he did in olden days.[34]

Political Prisoner Shares Dungeon Life

Where the Hutterites decline to speak, others sometimes speak for them. One of the most vivid descriptions of life in the dungeon comes from Philip Grosser, a Jewish conscientious objector from Boston who was no stranger to persuasion by force. He had registered for the draft as an objector and then refused to report for a medical examination. After his arrest, Grosser declared his determination not to participate in the military. In early 1918, he found himself in a stand-off with officers at Fort Andrews in Boston, who beat him with a rifle butt and chained him to the bars of his cell so that he had to stand on tiptoe, all in an effort to persuade him to serve as a soldier. He was sentenced in the summer of 1918 to thirty years of hard labor, beginning at Fort Jay on Governor's Island in New York. Soon he was transferred to Fort Leavenworth, where his stay overlapped with that of the Hutterites and where he participated in a prisoners' strike in February 1919.

In June 1919, under armed guard, he and thirty-two other prisoners traveled for three days and three nights, from Leavenworth to Alcatraz. Though arriving six months after the Hofer brothers and Jacob Wipf had departed, his account of life in the underground provides a window on what the Hutterites had experienced. Like them, Grosser received a military order to work and to stand in military formation as soon as he arrived. Like them, he refused. In the face of Grosser's disregard of official protocol, Lieutenant J.J. Meskill, the executive officer, sentenced him to fourteen days in the dungeon and a bread-and-water diet. Grosser described the descent to a darkness that enveloped all:

> Sergeant Cole, overseer in charge, switched on the electric light and took me down a flight of stairs to the basement, hollowed out of the rock under the prison. He ordered me to take up a bucket, and when I wasn't quick enough he lifted his club and yelled, "I'll knock your God damn brains out!" He showed me into a cell, locked the iron barred door behind me, and I heard his footsteps going up the stairs as I was left alone in the dungeon. Then he switched off the lights and I found myself in complete darkness. I tried to investigate the place which was to be my abode for the next fourteen days. Attempting to walk through the cell I bumped my head against the ceiling.

Feeling my way, I found that the cell roof was arched and lower at the sides than a man's height, so that it wasn't safe to walk around in the dark. I sat on the door-sill waiting for something to happen.

After a while the lights were turned on and a guard came down with a few slices of bread and a pitcher of water. Trying to have a good look at my cell while the lights were still on I found that there was no furniture or toilet facilities; the only things that were to be seen were the pitcher of water, the few slices of bread, and the "old wooden bucket" which the guard told me would be emptied only once every twenty-four hours. The dungeon cells were under the prison, situated so that not a ray of daylight ever penetrated them. The air in the cell was stagnant, the walls were wet and slimy, the bars of the cell door were rusty with the dampness, and the darkness was so complete that I could not make out my hand a few inches before my face. It seemed eternity until the officer of the day and a guard came about nine o'clock in the evening. The cell door opened and the guard threw in a pair of lousy Army blankets, wholly insufficient, as was evidenced by the fact that four blankets were provided for the warmer and drier cells upstairs. The prison officer had to put a searchlight on me to note that I was "present and accounted for."

The light was switched off, and as no other prisoners were at that particular time confined in the dungeon I was left alone with the rats for company. The water and sewer system of the jails were located in the center of the underground dungeon in front of the cells and in case of accident, as the bursting of a pipe, a prisoner could have been drowned like a rat before anyone in the jail proper could have noticed it. I took off my shoes and coat and used them as a pillow, wrapped myself in two blankets, and with the concrete floor as a mattress made myself a nice comfortable bed. . . .

The things hardest to endure in the dungeon were the complete darkness, the sitting and sleeping on the damp concrete floor, and the lack of sight or sound of any human being. The eighteen ounces of bread was quite sufficient for the first few days, and towards the last I had some of the bread left over. The rats were quite peaceful and friendly. The fact that the dungeon was made a store house for the "ball and chain," straightjacket, wrist chains and other implements of medieval torture was not very pleasant.

After serving fourteen days in the rat-infested dungeon I was taken out in a weakened condition to the prison hospital. The prison doctor thought that eating too much bread was the cause of my sickness. I knew better. To place any human being in the "hole" for fourteen days, even if one were given a chicken diet, was enough to weaken him. It felt good to be given a soft hospital bed after the concrete floor as a sleeping place. The food, which was quite good in the hospital, was also a treat compared with the eighteen ounces of bread. Then the daylight and the association with human beings again made me feel as if I were on a holiday.[35]

By military law, the convicts could not be kept down in the dungeon longer than fourteen days at a time, and they required a normal diet during that interim before being placed back in the dungeon, to subsist on bread and water. Since Grosser continued to refuse to work—in his case, the order was to "make little ones out of the big ones" on the rock pile—he was forced to parade around the windiest side of the island for eight hours a day, escorted by a special sentry. At the end of fourteen days of marching, he returned to the dungeon. The Hutterites experienced a similar rotation into and out of the dungeon during the four months that they spent at Alcatraz.

A letter by another conscientious objector transferred from Fort Leavenworth to Alcatraz, apparently written to George Huddle, who was an advocate for conscientious objectors in San Francisco during the war, confirms many of the details in Grosser's account while adding others.[36] Alcatraz was said to be not much different than Fort Leavenworth in some respects. In both places, men and rats met as cellmates. Apart from the bread and water rations, the food was said to be better at Alcatraz than at Leavenworth ("No kick on the food" at Alcatraz—even without being invited to the Thanksgiving dinner for the hospital staff in 1918, which featured oxtail soup, oyster cocktails, roast suckling pig, nut dressing, giblet gravy, candied sweet potatoes, and cigars for dessert). Packages were welcome, except for stationery and cigarettes. Two outbound letters per month were allowed.

Alcatraz, though, placed a heavier burden on the men's psyches. "The place is smaller," the prisoner said, "and the surveillance consequently greater." There was a strictness of regulations, including no visiting with other prisoners except during mealtimes. Some prisoners inevitably found the conditions too oppressive, and wilted under psychological and physical coercion. "A few days ago a prisoner here became insane—shouting and shrieking and rattling his cell door during the night. Certainly, the oppression, repression, etc., here are more terrible than at L. [Leavenworth]. Locked cells, single cells, every man in his cell, and the silent system break many spirits." The dungeon, or "the hole," however, is a place all its own. The walls are wet and slimy, with "accumulations of filth and green moss." Prisoners sleep on bedrock or concrete floors. When they had trouble sleeping, some, like Grosser, played with the large rats that had free run of the prison.

Sanitizing a Portrait of Prison Life

The official version of life at the prison portrayed conscientious objectors as having a pretty good deal at the expense of the taxpayers. Under the headline "War Shirker Basks and Fattens at Alcatraz," the *San Francisco Chronicle* described a typical daily menu, which began with pork sausage and gravy for breakfast and ended with coconut cake at supper.[37] Even the men in the dungeon did not have it so bad, according to the report. "Weird tales have been told about these dungeons, which are said to be swarming with rats and ripping with moisture." Not so: "The cells are dark, but they are absolutely dry and wholesome, and are actually warmer than the cells above." Prisoners down below are allowed four blankets with which to sleep on the concrete floor, the report incorrectly noted.

Church attendance was compulsory, but Grosser refused to go, perhaps seeing this as simply one more effort by the military to exercise control over prisoners' lives. As a Jew, he may have objected to the overt Christian themes that shaped each service. Grosser said that he was not alone in choosing to resist the services:

Before we came, one episode was brutal. The three Hofer brothers told the chaplain they preferred not to attend services. He attacked one of them, shook him, dragged him around, knocked him down and as the boy stood up, he slapped his face. Then, he attacked the other two, one by one. Finally he repented: saying to the sergeant, "I should not have beaten these boys. I

Spiral staircases provided access to the upper tiers in the cellhouse,
which contained six hundred one-man cells.
Golden Gate National Recreation Area, Park Archives, Alcatraz Field Collection III
(GOGA–35173)

should have called an overseer to do it!" He told these Christian protesters
that they should be shot, drowned or choked to death.

Chaplain Ossewaarde is the only person identified by name as having
struck the Hutterites while they were at Alcatraz. Alice Park, who visited
conscientious objectors at Alcatraz at the behest of the National Civil Liberties Bureau, referred to a guard named Lane who "was especially cruel to
the Hofer brothers" and told Grosser that he would "beat his brains out"
when Grosser wanted to shave first and then take a bath, instead of taking
his bath first as Lane ordered.[38]

Yet another account suggests the volatility of those in charge. Reading
was not encouraged, even though books and light were plentiful above

ground. The library privileges were one book per week. Grosser said: "I estimate that one prisoner in four uses books there—which is a good enough percentage to justify a great number of books per week, surely. There is nothing else to do but read—every man in his own cell when not working, and no talking except at meal times." One inmate, identified only as Toni, tried to study after a bugle call signaled the end of free time at night. He was pulled from his cell, beaten, and placed in the dungeon for twenty-four hours.

Preying on Prisoners

In their letters, the Hutterites make no mention of abuse suffered at the hands of other prisoners, though that was certainly a possibility, especially given the commitment of the Hutterites to nonresistance. Walter Stack, who arrived at Alcatraz in 1925, had enlisted in the army after the war at fifteen (lying about his age to gain early entry) and then went AWOL while in Plattsburgh, New York. When he was caught, he was shipped to the Philippines to finish out his term. But he really wanted to go home. So when his commanders gave him the choice of serving the remaining two years in the Philippines or nine months in the Disciplinary Barracks on Alcatraz, he entered the Rock as prisoner No. 15331.

Assigned to work in the rock quarry on the west side of the island, he soon came to fear more than the strenuous labor. Years later, he vividly remembered the physical attacks and rapes that he witnessed during those two months at the quarry, where seclusion promised privacy and protection. "I was the most terrorized there I ever felt in my life," he said. "There were lots of wolves there. You know, older guys who would get their guns off on some young kid. They did it to some kids so much, they kind of turned them into women."[39] At seventeen, Stack might have been a target himself. But he strategically placed rocks to be used as ammunition should he come under attack. After two months of cutting and hauling rock, he graduated to work in the prison laundry.

Wilbert Rideau, an award-winning journalist who served forty-four years in Louisiana prisons after killing a woman during a bank robbery, described a similar reality of prison life, albeit in a different time and place. There were men who preyed, men who became their sex slaves, and men who kept to themselves. But arguably the most damaging treatment could be inflicted when no other human being, absolutely no one, was around. He, too, knew solitary confinement:

> This is my reality. Solitude. Four walls, gray-green, drab, and foreboding. Three of steel and one of bars, held together by 358 rivets. Seven feet wide, nine feet long. About the size of an average bathroom or—and my mind leaps at this—the size of four tombs, only taller. I, the living dead, have need of a few essentials that the physically dead no longer require—commode, shower, face bowl, bunk. A sleazy old mattress, worn to thinness. On the floor in a corner, a cardboard box that contains all my worldly possessions— a writing tablet, a pen, and two changes of underwear. The mattress, the box, and I are the only things not bolted down, except the cockroaches that come and go from the drain in the floor and scurry around in the shower. This is my life, every minute of the year. I'm buried alive.[40]
>
> . . . I turn from the window and walk slowly toward the heavy steel door. I'm restless again. One . . . two . . . three . . . four . . . five . . . turn. Walk back. One . . . two . . . three . . . four . . . five . . . stop.
>
> Suddenly, adrenaline is coursing through me. I freeze, like a feral cat who spots a stray dog. It's the walls! They're closer! They're moving in on me, closing up the tomb. Panic is suffocating me. This is what they want; they want to kill me. Somehow, I will my muscles to relax, and my mind follows.
>
> Yeah, I've seen men broken, destroyed by solitary. Some have come to fear every shadow. Others have committed suicide. Some men would do anything to escape this cell. Some feigned insanity so they could go to a mental institution. Even more cut themselves, over and over, until the Man, fearing a suicide on his watch, moved them out of solitary. Others stayed doped up, whenever they could get dope. Engaging in such tricks, though, is beneath my dignity; it's unmanly. I am stronger than this punishment.

The practice at Alcatraz of confining inmates with their hands shackled above their heads to a high bar on the cell doors officially ended on December 6, 1918, about two weeks after the Hutterites had been transferred to Fort Leavenworth. Beginning the next month, the Disciplinary Barracks at

Alcatraz put in place cages that the government called "vestibule doors" (the *New York Call* and the National Civil Liberties Bureau referred to them as "iron torture cages"). Men were forced to stand in these cages, twenty-three inches wide by twelve inches deep, inside their cells. The National Civil Liberties Bureau lodged immediate and repeated protests, arguing that "inflicting physical suffering as a means of enforcing obedience" by squeezing prisoners into boxes was no different than manacling prisoners to cell bars, which Baker had only recently halted.[41] Within a few months, this treatment too, was ended.

Though the methods of incarceration evolved, solitary confinement always remained an option at the disposal of wardens during the war. Years later, after Alcatraz had been converted to a federal prison, the first man to be sent into solitary confinement in the basement was Leo McIntosh, No. 74, who was serving five years for auto theft. He arrived at Alcatraz on August 8, 1934, and one month later, after he refused to stop talking in the cellhouse, he was placed in D Block isolation; even so, he yelled at other prisoners. So he was taken to a lower solitary cell for nineteen days. There he scratched a line on the wall of the cell to mark each passing day.

Another prisoner, Charlie Berta, was placed in a dungeon cell in 1934 for "sending out defamatory comments, agitating and promoting trouble, making slanderous remarks about guards and hollering at officers on the wall." Berta described his time in lower solitary under D block, where he stood handcuffed to the door, much as the Hutterites had been:

There was no beds, you slept on the bricks, but it was warm. I had a jumpsuit. You didn't need nothing. You got bread and water, but there was no running water. You had a shit bucket but after a couple of days you had no bowel movement because you didn't take nothing in. The light was not a very strong light in the hall; no guards were stationed down there. When they'd come down you'd know it—there was a slight draft—you could feel it—and you knew somebody was coming down.[42]

Washington Ends Dungeon Confinement

In 1935, seventeen years after the Hutterites were imprisoned, the federal government wanted to be done with the dungeons and would certainly not brook the chaining of men in them. During a visit to Alcatraz, a representative of Sanford Bates, the superintendent of U.S. Bureau of Prisons, found several men chained in the dungeon. Bates immediately fired off a letter to Warden James A. Johnston to make sure that he understood that penal policy had changed:

> The use of chains in this manner is specifically and definitely disapproved. We have provided Alcatraz with every practicable scientific device to make it secure, and I cannot bring myself to believe that it is necessary to resort to the antiquated practice of chaining men.
>
> I think it is very undesirable for us to use the old dungeons as punishment cells. If you feel that we have not provided sufficient or suitable isolation facilities, please submit at once estimates on the cost of remodeling cells in the unused portions of the building in such a way as to adapt them to fulfill the need which you are now meeting by use of the dungeons.[43]

While the handcuffing of inmates in standing position ended, records show that the dungeon cells remained in use. Bates, clearly concerned about the risk of negative publicity, even sent a follow-up letter to Johnston, asking for his assurance that "there is no stringing up by the wrists or otherwise; they are using the old cells in the basement only as a last resort; that our most severe means of punishment is solitary confinement for short periods, meaning from three to 10 days." More public scrutiny followed as reports leaked out of self-mutilation and mental illness on the part of men kept in isolation (one parolee claimed to have known fourteen convicts who went insane at Alcatraz). Writing his memoir a few years later, Warden Johnston indicated that he was ashamed of the dungeons and used them only when absolutely necessary.[44]

The last inmate to serve time in the dungeon was Berta, who had been convicted of mail robbery and aggravated assault, prone to attacking officers and prisoners alike. During one of Berta's many visits to the dungeon, an associate warden named Miller kicked him down the stairs, with Berta thrashing in return. Berta was left handcuffed in a standing position for eight hours. Miller himself came to remove the prisoner and put him in a standard isolation cell upstairs. Soon afterward, Johnston and Miller ordered that the bars be removed from the cells and the dungeons be banned. The bars were removed with welding torches in 1938.[45]

Case against Solitary Confinement

Long before the dungeons at Alcatraz closed, and well before the four Hutterites arrived in chains, the federal government knew the harm that solitary confinement could cause. The United States Supreme Court nearly declared the punishment unconstitutional in a case in 1890 in which a Colorado murderer, James J. Medley, had been held in isolation for a month, awaiting his execution. Writing for the majority, Justice Samuel F. Miller underscored the "serious objections" to the practice of solitary confinement raised by experiences in Maryland, Pennsylvania, and other states:

> A considerable number of the prisoners fell, after even a short confinement, into a semi-fatuous condition, from which it was next to impossible to arouse them, and others became violently insane; others, still, committed suicide; while those who stood the ordeal better were not generally reformed, and in most cases did not recover sufficient mental activity to be of any subsequent service to the community.[46]

Miller noted that Great Britain had also kept death-row prisoners in isolation but ended the practice when the public decided that solitary confinement represented "a further terror and peculiar mark of infamy" that was too extreme.

For the better part of the twentieth century, in keeping with the court's outlook, the United States used solitary confinement relatively sparingly, and only rarely for long term. Alcatraz of the 1930s became symbolic of the exception. But the consensus among prison policymakers has shifted in recent decades. Correctional administrators have become much more aggressive in using segregated confinement, in part because of overcrowding that threatens discipline and violence and in part because of an absence of alternatives. What does one do with incorrigible inmates?

States like Mississippi have embraced high-tech "supermax" prisons, designed for mass solitary confinement (12 percent of the state's prisoners overall are in supermax). As two psychologists, Craig Haney and Mona Lynch, put it, "It is likely that at no point in the modern history of imprisonment have so many prisoners been so completely isolated for so long a period of time in facilities designed so completely for the purpose of near total isolation."[47] In some cases, prisoners are locked down twenty-four hours a day in cells without natural light; they have no contact with other prisoners; when permitted to use a concrete exercise pen, perhaps for an hour every other day, they do so alone; radio and television are banned; visits with family, when permitted, are infrequent.

The flourishing of solitary confinement offers researchers a living laboratory to study what happens when people are starved for companionship. After reviewing dozens of studies conducted since the 1970s, the psychologists Haney and Lynch concluded that while the effects of solitary confinement vary, every study documented psychological damage among the inmates who were held for longer than ten days. As they said, isolation "takes the pains of imprisonment" and intensifies them. A list of the damages includes chronic anxiety, insomnia, panic, difficulty concentrating, impulsive anger, memory lapses, hallucinations, self-mutilation, and suicide. Electroencephalogram (EEG) studies have found a slowing of brain waves after a week or more of solitary confinement.

Haney and Lynch believe that "conditions of total social isolation and extreme sensory deprivation (e.g., darkness)"—in other words, the manner in which the Hutterites were kept for two weeks at a time—should be prohibited entirely. The isolation must have held a special pain for the Hutterites, who had been raised so explicitly in community. Indeed, their identity as Hutterites was understood only within the communal order. In prison they were asked to embrace an individualism that at home represented a worldly temptation.

In 2006, a bipartisan national task force, the Commission on Safety and Abuse in America's Prisons, completed a yearlong investigation of prison conditions. The commission called for ending long-term isolation. Beyond ten days of such incarceration, the commission said, the harm to inmates is clear. All people require "regular and meaningful human contact."[48] To deny inmates that social need, in other words, is to accept legalized torture.

In 2011, the group Psychologists for Social Responsibility objected to the "inhumane" solitary confinement of Bradley Manning, an army intelligence analyst who was then awaiting trial on charges related to giving troves of classified information to WikiLeaks. As the open letter noted, "history suggests that solitary confinement, rather than being a rational response to a risk, is more often used as a punishment for someone who is considered to be a member of a despised or 'dangerous' group."[49]

War Department Reviews Trial

While the Hutterite men remained locked up at Alcatraz, the Office of the Judge Advocate General in the War Department reviewed their trial that had taken place at Camp Lewis on June 10. Samuel Ansell, the acting judge advocate general, released his findings on September 30. He had reviewed the facts, noting that within a few hours of their arrival at the camp on May 28 and before the uniforms had been issued, the men were ordered to fall in with their squad. The purpose was "merely to have the men line up so that they might be checked"—it had nothing to do with combatant service.[50] And when they were ordered to fill out the enlistment and assignment cards on June 2, Ansell said, it was just to provide basic information like place of birth and age and not to advance the war effort. General Ansell wrote:

> The command . . . to sign the enlistment and assignment card, was one which the accused were bound to obey, regardless of their status as conscientious objectors. It is essential that every soldier furnish his superiors with the information necessary to the completion of his record, and for his identification as a member of the Military service. It is for this purpose that the enlistment and assignment card is used. . . . To dispense with this in the case of any man would throw the system of military records into disorder and would be productive of the utmost confusion. . . . There is nothing in the signing of such a card that can in any way prejudice the status of one who claims to be a conscientious objector and it manifestly could not have been

the intent of the Executive Order of March 20, 1918, to exempt him from this duty, whatever his status under the terms of that order.

Ansell went on to note that a subsequent directive, issued by the adjutant general of the army on July 30, seven weeks after their trial, made it clear that conscientious objectors should be told directly that providing personal information upon their arrival in camp would not affect their status as an objector. Because the directive came after the trial, though, the commanders at Camp Lewis were in no way required to offer a similar explanation to the Hofer brothers and Jacob Wipf (and the implication is that they did not do so). Ansell sustained the findings and the sentence of the court. The Hutterites, he concluded, had received a fair trial.

Only a few months later General Ansell condemned the court-martial system. Testifying before the Senate Military Committee, he said: "For forty years the army has been cursed with red tape in its court-martial proceedings. Terrible injustices have been inflicted upon small offenders. The whole system is wrong."[51]

Chapter Six

Enemy on the Home Front

*We know of no place to go. We are surrounded by the king's lands.
In every direction we would walk straight into the jaws of robbers and
tyrants, like sheep cast among ravenous wolves.*
—Jakob Hutter

District Attorney Targets Amish and Mennonites

The letter that appeared in the *Budget*, a newspaper that went to Amish homes across the country, began on a religious note and then turned casually to the weather, easing into the grave subject at hand:

A greeting in our Saviors name. People are all well excepting some colds. The weather is cool again. We're having more rain than usual this spring. Oats fields are nice and green much more barley is being put out this spring than usual on account of the wheat failing. A few farmers think they have some wheat that will be harvested, some corn is planted.

As we are living in an age of time when the gospel is preached over a wider area than ever before, but in what state of affairs the world is in? A world war, never since the time of Julius Caesar was so large a portion of the civilized nations at war, never were such destructive weapons used to destroy life, never were the nonresistant people put to a more trying test in our country . . .

Now we are asked to buy Liberty Bonds the form in which the government has to carry on the war. Sorry to learn that some Mennonites have yielded and bought bonds. What would become of our nonresistant faith if our young brethren in camp would yield.[1]

The writer, Mannasses E. Bontrager, an Amish bishop with a 106-acre farm near Dodge City, Kansas, apparently wanted nothing more than to shore up the faith of the 3,600 subscribers to the newspaper. In the letter, which was published on May 15, 1918, a week before the Hutterites left for Camp Lewis, Bontrager expressed both regret that some Mennonites were compromising by buying war bonds and an implicit fear that Amish would follow suit.

Representatives of the historic peace churches were, indeed, divided over how to respond to these appeals to finance the war. In the Mennonite Church, for example, one national publication, the *Gospel Herald*, opposed the bonds on the grounds of military participation, while another publication, the *Mennonite*, saw the purchase as acceptable, rendering unto Caesar the things that were Caesar's. Those members who bought bonds often gave them to the Red Cross or another relief fund, or even to their own churches, aiding the government but for a worthy cause.

The editor of the *Budget*, Samuel H. Miller, who himself was a Mennonite minister, was away from his Ohio office when the letter from Bishop Bontrager arrived; his printer, A.A. Middaugh, elected to publish it. The American Protective League for Wayne and Holmes counties, a patriotic watchdog group nominally attached to the Justice Department, quickly swung into action. One of the league's citizen volunteers discerned a threat to the nation lurking in the letter to the Amish community and contacted the U.S. Justice Department, which relayed the information to District Attorney Edwin Slusser Wertz of Cleveland.

On July 7, 1918, a grand jury indicted Miller and Bontrager on five counts of violating the one-year-old Espionage Act, which prohibited any interference with the mission of the armed services, including recruitment. F.B. Kavanagh, the assistant U.S. attorney who signed the indictment, characterized the letter as an example of "fanatical anti-war teachings."

The trial began on August 17, with the temperature hovering around 90 degrees. Miller, who was present without a lawyer, had earlier pleaded not guilty. Though he could have fought the charges, especially given that he neither wrote the letter nor signed off on its publication, he agreed to a plea bargain in which the government dropped four charges and he pleaded guilty to one—attempt to cause or incite insubordination, disloyalty, mutiny, and refusal of duty in the military and naval forces of the United States. Bishop Bontrager pleaded similarly. They were both fined five hundred dollars, plus court costs. Miller spent several days in jail until he raised the money to pay the fine.

Wertz, a former Democratic state lawmaker who had served in the Spanish-American War, was on a roll. During the same week in which Miller was indicted, the district attorney brought sedition charges against Eugene V. Debs, the leader of the American Socialist Party and a four-time presidential candidate (who tallied 901,873 votes in 1912). Debs was arrested in Cleveland on July 1, two weeks after a speech in Canton, Ohio, in which he had said that the United States and its allies had the same purpose as Germany and the Central Powers in going to war: plunder. Decades earlier, in 1893, the Pullman's Palace Car Company had used wage cuts and layoffs to take advantage of employees, prompting a strike that vaulted Debs into political leadership. Once again he saw American lives being sacrificed in the pursuit of profits, and this time people were being asked to pay the ultimate price.

Debs, who was accustomed to speaking his mind before overflowing crowds across the country, apparently spoke too honestly in Canton. He was weak from illness, but he rose in the heat, dressed in a jacket and vest, to condemn the politicians who had declared a war that others were being asked to fight. "If war is right," he said, "let it be declared by the people—you, who have your lives to lose." The prosecutor in Ohio once again heard "language intended to incite, provoke, or encourage resistance to the United States and to promote the cause of its enemies." Wertz indicted Debs, even though a special assistant with the Justice Department in Washington had recommended against it.

Debs was found guilty of the encouraging resistance count and of two others on September 15. At his sentencing, Debs said: "I hope I am laying no flattering unction to my soul when I say I believe the soldier has no more sympathetic friend than I am. Could I have my way there would be no soldiers."[2] Before sentencing Debs to ten years in prison, Judge D.C. Westonhaver responded: "I do not regard the idealism of the defendant as expressed by himself as any higher, any purer, or any nobler than the ideals and the idealism of the thousands upon thousands of young men that I have seen marching down the streets of Cleveland to defend the Constitution and the laws of their country and its flag." Debs appealed his case to the Supreme Court, which upheld the conviction.

Wertz turned his eye to another potential target: 181 bishops, ministers, and deacons in the Mennonite Church. The church leaders were all signatories to the denomination's most comprehensive statement against the war. In August 1917, three months after President Wilson and Congress had declared war, these delegates had gathered at the Yellow Creek meeting-house near Goshen, Indiana, to underscore their traditional nonresistant stance, reminding especially the young people that the church had "continually stood for the surrendered life, a consistent separation from the world, and an attitude of peace toward all men." Young men should report when drafted, the delegates said, but state their unwillingness to serve under the military arm of the government, even as noncombatants.

Wertz prepared for a grand jury indictment, finding in the Yellow Creek statement yet another clear violation of the Espionage Act. While the case against the *Budget* drew limited press coverage, a massive indictment of Mennonite leaders would ensure Wertz a national stage on which to punish this Germanic sect of pacifists and send an unmistakable message to any other Americans who might share their views. In August 1918, while prisoners 15237, 15238, 15239, and 15240 remained in the dungeon at Alcatraz, Wertz pressed the Justice Department for permission to prosecute; to his chagrin, he met with stiff resistance. Officials in Washington said that the Yellow Creek statement did not suggest that Mennonites would try to dissuade their neighbors from fighting; they were only urging their own young men to follow the church's teachings.

Military Intelligence Identifies Anabaptist Threat

The War Department was also concerned about the church groups that were filling the camps with so many young men who were unwilling to fight. The department's Military Intelligence Division commissioned a report specifically on the Hutterites, the Mennonites, and the Amish.[3] The report, overseen by Captain R. J. Malone,[4] an intelligence officer in Washington, was part of a larger effort to address the security risks posed by pacifists or by enemies of the state operating in the guise of pacifism. Though the Military Intelligence Division led the investigation, several other agencies assisted in monitoring the Anabaptist church groups: the Bureau of Investigation—a forerunner to the Federal Bureau of Investigation—which had fewer than three hundred agents on staff at the outset of the war; the American Protective League; and state and local Council of Defense organizations.

The division's research techniques involved opening mail, monitoring phones, and recording private conversations with dictograph machines, casting a surveillance net that prefigured the anticommunist witch hunts led by Senator Joseph R. McCarthy in the 1940s and 1950s and the surveillance campaign that targeted civil rights leaders and other dissenters in the 1960s and 1970s. One intelligence official suggested that trained operatives should pose as conscientious objectors at Fort Leavenworth to get a true reading of sincerity and to ferret out any plots among both the political and religious objectors. The operation envisioned one spy for every fifty conscientious objectors. The moles would have to be intelligent and resourceful; they should be familiar with the cultures of the various dissenting groups, whether the Hutterites or the International Workers of the World.

The spy network may never have been installed at Leavenworth, but it is clear that many intelligence officials saw a conspiracy being carried out by "dangerous, disruptive and unpatriotic" Anabaptists.[5] The officials suspected that these church members were less antiwar than they were pro-German. The investigators concluded that seventy to eighty percent of the objectors at the four camps with the highest concentration of Anabaptists (Dodge, Riley, Pike, and Jackson) were insincere in their convictions. The men were deemed insincere because they would not accept noncombatant duty as defined by President Wilson. The test of sincerity became a willing-ness to obey military orders.

Allan Teichroew, an archivist in the Library of Congress who later un-earthed the Malone report, commented: "Thus evolved a paradox worthy of Joseph Heller's Catch 22: a pacifist who compromised and served was a pacifist, while a pacifist who did not compromise and refused to serve was not a pacifist."[6] Marlborough Churchill, the newly appointed head of the Military Intelligence Division, said: there is "absolutely no question or doubt about the fact that the activities of the Mennonites and Amish reli-gious organizations are doing as much harm with their pacifist and antiwar views as any similar organization in the country today, and that their actions ought to be silenced at once."[7] A.B. Bielaski, chief of the Bureau of Investi-gation, concurred, suspecting that Mennonites might be a covert front for a pro-German underground, perhaps even an international movement.

The Malone report, which was released early in 1919, suggested an iron-clad case against Bishop Aaron Loucks of Pennsylvania, a church leader who was portrayed as orchestrating Mennonite resistance to the war effort and encouraging sedition among Mennonites and Amish; he logged thou-sands of miles during the war to counsel men in training camps and to speak with military officials. Investigators pointed to a sermon that Loucks delivered in Tiffin, Ohio, for example, in which he was said to have charac-terized Americans who were seeking to raise funds for the war as a "crowd of cigarette smoking suckers gambling in War Thrift Stamps." In their view, Loucks was the ringleader of a vast plot to stymie the war effort and the Yel-low Creek participants were his co-conspirators.

The report also expressed concerns that Mennonites, Amish, and Hut-terites were communists or socialists bent on an overthrow of capitalism. "It would seem," one agent wrote, "that their doctrine is of a highly pacifist nature, and that their influence is close akin to the Bolsheviki movement in Russia, which influence they hope to spread in the United States." Apart from wildly inaccurate reporting, the conclusions in the report are notice-ably short on nuance. "The Mennonites and kindred sects are strict com-munists." "As farmers, the Mennonites are 100 percent efficient—as mili-tants, 100 percent deficient." The analysts also reveal a weakness for folksy generalizations about a people who would not seem capable of representing a national threat even on their best days: "The individual Mennonite draftee is in general narrow, bigoted, pig-headed, ignorant, slovenly, and selfish; he is unaccustomed to thinking for himself but follows stupidly along the lines of the traditions of his clan. Whether a sincere Objector or just plain 'yellow' need not concern us here. He is at any rate, mighty poor material for the army."[8]

The Military Intelligence Division conducted its fullest phase of the investigation during the war as an inquest into the activities of Bishop Loucks and several ministers in the area around Camp Dodge, Iowa, certain that these men had initiated a vast conspiracy to undermine the war effort. But neither the prosecuting lawyers in the attorney general's office nor the civilian leaders in the War Department agreed with the conclusions. Just as they had rebuffed Wertz's prosecutorial ambitions, so too Justice Department officials blocked investigators in the intelligence agency.

The War Department's policy, according to Alfred Bettman, a prosecuting attorney, "recognizes the conscientious objector as a fact, and not as an illegal fact. . . . To prosecute any man who simply adjusts himself to the War Department's program or to prosecute any legitimate leader of the [Mennonite] sect for advising a bona fide member of War Department's [conscientious objector] program to stick by the tenets of his church, would, it seems to me, be unfair and inconsistent with the War Department's policy."[9]

The intelligence division never marshaled enough evidence to persuade the Justice Department to bring a single Mennonite to trial, let alone the 181 supporters of the Yellow Creek statement. The Military Intelligence Division was not a factor in the two cases in which Mennonites were convicted during the war: the plea bargain of two church members over the letter published in the *Budget* in Ohio, and a September 1918 trial in West Virginia in which two defendants, Bishop Lewis J. Heatwole and a home missionary, Rhine W. Benner, were found guilty of violating the Sedition Act by obstructing the sale of war bonds (and were fined a thousand dollars).

Government Appeals to Patriotic Soul of a Nation

Though the leadership of the departments of war and justice may have limited the formal prosecution of Mennonites and other peace church members during the war, other forces of coercion rippled across the nation. On the eve of going to war, President Wilson had warned that social institutions, human labor, and public opinion would all have to be mobilized. However unpopular the war may have been during the years of neutrality, once the nation resolved to take sides, he said, all Americans would have to lend a hand in the effort. The battle abroad demanded conformity at home. Being a good citizen meant conserving food, flying a flag, buying war bonds, joining voluntary associations, and standing ready to fight (if you were a man between the ages of 21 and 30). These contributions to the state became the duty of every citizen. Americans were "obliged to volunteer in a culture of coercive voluntarism."[10] For those who refused, the consequences could be grave.

When the mobilization for the war began, the opening engagement came in the field of public opinion. Many Americans had vigorously opposed directly taking sides and remained at odds with official policy. After April 1917, differences of opinion were unacceptable. President Wilson used his own formidable rhetorical skills to rally Americans and sway public opinion. This was not war for war's sake, he said; it was a war for democracy, a war to halt the bestial Hun, and a war to end war. In a Flag Day address in June, the president put peace advocates on notice: "Woe be to the man or group of men that seeks to stand in our way."[11]

Wilson created the Committee on Public Information, a federal propaganda agency armed with writers, photographers, historians, and entertainers. Led by George Creel, who reported for duty with a "white-hot" patriotic fervor, the committee presented the war as a popular and righteous crusade against an evil enemy; doubters and slackers had better get on board. The committee published more than thirty pamphlets in support of the war, and dispatched a special division of Four-Minute Men, more than 75,000 volunteers ready to talk quickly to stir enthusiasm in schools, theaters, union halls, and social clubs. Though the committee promised to use facts to make its case, as time went by the propaganda machine took more liberties in promoting the cause, as when the committee endorsed films like *The Prussian Cur* and *The Kaiser, the Beast of Berlin*.

Meanwhile, Thomas W. Gregory, the United States attorney general, empowered a network of citizens groups to seek out disloyalty among neighbors, colleagues, and friends. These citizen-detectives included the American Protective League, the American Defense Society, and the National Security League. Gregory helped to organize the first of these, whose members carried cards identifying themselves as "Secret Service Division" agents, suggestive of a crackerjack federal spy team. Gregory, an antitrust lawyer from Texas, boasted that he had several hundred thousand private citizens working for him as part of the American Protective League and other patriotic organizations.[12] America's ethnic groups, especially those holding an attachment to the German language and culture, loomed as prime suspects. "Never in its history has this country been so thoroughly policed," Gregory said. His ally, George Creel, added: "Not a pin dropped in the home of anyone with a foreign name but that it rang like thunder on the inner ear of some listening sleuth."

The postmaster general, Albert Sidney Burleson, who was also from Texas and shared Gregory's inclination to deal forcefully with any perceived threats, launched a crusade against war dissenters through espionage laws. In laying the groundwork for a successful prosecution of the war, Congress had passed the Espionage Act in 1917, shortly after the United States entered the war, and then added complementary amendments through the Sedition Act in 1918. The Espionage Act prohibited statements that might hamper the war effort and authorized the postmaster general to ban any material that violated the act, or that advocated treason, insurrection, or forcible resistance to U.S. law. The Sedition Act aimed to further silence challenges to the government's authority by political groups and others.

Burleson needed no encouragement in waging a campaign against pacifists, radicals, and the foreign-born; he quickly established himself as the "foremost official enemy of dissidents."[13] Burleson said he would not prevent the mailing of socialist publications unless they carried treasonable or seditious content—and famously added, "the trouble is that most Socialist papers do contain such matter."[14] Ethnic publications found their second-class mailing privileges eliminated without just cause; many foreign-language papers elected to simply close shop when the Trading with the Enemy Act required them to file English-language translations of all articles relating to the government or the war.

If truth is the first casualty in war, freedom of speech is the second. About two thousand people were arrested for violating the Espionage Act or the Sedition Act, and nearly half of them were convicted. The first case to reach the Supreme Court was *Schenck v. U.S.* in 1919. Charles T. Schenck, the general secretary of the Socialist Party, and another party member were convicted for distributing about fifteen thousand leaflets to military recruits; the leaflets urged the draftees not to serve, denouncing the war as a guise under which big business would profit. The Socialists claimed the right to speak out under the First Amendment; the court begged to differ, noting that free speech is never absolute. The opinion by Justice Oliver Wendell Holmes Jr. offered this test: "The question in every case is whether the words used are used in such circumstances and are of such a nature as to create a clear and present danger that they will bring about the substantive evils that Congress has a right to prevent." The Supreme Court upheld every conviction that it considered.

The drive for unity included a campaign to "Americanize" the waves of immigrants who had flowed into the United States in the decades before the war. In 1917, one-third of the nation's population had been born overseas or had a parent who was an immigrant. An effort to educate and equip immigrants was under way well before the war in schools, settlement homes, and factory floors (the first sentence to be mastered at Henry Ford's factory school for immigrants was this: "I am a good American").[15] As the war proceeded, the impulse to educate immigrants—to give them the tools to find work and successfully integrate—gave way to increasingly harsh repression. The goal became "100 percent Americanism," often with a sneer for those who were not.

As might be expected, among the foreign-born the most suspect immigrants were German-Americans. But the plummeting of their ethnic stock caught many immigrants off guard; before the war, Germans had been "probably the most esteemed immigrant group in American, regarded as easily assimilable, upright citizens."[16] By 1918, secret agents of the American Defense Society operated in states like South Dakota, where, not far from the Hutterite colonies, ears listened for the sound of German. The group openly advertised for supporters and urged citizens to "telegraph, write, or bring us reports of German activities in the district."[17]

Mobs Turn against Neighbors in Montana

Montana may have been the worst state in the nation in which to have had the misfortune of being German-American and of being unconvinced about the merits of the war. Those who did not stand foursquare with the nation invited the fury of their neighbors and the full weight of laws strengthened for wartime. Seventy-nine Montanans were convicted under state law for speaking out in ways considered illegally critical of the United States.[18] The state approved its own sedition law early in 1918, the template for the federal law that would follow. Montana's version made it a crime to say or publish anything "disloyal, profane, violent, scurrilous, contemptuous, slurring, or abusive" about the government, soldiers, or the American flag.[19] But what was "disloyal"? When would an honest opinion be construed as putting the nation at risk?

A traveling wine and brandy salesman, Ben Kahn, learned how narrow the acceptable bounds were; he was sentenced to seven-and-a-half to twenty years of hard labor in prison (he served thirty-four months) after characterizing wartime food regulations as a "big joke."[20] An undercover agent on assignment for the prosecutor in Helena socialized at a German beer hall; the comments he elicited on the war convicted eight men, four of whom went to prison.

Nearly a century later, Montana recognized its misplaced zeal, when Brian Schweitzer, as governor and a descendant of ethnic Germans who migrated to the United States from Russia in 1909, posthumously pardoned seventy-eight people. One person who traveled to attend the ceremony in 2006 was Fay Rumsey, a ninety-year-old daughter of a convicted seditionist. She and her eleven siblings had been put up for adoption after her father was imprisoned during the war and the family farm failed.

In Montana, a Mennonite minister came close to being lynched. The sheriff told John Franz, the pastor of a church near Bloomfield, that he was asking for trouble by teaching Bible classes in German to local Mennonite children. Franz ended the classes. But one dusty Saturday in April 1918, the sheriff and a dozen vigilantes (among them two attorneys and a banker) grabbed him at a school meeting and pushed him into a waiting car. Trying to stop the men, Franz's wife held fast to the door handle and glimpsed a rope and shovels inside. The abductors, who had been drinking, pushed her to the ground.

The men took Franz to a canyon, parking underneath a large poplar tree, suitable for a hanging. They ordered him out of the car. They looped one end of the rope across a large branch and tried to put the noose around Franz's neck. He resisted while making his case. He pleaded with the men to try him in court rather than convict him in the canyon. He appealed directly to the sheriff: "You don't want a record of this hanging to go down in the history of the county, do you?"[21] The sheriff at last thought better of the vigilante justice. They returned Franz to jail to await a formal court hearing; he was released after posting a $3,000 bond and promising not to use the German language.

That same month, near St. Louis, Robert P. Prager, a thirty-one-year-old miner and socialist who was born in Germany, was not so fortunate. He had tried to enlist in the American Navy but was rejected for medical reasons. The trouble came when he applied to join a miners' union; several miners said that he had spoken ill of the United States and positively about Germany. A mob of several hundred people tracked him down one night. He was stripped, bound with an American flag, led barefoot through town, and hanged from a tree after midnight, his feet dangling ten feet from the ground. Public sympathy lay with the aggressors. In less than twenty-five minutes, the jury returned a verdict of not guilty to those who led him to his death.

This was not the first such lynching. Earlier in the war, a band of masked men in Montana had abducted Frank Little, a member of the executive board of the Industrial Workers of the World and a critic of the United States government. Little wanted to organize workers in the Butte Copper mines. During a speech to miners, he had referred to American troops as "Uncle Sam's scabs in uniforms."[22] He also said: "If the mines are taken under federal control, we will make it so hot for the Government that it will not be able to send any troops to France." Six men hustled him from a lodging house during the night of August 1, 1917. They tied him to an automobile and dragged him through the streets, scrapping bare his kneecaps. Then they strung him up along a railroad trestle, where he died, fourteen feet above the roadway, on the outskirts of Butte.

Persuasion by Tar and Feathers

The popularity of war bonds made it relatively easy for communities to identify those who were holding back financial support and then take measures to ensure compliance. Perhaps the brunt of the hysteria was felt by Mennonites in Kansas, a state that had worked hard to entice Mennonite migrants decades earlier. The state legislature in 1865 promised exemption from military service for anyone with scruples against war; back then, the state wanted Mennonites for their expertise in farming. By World War I, the state had forgotten its invitation—or at least wanted to rescind the terms. Mobs set out to punish pacifists in the spring of 1918, relying on a favorite scare tactic: tar and feathers.[23]

The third Liberty Loan drive, held on April 6, stirred up the hyperpatriots of McPherson County, which was the first county in the state to publish a list of slackers (in November of 1917). McPherson did well in the loan drive, selling more than its quota, but a group of about forty men thought they could do better. On the night of April 22, they drove out to the Walter Cooprider farm in Groveland Township. Cooprider was the son of a Civil War veteran who had married a Mennonite widow and converted to the faith; he had refused to buy bonds. When the men arrived at the farm, they cut the telephone wires. They put on masks and surrounded the house. The mob called him from the house and issued an ultimatum: buy bonds or be tarred and feathered. Despite their demands, Cooprider said that he could not buy bonds because of his religious convictions. A son, George, volunteered to substitute for his father, who had not been in strong health. They applied warm roofing paint to George's head, neck, and shoulders and then directed him to lie down and roll in a bed of feathers.

The men drove on, now past midnight, to the homes of Daniel Diener and his son, Charles, ministers at Spring Valley Mennonite Church. The mob was angered not only about their failure to buy bonds but also because

Charles Diener had removed a flag that had been nailed to the church during the day. The younger Diener received the tar and feather treatment first. The men drove on to Daniel Diener's home and pulled him from bed to be smeared in tar. Two days later, Walter Cooprider bought bonds, but the Dieners held out. On June 3, the vigilantes returned to Daniel Diener's house; he agreed to write a check for $50 to the Red Cross. The next day he put a hold on the check and met with Liberty Loan officials to work out an alternative contribution to the Friends Reconstruction Service.

But the neighborhood enforcers returned to Daniel Diener's house on June 10 in no mood to bargain. They stole money and a watch, ransacked the house, painted the house and car yellow inside and out, stripped him and whipped him with a strap, and applied roofing paint and feathers. At Charles Diener's house, the men did the same. The mob threatened to kill both men if they were forced to come back again. Faced with this extralegal violence, the Dieners bought bonds.

The mob in this case, as in so many, was composed of neighbors and community leaders, people who in an earlier time would have been regarded as friends. Charles Diener had recognized, if only by voice, the auctioneer, the produce man, and other business owners. The state did not express much outrage. The governor, Arthur Capper, set the tone for Kansans. Not long after the attacks on the Dieners, he commented on the so-called disloyalists: Capper said he had "advised one man to either invest in Liberty bonds or leave the state," and that as governor he would "insist upon thorough loyalty or removal from Kansas."[24] While Capper had plenty of company among national and state leaders in declining to speak out against mob violence, some officials in positions of authority did stand up to mobs, for which John Schrag in Kansas would be thankful.

A group of zealous patriots became fed up with Schrag, a prosperous Mennonite farmer who had declined to buy bonds. On November 11, the day the Allies and Germany signed an armistice, the citizens of Burrton decided to challenge Schrag directly.[25] Men piled into five cars and drove eleven miles to the Schrag farm, intending to draft him for an Armistice Day celebration in town.[26] After ransacking a barn and machine sheds, the men forced their way into the house and found Schrag; he went along without protest.

A crowd gathered around him in Burrton, demanding that he buy war bonds. He offered to donate money to the Red Cross and the Salvation Army, but that would not do. They ordered him to salute the American flag and lead a parade through town. He refused. At that point, someone apparently thrust a flag into his hand, and the flag fell. Cries arose that he had stepped on the flag. The enraged mob painted him in yellow, covering his scalp and rubbing it into his beard and splashing it on his clothes. One of the men in the mob secured a rope from the hardware store and looped it over Schrag's neck. They marched him down near the city jail, alongside a tree, intending to hang him.

All the while, Schrag, a short, heavyset man, offered no resistance. Tom Roberts, the head of the local Anti-Horse-Thief Association, managed to get Schrag inside the jailhouse and blocked the door, flashing a gun and warning, "If you take this man out of jail, you take him over my dead body." A Harvey County sheriff transferred Schrag to the county jail for safekeeping and to await trial on charges of violating the Espionage Act by desecrating the flag. Schrag would later be found not guilty and Mennonites and others of German descent quietly began an economic boycott of Burrton; one by one, they pulled their money from the local bank and opened accounts in neighboring Buhler, Hesston, and Newton.

Churches in the Crosshairs

Vigilantes also targeted property, especially churches, to ensure conformity. In the spring of 1918, a month before the Hofer brothers and Jacob Wipf packed for Camp Lewis, arsonists went after the Mennonite church in Fairview, Michigan, a small community in a part of the state known for its sandy soil and severe winters.[27] Fairview is in Comins Township in Oscoda County, about three-fourths of which lies within the Au Sable State and Huron National forests. The church had grown from about thirty-five members in 1901 to more than 200 by 1918. Mennonites appeared to be well liked and respected by many of their neighbors, with several church members having been elected to public office. But resentment had been building in the months before the torching of the church, over both the Mennonites' stance on warfare and also their success as Democrats in winning local elections.

William F. McNeeley, a local game warden and president of the Oscoda County American Defense Society, wrote a letter to Comins Township residents in advance of the April elections in which he likened conscientious objectors to "copperheads at our back using their poisonous fangs at every opportunity."[28] He concluded the letter: "At the next session of the legislature the American people are going to demand that conscientious objectors and pro-Germans should be disenfranchised, and there is not the slightest doubt but that it will be done. In the meantime go to the polls and vote for Americans."

On April 1, Election Day, Republicans defeated Democrats at the polls, including the Mennonite candidates. Three nights later, McNeeley and Edwin Goodwin, the publisher of the *Oscoda County Telegram and News*, set fire to the wooden church building. One poured a flammable liquid, and the other struck the match. The sheriff was not inclined to investigate. The church members did not help themselves in that regard; they did not believe they should seek redress in court or fight back. By 1919, the Mennonites had rebuilt the church. The arsonists, meanwhile, escaped prosecution as the investigation stalled amid political maneuverings.

Advocate for the Imprisoned Pacifists

Given the widespread hysteria, the safest approach for pacifists or opponents of the war was to avoid attention. But some advocates would not be cowed into silence. One of the most tireless campaigners on behalf of conscientious objectors was Jacob G. Ewert, a journalist and a professor of comparative philology at Tabor College in Hillsboro, Kansas. Though left paralyzed and confined to bed because of rheumatism, Ewert welcomed hundreds of visitors to his home during the war and kept up an extensive correspondence with young men in the training camps, urging them to refuse to take up arms. He operated what he called a private "Civil Liberties Bureau" for Mennonites of the West.

Even at the risk of running afoul of the Espionage Act, he denounced Liberty Bonds in his column in the *Vorwaerts*, a German-language newspaper that he edited in Hillsboro. As a Mennonite, he also called on denominational leaders to be more forceful in challenging the treatment of conscientious objectors, especially the kind of prison abuse to which the four Hutterites had been subjected at Alcatraz. Many church leaders were reluctant to mount an aggressive protest, not wanting to appear disrespectful of the government or invite prosecution. Ewert, a Socialist and a member of the National Civil Liberties Bureau, did not view reticence as an option.

When he learned about the Hutterites' imprisonment at Alcatraz, Ewert turned to verse to pay tribute to the men. The poem began:

Four bearded men there stand in chains,
With hand-cuffs fastened to the bars
Their arms stretched up, with fev'rish pains,
With bruises not yet changed to scars,
They barely reach the slimy floor
With their bare feet: in underwear,
Their shiv'ring bodies, weak and sore;
And yet their hearts are strong in prayer.

All's still, while dark and heavy gloom
The dungeon fills, and silence reigns
O'er Alcatraz, this living tomb,
Where life is crushed with cruel chains.
How could they live with bodies frail—
No blanket on the clammy floor—
Just bread and water, often stale,
And just so much, and no ounce more?

At stated times the keepers come
And bring the scanty food and drink;
But not sufficient 'tis for some
To hold their lives back from the brink.
Oh, yes! There's something else besides
The keepers give these heretics;

But their report securely hides
The shameful cursings, clubbings, kicks!

All's still again; when left alone
They pray for grace to bear it all:
No words we hear, but just a moan
Or cry of pain that would appall
'Most any heart not made of stone.
But no sound thru the dungeon wall
Is heard, except the constant splash
Of waves that on the island dash;
And thru the crumbling mortar seep
The briny waters of the deep.[29]

With the end of the war in sight, the Hofer brothers and Jacob Wipf were headed to Fort Leavenworth, where they would be imprisoned with the vast majority of the nation's conscientious objectors. There they would meet Erling Lunde, a war objector on political and moral grounds who had been court-martialed earlier that year for refusing to obey orders. Lunde's father, Theodore, who owned a piano hardware company in Chicago, American Industrial, would soon be in contact with Jacob Ewert. United in their outrage over the treatment of conscientious objectors, the bedridden professor and the piano maker would ensure that the news of the Hofer brothers and Jacob Wipf reached the world.

Chapter Seven

Midnight at Leavenworth

Yea, before we would knowingly wrong a man to the value of a penny,
we would rather lose a hundred pounds; and before we would strike our
greatest enemy with the hand, to say nothing of the gun or sword, as the
world does, we would rather die, and let our own lives be taken.
—The Chronicle of the Hutterian Brethren

Cheering the Armistice, Staying on Alert

San Francisco celebrated the armistice with a human chain of five thousand people, who gathered at the Civic Center, still wearing flu masks as a precaution. Like so much of the rest of the country, the city was just emerging from the worst of an influenza epidemic when war, at least on paper, came to end on November 11, 1918. So the people of San Francisco offered up a muffled rendition of "Auld Lang Syne" in an impromptu chorus, swinging their clasped hands in time to the music and punctuating the end of the song with the American war cry "Yip!"

Up north along the coast in Washington State, near where the Hutterites had started their detention, Tacomans also streamed from offices and factories to revel in the news. The giant American flag that proved too big for a pole on Memorial Day finally made its appearance, as staff members of the *News Tribune* unfurled the flag from the top of their headquarters at the Perkins building. From the cornice above the sixth floor, the flag touched down near the sidewalk. A reporter with a sentimental eye captured the scene: "A cheer rose from the throats of the crowd at 11th and A and a band struck up 'Keep the Home Fires Burning.' Not a dry eye remained in the crowd and, with hats over their hearts, Tacoma declared that the Great War was over."[1]

The armistice signed by the allies and Germany signaled a victory for the United States, but troops (and their anxious families at home) who expected an immediate withdrawal from Europe were in for a disappointment. The American military machine would remain in place in France without relaxation pending German compliance with the terms of the armistice, including the immediate removal of troops from France and other territories. Secretary Baker said: "The signing of the military armistice enables us to suspend the intensive military preparation in which the country was engaged. It does not, however, signify the formal end of the war."[2] Readers of the *Examiner* in San Francisco were reminded that however strong the convictions of the four Hutterites, however righteous their stance, other American young men were continuing to shed their blood on behalf of the nation. Two days after the armistice, the army reported 482 deaths on that day alone, bringing the total number of casualties since the war began to 25,096.

Three days after the armistice the Hutterites left Alcatraz, still in chains. Under overcast skies that threatened a chilly rain, they boarded a train for the disciplinary barracks at Fort Leavenworth, Kansas. The reason for the transfer at this time is unclear, especially since the army would send many conscientious objectors the opposite direction, from Leavenworth to Alcatraz, in the coming months. Security ratcheted up for the men when they began this leg of their journey in detention on November 14. In traveling to Alcatraz, four officers guarded them. This time six officers, all sergeants, accompanied the Hutterites, who were once again chained in pairs.

The Hutterite men traveled by train through Texas, en route to Fort Leavenworth. The trip took four days and five nights. Michael Hofer wrote his last letter from the train, near the end of the trip. If taken at his word, he was in good health. But the multiple references to the afterlife suggest otherwise:

Grace and peace be with you. I want to write to you that we are now on the way to Fort Leavenworth. We don't know, however, what will become of us

Residents of Tacoma, Washington, celebrated the end of the war with a flag that proved too large for a pole at Camp Lewis.
Tacoma Public Library

there. Only God the almighty knows if we will see each other again in this world, for we go from one affliction to the other. We plead earnestly to God, for he has promised us that not a single hair falls from our heads without his will. And if we do not see each other again in this world, then we will see one another in the next world.

Dear spouse, I have received two letters from you and one from dear brother Peter. You can imagine that I wept when I read that you are sick, along with our dear little daughter. Don't go leave the house too soon. Keep yourself warm.

I am still healthy in body and soul and wish for you the same, and for all the brothers and sisters—which is the greatest treasure that a human could receive here on earth. Now I will close with a heartfelt greeting to all the brothers and sisters in the community. . . . And I remain your sorrowful husband. Michael Y. Hofer, until death.[3]

Joseph, likewise, wrote his final letter home to Maria while in chains as the train crossed the Southwest. In a note colored by end-time imagery, he conveys his certainty that they will not be reunited again on this earth, but only in heaven:

> My dear wife, since we will no longer see each other in this troubled world, then we will see each other yonder through the power of God. With this we must be satisfied with that which God allows to happen. And he will not lay upon us more than what we, with his strength, can endure. . . .
>
> And when you look at our scrawling you can well imagine how low our spirits are, for we are where the waves are roaring and in that time when the seas throw up the dead—if you can only see this in the right way.
>
> This is all for this time, my dear wife. For this is not a good letter at all, since the train shakes and bounces so much. Now to close. My best greetings to you and our dear children, father and mother and all the brothers and sisters in the faith.[4]

Marching to the Barracks in a "Cruel Manner"

The men arrived at Fort Leavenworth, on Tuesday, November 19, at 11 at night, fully spent. David Hofer recounted their difficulty in traveling any farther:

> We were marched through the streets, up the hill to the barracks, carrying our suitcases, and other luggage. When we arrived we were worn out and very sweaty and warm. We were told to undress. We did so, and were required to stand in the chilly night air in our sweated underwear for two hours before the warden came with prison garments. At 5 o'clock the next morning we were required to appear again and wait for some time in the sharp morning air. Michael and Joseph complained of sharp pains in their chest, and were taken to the hospital, sick.[5]

By some accounts, officers herded the men along like cattle from the train station to the military camp, menacing them with the sharp edges of bayonets. A narrative based on an interview with David Hofer provides this

A week after the armistice, the Hutterites arrived at Fort Leavenworth, Kansas,
shown here in 1920.
Courtesy of Frontier Army Museum, Fort Leavenworth, Kansas

detail: "They arrived at Leavenworth at 11 o'clock at night and were driven through the middle of the street, under much noise and prodding with bayonets, as if they were swine. Chained together at the wrists, carrying their satchels in one hand and their Bibles and an extra pair of shoes under the arm, they were hurried on, in a cruel manner, up the hill toward the military prison."[6]

A military officer's report took issue with that account, after word spread that the men had been manhandled with bayonets.[7] The report said that one sergeant and four privates met the Hutterites at the train station that night. The soldiers escorted them on a walk of about three hundred yards, up a hill to the barracks. They walked fast and so did indeed work up a sweat, but there was no one who threatened them with bayonets, according to the report, said to have been confirmed by Jacob Wipf. When the four men arrived at the base, they got cold because they had left their gloves and coats in the guard's office and had to stand with their coats off outside in the yard for about twenty minutes while the sergeant put their things away. The report rebuts David Hofer's account: "They did not stand anywhere at any time for two hours in their underwear."

A few weeks later Colonel Sedgwick Rice, the commandant at Fort Leavenworth, sought to put the alleged mistreatment to rest.[8] He said that guards who escort prisoners to the fort are never armed with rifles or bayonets, but only with revolvers. Moreover, he said, prisoners are immediately put to bed when they come in on the midnight train. All of the formalities of checking them in and issuing clothing are put off until morning.

The harsh particulars of their welcome aside, the men entered a massive prison that night, enclosed by a stone wall that varied from fourteen to forty-one feet high. The U.S. Disciplinary Barracks was known as "the castle," owing to a dome at the center of an octagonal hub. From that gray dome eight wings branched out, each one eight tiers high. Prisoners who would not work were kept in solitary confinement in the lower level, below ground, in cells about five feet by eight feet. Near the castle was the hospital and medical clinic. The prison held several thousand inmates that winter, with about five hundred men kept in locked cells and the rest assigned to open cells or temporary barracks.

Ernest L. Meyer, a conscientious objector from Wisconsin, arrived at Fort Leavenworth two months before the Hutterites. Like them, he approached the prison shortly before midnight, walking from the train station.

We left the train, bowing under our duffle bags, and filed along a gravel path leading through a park. Reversing the more popular quest, we searched for an entrance to the prison. Our guard, the good sergeant, was as unfamiliar with the grounds as we were, and we aided cheerfully in scouting the dreaded goal. At length, in the darkness, we came to a great wall on which at intervals loomed turrets mounted with brilliant searchlights that swept the crest of the brick barricade. A dog barked loudly somewhere. Sentries popped out of the turret directly overhead and in response to a query by our sergeant shouted directions. We marched silently around the base of the wall. Looking up we saw barred windows, a number of which framed

S. Disciplinary Barracks-Ft. Leavenworth Kans.

*The U.S. Disciplinary Barracks, with a dome at the center, was known as
"the castle."*
Courtesy of Frontier Army Museum, Fort Leavenworth, Kansas

white and motionless forms. We came to a great arched gateway, also heavily barred. We were let into a narrow, separate section of the great gate by a
keeper provided with an enormous key.[9]

A Model of Productivity

Alcatraz presented itself as a school of second chances; Fort Leavenworth
intended to be the model of an efficient factory. By 1918, the Disciplinary
Barracks at Fort Leavenworth was a self-supporting hub of productivity,
with prisoners fanning out across the property to their respective jobs, not
unlike a Hutterite colony in some ways.[10] The agriculture unit, which was
even called the farm colony, included dairy, poultry, and hog operations; a
canner; a garden; and a greenhouse. The farming operation was expansive.
For the fiscal year ending July 1, 1918, Leavenworth counted hundreds of
productive acres: wheat, 320; barley, 103; alfalfa, 103; potatoes, 109; toma-
toes, 10; melons, 10; and more. The operation included 182 head of Hol-
steins, each of which was milked three times daily.

One prisoner, Arthur Dunham, recalled entering the Disciplinary Barracks "under an archway that reminded one of a medieval castle."
Courtesy of Frontier Army Museum, Fort Leavenworth, Kansas

To illustrate what could be accomplished with prison labor, Colonel Rice noted that Fort Leavenworth had manufactured 1,866 brooms during 1918 at a cost of only $43.95 for supplies, equal to a few pennies per broom. The corn for the brooms came from sixteen acres of land harvested in 1916, and two prisoners working with crude machinery had turned them out. If the prison devoted more equipment and men to the enterprise, Rice figured, they could expand from two thousand brooms a year to two thousand a day. Elsewhere, a cold storage facility churned out twenty-five tons of ice daily, easily enough to keep the entire post well supplied. A tailor's shop produced almost 22,000 civilian and military garments that year; pressing was also handled on site at the dry cleaning plant.

During a visit to Fort Leavenworth in August, three months before the Hutterite men arrived, Secretary Baker spent the afternoon driving around the reservation and touring the vocational training farm with Colonel Rice. Rice was a bear of a man, but he was not one to bully the prisoners or be

By 1918, the Disciplinary Barracks at Fort Leavenworth was a self-supporting hub of productivity, including a shoe shop.
Courtesy of Frontier Army Museum, Fort Leavenworth, Kansas

anything but gracious with visitors. He welcomed the chance to show off what he regarded as a well-run institution, whether it be a Washington official or a local reporter who came calling. Even Roger Baldwin, who visited the prison twice as the head of the National Civil Liberties Union, came away convinced that Rice was a progressive commandant, the "chief good point" at the camp.[11] In making the rounds with Baker that August, Rice also put forward a "generous and kindly" face.[12]

The visit went well. Baker made clear his conviction that every prisoner should be put to work: "The farm will help develop the physical side of prisoners, which appears to be very important. . . . The success of the post lies in the efforts that are made to develop men and to keep them from going to waste, and to make useful citizens of them."[13] Once back in Washington, Baker exchanged several friendly letters with Rice, often touching on the subject of dog named Yank that Rice had given to Baker's family as a gift (and that Frederick Keppel, the assistant secretary of war, had personally brought back from Kansas). "I have just returned from abroad and find that Yank is already a member of the family, being the constant play-fellow of my three small children," Baker mentioned in one letter.[14]

For Many Conscientious Objectors, Prison Work Is Agreeable

Many conscientious objectors were ready to take advantage of the opportunity to be productive. In the training camps earlier, surrounded by soldiers in uniform who were preparing to engage in direct combat, men who had scruples against war often felt that any labor was contributing to the military machine, even if indirectly. But now that they were in prison, having been dishonorably discharged, the war had receded. For the conscientious objectors who accepted jobs at the prison, the conditions in some respects seemed comfortable.

Elmer Liechty, a twenty-six-year-old Mennonite who was sentenced to ten years at a court-martial at Camp Taylor in Kentucky, was transferred to Leavenworth in November, just when the Hutterites arrived. He said inmates were allowed to have church services on Saturday afternoon as well as on Sunday morning. During the week he helped to unload baled hay and do other chores at the prison. In a letter home, he thought it worth commenting on dessert: pumpkin pie for the third time. "We get clean bed sheets every week and clean underwear twice a week and we don't do our own washing. What do the people say about me being a prisoner?"[15] Liechty did not work when he reported to Camp Taylor in Kentucky, but he reasoned that since he had been court-martialed, he was no longer a soldier; beyond that, he said, the work at Leavenworth did not furnish money or matériel for the war.

Emanuel Swartzendruber, a Mennonite from Michigan, also agreed to work once he arrived at the prison camp. In effect, he had come full circle. When he reported to Camp Greenleaf in Georgia, on March 5, 1918, Swartzendruber started out on kitchen duty, peeling potatoes and washing dishes. But he soon had misgivings. As he said, "I am not opposed to work, but I can't be a member of the army."[16] A sergeant did all that he could to change his mind, ordering Swartzendruber and three other objectors to tear down an outhouse. After the building was removed, the sergeant said:

"Now we'll show you what your Jesus can do when you are in our hands."
Soldiers threw one of the men into the cesspool, where he stood, chest-deep
in muck. They shoveled excrement on his head, saying, "I baptize you in the
name of Jesus."

After Swartzendruber helped to clean off the man, it was his turn. The
sergeant escorted him to the cesspool and asked him three times whether
he was ready to serve. Swartzendruber answered once—a certain no. So the
soldiers lifted him by his legs and dumped him head-first into the waste
pool. He heard someone cry out, "Don't put him any further, you'll kill
him!" When the men pulled him out, the sergeant shook his head, not saying a word. Finally, he said, "Go and wash." Swartzendruber was sentenced
to ten years of hard labor, arriving at Fort Leavenworth in September. There
he filled silos, stripped broom corn, and picked acorns.

Albert Voth, a Mennonite from Kansas who had been court-martialed
at a camp in southern Texas for refusing to perform any kind of military
service, and then sentenced to twenty-five years, recalled how welcoming
Fort Leavenworth appeared after the camp.

> Paradoxical as it may seem, my first impression on entering the prison gates
> at Leavenworth was one of genuine relief. Others in our group concurred in
> this. The mental pressure of uncertainty and countercurrent events in camp
> had become so increasingly severe that at times one's rationality seemed in
> question. Here suddenly the atmosphere was changed. Prisoners were sim-
> ply dressed and clean in appearance. The white walls seemed peaceful, and
> above all there was a certain attitude of natural ease in evidence around us
> which we so badly needed.[17]

The prison chaplain met with them and offered to serve as the "prisoners'
friend" in so far as he could. "Then, drawing himself up into an air of severity, he went on to say 'but those among you, and you know whom I mean,
who have refused to participate in this most holy of holy wars—well, I will
refrain from saying what I would like to say—that is all.'"

Prison, despite Voth's favorable first impression, was still prison. The
food was hard to eat, especially when worms appeared in the stew. Fights
and sexual activities were on display. Voth was assigned to work in the farm

fields, part of a crew of six men who labored under shotgun surveillance. After three months he was offered a job as a library assistant, supervised by the chaplain. In time, they became friends. Voth learned to know other prisoners as well, including socialists with doctoral degrees. "I had expected to see hardened, sullen men," he said. "Instead, I was impressed with the many intelligent, normal faces all around me."

Solitary Confinement Brings a Change of Heart

But for men who refused to work at Fort Leavenworth, conditions quickly worsened. Arthur Dunham arrived as an "independent liberal Christian"— and a pacifist.[18] While studying political science at the University of Illinois before the war, he had what he described as a second conversion: "I felt that I had found a real basis for a vital Christianity in the principle of Love as the motive for every individual act and every group relationship. In religious social service work I had begun to try to work out some of the implications of this principle."

He resigned from the Presbyterian Church in protest against the church's support of the war and became a member of the Society of Friends. As Private Dunham at Fort Riley in Kansas, that meant refusing to pick up a rake to clean the parade grounds. The day after the armistice was signed, he was court-martialed and sentenced to twenty-five years, to be served at Fort Leavenworth.

> The great iron gates swung open. We passed in, between the two gates, under an archway that reminded one of a medieval castle. A young man—a strange-looking man in an ill-fitting brown suit and a visored cap—moved silently by with a lantern, sparing us just a glance. We turned into the little room to our right, and we faced a bulletin board. "U.S.D.B.—POPULATION 3125" . . . We were prisoners, in the largest military prison in the United States—Fort Leavenworth.

Dunham quickly caught on to the drill. That first night, he claimed a cot in the corridor in the sixth wing basement. When a bell clanged, the men in cells sprang forward to the doors, armed folded, standing silently. The

The mess hall could serve 1,500 men at a time; even so, to accommodate all the
men, meals were served in two shifts.
Courtesy of Frontier Army Museum, Fort Leavenworth, Kansas

men in the corridor stood as well, just outside the doors, facing the same direction, arms folded. The officer of the day took a walking count, and soon afterward someone called "lights out."

At six in the morning Dunham's unit marched into an immense mess hall, with a capacity of 1,500. To accommodate all the men, meals were served in two shifts. The officer of the day sat at a desk, on a small raised platform. About fifteen guards, armed with clubs, kept watch around the mess hall. The prisoners all sat facing the same door, eight seats in a row before a foot-wide wooden table. The waiters went up and down the aisles, passing out large tin containers. Once a day there was "slum," a version of beef stew, heavy with potatoes and carrots.

When unpacking, the only personal book prisoners could keep was a Bible. All clothing was taken, replaced by black and brown prison suits, with numbers painted, about three inches high, across the overcoat, raincoat, coat, shirt, and working blouse, and across each trouser leg, about four inches above the knee. White numbers went to men in first class ("entitled to all the privileges of the institution," as an assistant executive officer put it); red, in second class; and yellow, in third class. Each man also received a dog-eared cap with a visor and a pair of large, clumsy shoes. "We broke into laughter as we looked at each other," Dunham said. The men also were given a book of rules (one of which said, "You will be known by number while here"). Dunham became No. 15336.

During his orientation, No. 15336 was part of a group of about six men waiting outside the chaplain's office. When the chaplain suddenly appeared, he found the men seated on benches instead of standing at attention, and the guard standing with his hands in his pockets. The chaplain was not happy. "I suppose if the colonel himself came along, he'd find you in that position," he bellowed. "Have these men stand up!" Once inside his office, the chaplain assumed the voice of spiritual guide: "This is not the place of lost hope—it is the place of another chance."

When asked by a lieutenant what work he would do, Dunham said, "I cannot conscientiously do any work here." Verification came the next day. After breakfast, the new men waited in the prison yard. A corporal arrived and led the men to a tool room where he handed out several brooms. When Dunham stood back, the corporal said, "Come on, step up and grab a broom; don't be bashful!" I answered, "I explained to the Executive Officer yesterday that I intended to refuse to work here; I'll take the penalty." "All right," the yard corporal said, "stand over there against the wall." Several other objectors joined him at the wall, while others went out to clean the yard.

One by one the men were taken to see an executive officer, a Captain B. He looked up and said, "You are charged with refusing to do any work at all. Is that right?" "Yes sir." They returned to the clothing room, where the white numbers were painted yellow (signifying that they had now become dangerous prisoners). The painter, himself a prisoner, seemed fully exercised about being caused a "hell of a lot of trouble by you damn slackers." The guard added, "Well, if I ever meet a C.O. in civil life, either he'll get beat up or I will!"

Dunham was sentenced to fourteen days of solitary confinement, on a full diet if he worked on the rockpile, or, if not, given bread and water and handcuffed to the bars nine hours a day. He declined all work, including breaking rocks. He entered the cell on a Saturday night. "I placed my hands through the bars of the door, and for the first time the steel handcuffs closed over my wrists. For a moment I caught a glimpse of a guard grinning malevolently at us; then the wooden door closed, shutting off most of the light and deadening all sounds. I was alone in the Hole."

The cell was about eight feet long by five feet wide, and eight feet high. The walls were of brick, the floor concrete. About six inches in front of the steel bars was a wooden partition, shutting out light and fresh air, except what came through screens at the top and bottom of the door (the screens were about six inches wide and fourteen inches long). In each cell there was a washbowl, a toilet, three blankets, and a tin cup. The primary furnishing was a wooden bed: a single board, about eighteen inches wide and not quite six feet long. At meal time, three pieces of bread and a cup of water passed through the bars.

On Monday morning, the regular shift began. The men were awakened at 6, given breakfast, and handcuffed to the bars at 7. From 12 to 12:30 the handcuffs were removed, for lunch; from 12:30 to 4:30 they were strung up again. In solitary, no books were allowed, not even a Bible. Even so, it would have been impossible to read except at mealtime or maybe in the evening if the guard left the door open. The men could talk from cell to cell, but it was hard to hear once the wooden doors were closed. In a typical week, the prisoner would never leave his cell except on Saturday afternoon, when the cells were cleaned and the solitary prisoners went to the washroom for a bath and a shave.

> No doubt it is a mark of immaturity of character, but I must confess that two or three times that week the conditions of the solitary were so far psychologically effective as to produce the blackest fits of mental depression that I have ever experienced. Personally, I always felt that this mental effect was the most real torture of the Hole. No doubt the other men had similar experiences; we did not discuss such symptoms, but always alleged that we were "getting along fine," in answer to shouted questions from each other.

After nine days in solitary, Dunham and several companions agreed to work. They reasoned that the war was over, so in no way were they contrib-

A row of cells in the 1914 wing of the Disciplinary Barracks appears much as it did when the Hutterites were held there in solitary confinement. The barracks were razed soon after this photo was taken in 2002. Mennonite World Review

uting to any killing field. They also believed that staying in solitary would break their health. No. 15336 was painted red, consigned to shoveling dirt and carting it off in wheelbarrows. Years later, Dunham regretted his decision: "I believe now that my reasoning was fallacious. I believe that it would have been braver, more logical, and more consistent to have persisted in my refusal to work and to have remained in solitary. I regret the weakness which caused me to compromise, and I doubly honor those who refused to compromise."

Hutterites Steadfast in Refusal to Work

In the week before the Hutterites arrived at Fort Leavenworth, the National Civil Liberties Bureau appealed to Secretary Baker to intervene on behalf of conscientious objectors in solitary confinement at the prison. The letter described men hanging by their wrists from cell doors for nine hours a day, sleeping on cold cement floors, subsisting on bread and water. Bureau officials objected to the "use of torture in our prisons for any offender whatsoever or for any offense. It is inconceivable that a humane people like American[s] and a liberal administration like your own can continue to tolerate such form of punishment."[19] Bureau files show no record of a reply from Baker.

Noah Leatherman, a Mennonite who was raised in Kansas, was at Fort Leavenworth when the Hofer brothers and Jacob Wipf arrived. He spoke with them in German that night—they appeared to be in "pitiful condition"—and then never again.[20] They made it clear that they would not work at Leavenworth, just as they had refused any assignments at Alcatraz and at Camp Lewis. For his part, Leatherman, No. 15161, headed out to the fields, gathering grain, corn, beets. He had arrived at Leavenworth on November 13, sentenced to twenty-five years for having refused an order to cut weeds and grass with a scythe at Camp Funston in Kansas. He agreed to work at Leavenworth, he said, since it no longer felt as if officials wanted to turn him into a soldier; the war was over. He also admitted that he was not eager to face the solitary cells in the basement of the sixth and seventh wings ("I may have yielded somewhat here through weakness of flesh").

The three Hofer brothers and Jacob Wipf, who had been confined together since their arrival at Camp Lewis in May, finally separated at Fort Leavenworth. One day after their arrival on November 21, Jacob Wipf was admitted to the hospital, suffering from what doctors diagnosed as acute intestinal fermentation; he was returned to duty on November 25. Wipf, when he was well, and David Hofer—who appears to have been the only one of the men to have arrived in reasonably good health—were placed in isolation cells, their hands shackled high up through the bars of the doors. In this way, they stood for nine hours each day, just as Dunham had. They received only bread and water.

David Hofer soon asked to send a telegram to his family, warning them that his brothers were in grave condition. Their wives, and most likely their father and a brother, left the home colony in South Dakota immediately. Their arrival was delayed when they were mistakenly directed by a railroad agent to the wrong fort in Kansas, Fort Riley, about 126 miles from Leavenworth.

Family members tell a story, perhaps apocryphal, that when the wives got off the train at the station near Fort Riley, likely in Junction City, a kind stranger approached, like a guardian angel on a biblical mission.

> They stood there in the street of that little town and didn't know what to do. When it began to rain, they moved inside to a restaurant. Here they were in a strange place, not knowing the whereabouts of their husbands, despairing, not knowing what to do.
>
> Suddenly a man stopped by their table and began to visit with them. He asked who they were and what they were doing there, so the women told him their troubles. He listened until they were finished.
>
> Then he told them, "Your husbands have been sent to Fort Leavenworth in Kansas. I will go with you to the train station and help you get tickets. When you get to Fort Leavenworth, it will be evening and you will have to walk a mile to the prison. When you get there the guard will say, 'It is too late. Come back in the morning.' But you must insist on seeing your husbands and then he will let you in."
>
> The women trusted the man and went with him to the train station. Soon after they had bought their tickets, the train came in. The man helped them board the train with their luggage, and when the women turned to thank him, he was gone. They never saw him again.[21]

A Deadly Plague Sweeps through the Prison

Though delayed by a day, the wives arrived at Leavenworth in time to see their husbands, Joseph and Michael; Joseph was barely able to communicate. He died at 8:35 the following morning, November 29, in the barracks hospital at the age of twenty-four. The guards said that family members could not see him. But Joseph's wife, Maria, perhaps remembering what the stranger had said, pushed past the guards and demanded permission from the head officer to see her husband. He relented. With tears in her eyes, she approached the coffin, which was set on two chairs. When the lid was opened, she found Joseph in death dressed in a military uniform that he had steadfastly refused to wear in life. Jacob (J.D.) Mininger, a Mennonite minister from Kansas City who served as a pastor to the conscientious objectors at Fort Leavenworth, visiting each week, was with Joseph when he died. Mininger later said, "If ever I saw a person die as a real Christian and pass from this life into a better world, it was Joseph Hofer."[22]

Michael Hofer died a few days later, at 3:40 p.m. on December 2, in the barracks hospital. He was twenty-five. His last words were said to be: "Come, Lord Jesus, into thy hands I commend my spirit."[23] David Hofer was there when Michael died, as was Mininger. Mininger happened to have an apple in his pocket and offered it to David, who said, "Thank you. All I get is bread and water."[24] At the family's pleading, prison officials did not place Michael in military dress when they prepared his body for immediate shipment home by train.

The Office of the Surgeon of the Disciplinary Barracks listed pneumonia as the cause of death for both men, a common designation for the "Spanish" influenza, which was sweeping through the prison just when the men transferred from Alcatraz. As Colonel Rice later said, "These prisoners arrived during the epidemic of influenza."[25] The epidemic had also spread across San Francisco while the men were still at Alcatraz, leading authorities there to close schools and require that masks be worn in public for several weeks in October and November.

Rice made a point of noting that neither prisoner was in solitary confinement or was undergoing punishment for any violation of barracks rules in the days immediately preceding their deaths; they had been hospitalized as soon as they arrived from Alcatraz. The annual report for the year showed a surge in deaths that fall and winter, many related to the influenza: July, one; August, none; September, none; October, fifty-nine; November, seven; and December, four.

The 1918–1919 influenza pandemic, likely the deadliest plague in human history, infected 500 million people, or one-third of the world's population, and killed more than 50 million, far more than died in the war.[26] Investigators today put the death toll in the United States at about 675,000 people.[27] The virus was highly contagious and easily spread. The incubation period was twenty-four to seventy-two hours, and soldiers with influenza could infect others before they felt any symptoms (the average time from first symptoms to death was about ten days). The symptoms included head-aches, body aches, fever, cough, fatigue, and chills, possibly progressing to pneumonia.

Researchers remain puzzled about why the 1918 pandemic was so fatal. In the winter and spring of that year, a few countries reported influenza outbreaks, but the virus was hardly a killer. Then in the summer, several countries, mainly in northern Europe, began to tally victims, perhaps sig-naling the start of the influenza pandemic. A highly fatal influenza wave swept across the United States from September to November 1918, when the Hutterites were imprisoned at Alcatraz and transferred to Fort Leaven-worth. A second wave struck many countries, including the United States, early in 1919.

Prisons like Alcatraz and Leavenworth offered optimal conditions for the spread of the virus. In the words of infectious specialists, they featured "increased crowding indoors" and "imperfect ventilation due to closed win-dows and suboptimal airflow."[28] The prisons could not follow the lead of schools and other public places, which simply closed as a public health strategy. Just before they fell ill, the Hofer brothers had traveled by train from Alcatraz to Fort Leavenworth, confined in a space with less ventilation than any barracks or prison.

Moreover, all of the prisoners at Leavenworth appear to have been at a greater risk because of their age. Historically, the curve of influenza deaths is U-shaped, with mortality peaking among the very young and the very old. A plotted line for the 1918 worldwide pandemic shows a spike among young adults in their twenties and thirties, the prime years for military ser-vice. The age graph of the dead in 1918 advanced two places in the alphabet, resembling a W.

The virus, however frightening its reach, passed through the major-ity of people as viruses usually did, with several unpleasant days followed by recovery. "This was influenza, only influenza," as John M. Barry wrote in *The Great Influenza*.[29] But in a minority of cases, the virus reached ex-treme virulence or led to pneumonia. Though most victims who died did not experience severe pain, some did. In *Pale Horse, Pale Rider*, Katherine Anne Porter, a reporter who caught the disease and was expected to die, drew upon her own experience for the description in the novella: "Pain returned, a terrible compelling pain running through her veins like heavy fire."[30] Lips, ears, and other body parts might turn a dark, leaden blue. Blood might trickle or even spout from the nose, mouth, or ears. The Hofer family shared no such detailed description of the brothers' physical condition in the last days.

Regardless of the military's official pronouncement on the cause of death and gaps in information about the case, the Hutterite church was convinced that the men died because of the manner in which they had been imprisoned in the weeks and months leading up to death. The official church history, the *Chronicle of the Hutterian Brethren*, states that Michael and Joseph Hofer "died in prison as a result of cruel mistreatment by the United States military."[31]

The National Civil Liberties Bureau shared that view. During a campaign to free the remaining conscientious objectors held at Alcatraz in 1919, the director, Roger Baldwin, telegraphed a newspaper executive in California: "Dungeon at Alcatraz Island and Treatment which killed Hofer Brothers is again being used on conscientious objectors at Alcatraz." A California pastor and researcher for the bureau, Robert Whitaker, also sought to counter denials on the part of Alcatraz officials: "The commandant in his official statement quoted in recent papers says that the statement made by visitors that there have been several deaths at the prison are untrue—that there has been only one death in five years. This is a quibble—the Hofer brothers died elsewhere—but they were killed by Alcatraz."[32]

David M. Morens, an epidemiologist in the National Institute of Allergy and Infectious Diseases who has studied the history of pandemics, noted various factors that could have left the brothers vulnerable to influenza, apart from being in the presence of hundreds of potentially virus-carrying men.[33] They might have had a vitamin deficiency linked to their diet at the colony, at Camp Lewis, or in the prison at Alcatraz (Dr. Morens was doubtful that even if the brothers received only bread and water in alternating two-week periods at Alcatraz, they would have suffered a major deficiency from that alone). Given the intermarriage among Hutterites, the brothers might have been genetically vulnerable to infection. Then, too, they were said to have been chilled on the night they waited outside at Fort Leavenworth (and during their time in the basement at Alcatraz).

In the end, Dr. Morens said, "Why these two men died is a mystery not easily explained by the conditions under which they lived. There is not going to be any smoking gun." What's also puzzling is that two brothers died. The mortality rate, even for soldiers living in cramped barracks, was under 5 percent. "Statistically," he said, "the death of both brothers was not likely under any circumstances."

Deaths Condensed to Eighteen Words

Back in South Dakota, a hometown weekly paper, the *Freeman Courier*, which was owned and edited by Jacob J. Mendel, printed the briefest of reports about the deaths of Joseph and Michael Hofer, not even including their names. A one-sentence notice appeared on page 8 as part of a series of dispatches from the Wolf Creek region: "The two sons of Jacob Hofer of Rockport died in a Wash. camp [*sic*] and were buried at home."[34] The subject quickly changed. The next item in the column read: "The Neu Hutterthal church decided to buy a paper cutter for Bartel of China"; and below that, "Sam K. Hofer is building a kitchen and auto shed."

Six days later, the paper reported on the arrival of David Hofer while correcting the earlier error on the place of death: "David Hofer, brother to the two who died at Leavenworth Kansas, was discharged and came home. They are from Rockport. They were transferred from Wash. to Cal. and from there to Kansas."[35] It's not clear why Mendel, whose parents were among the noncommunal stream of Hutterites who fled mandatory military service in Russia four decades earlier, would have downplayed such compelling news—perhaps out of deference to his advertisers and neighbors who supported the war effort. Mendel also served on the Hutchinson County Council of Defense, which opposed family deferments for communal Hutterites.

Whatever Mendel's religious convictions as a member of Neu Hutterthal Mennonite Church, his coverage in the *Freeman Courier* clearly leaned patriotic. In October of 1917, Mendel accompanied Martin M. Waldner to Camp Funston to visit Waldner's brother Peter and "all our boys."[36] The reporting trip came amid rumors, Mendel said, that conscientious objectors were being mistreated at the camps. In his dispatch, Mendel sought to reassure parents of the soldiers: "Knowing that some mothers are worrying because they are under the impression that their sons, dear to them, are mistreated and occasionally a story is circulated with unfavorable reflections upon the treatment they get. We wish to say and honestly and sincerely way down in the bottom of our heart that everything that can be done for the comfort of these men is done."

David Hofer recalled standing in his cell with tears streaming down his face after hearing that his brothers had died. With his hands chained fast, he couldn't wipe them away. He simply stood and wept. He also asked to be moved to a cell closer to Jacob Wipf. Instead, an official soon told him that he was being discharged and should gather up his belongings. David unsuccessfully tried to see Jacob before leaving for home, but a guard promised to pass along a note. David and Jacob would see each other five months later, in April, when Jacob was finally free to return to the colony.

David Hofer was released on December 4 (the order had been given on December 3, the day after his second brother, Michael, died). In January, in a letter to Jonas S. Hartzler, a Mennonite pastor and wartime delegate on behalf of the church, he reflected on the months of confinement: "I praise God for my release, but my soul goes out in behalf of the other prisoners who are confined there in ways that no human being should ever be asked to endure, much less people who have never been guilty of any crime, but because of their relation to Jesus Christ, could not possibly do all that they are asked to do, and because of that, are made to suffer so severely."

Confinement Ever More Solitary

Howard W. Moore, a conscientious objector who was raised on a farm in New York, ended up in solitary confinement at Fort Leavenworth, in a cell next door to Jacob Wipf's. He recalled: "On my second day in solitary I heard someone in the adjoining cell trying to talk to me. There was a space between the barred door and the cell partition, through which I could see an eye peering. Through this channel of communication I learned that my neighbor was Jacob Wipf, a member of the religious sect known as Hutterites."[37]

In "whispered conversations," Moore said, he pieced together an account of the four men from the Rockport Colony in South Dakota. Once hand-cuffing ended and Moore could write, he smuggled out an account of the Hutterites that was published in *The World Tomorrow*, Norman Thomas's Christian pacifist magazine. Moore's experience mirrored Wipf's rotation in and out of solitary confinement.

> After two weeks in solitary I was taken to the prison basement for a shower bath. Some of the other absolutist COs were there, Evan [Thomas] and the Eichel brothers among them; the brief meeting was a delight and our spirits were strengthened. Then we were conducted to the prison office and asked if we were now willing to work. One by one we refused and were sentenced to two more weeks in solitary, shackled as before for nine hours daily. But this time we were to receive full diet. I looked forward to my first meal in two weeks. It consisted of a plate of soupy beans, which the guard shoved under the cell gate and then deliberately spit into. If this was intended to curb my appetite, it was successful. I continued to live on bread crusts, the pièce de résistance of the various garbage that was offered to us.[38]

The prison was so full that convicted soldiers returning from overseas were being housed in corridors of the cell blocks. One offered Moore a memorable gift.

> These men, who worked in prison without question, could hardly be ex-pected to see the significance of the thirty pairs of shackled hands sticking out between the bars of the solitary cells. But some kind of sympathy appar-ently stirred a black man, who concealed a raw onion in his shirt and, at the risk of being put in solitary himself, threw it into my cell as he passed. It was a kindness I would never forget. I hid the onion behind the broom near the toilet, and although it was shared by a couple of rats it lasted nearly two weeks. A little piece rubbed on the crust made the bread more palatable.

Moore described several notable visitors. Jane Addams, the founder of Hull House in Chicago, the first settlement house for poor immigrants in the country, toured the wing where Moore, Wipf, and twenty-eight other conscientious objectors were manacled, asking each man about his health.

After the visit, the men received wooden pallets to lie on and army blankets. Soon afterward, Moore said, Colonel Rice likewise conducted an inspection tour.

> It was an episode worthy of comic opera. The colonel entered a few cells and bent over from the waist stiffly to avoid any contact of his immaculate uniform with our blankets, which he examined carefully through his pince-nez. Of course he found nothing, for bedbugs hide their blood-swollen bodies in wall crevices during the day. Had he stayed inside any of the cells for an hour he would have carried away a few bugs in his clothes.[39]

Day after day, the men stood chained to bars, a tedium broken only by daydreams. The night brought no relief.

> When the lights went out the bugs became more ravenous and the rats more active. There was no way to shut out the prison noises. Men talked in the corridors, their conversation mostly obscene and profane. Sharp cries came from the wing that held sexual deviants. And day and night I heard the cry of "Fight! Fight! Fight!" as regular as the ticking of a clock—the litany of some demented soldiers, perhaps a once healthy but sensitive young man whose mind had cracked under military pressures and like a broken phonograph record continued to repeat the same note . . . At last the morning light, like a gray mist, filtered through the barred windows. . . . There was a clang of bells, and the officer of the day made his rounds. The chains of the handcuffs rasped against the bars as they were applied to our wrists, and another day of standing in shackles began.[40]

War Makes Strange Bedfellows

The refusal to work at Fort Leavenworth brought together men of strikingly different life histories. Under peacetime conditions, the Hofer brothers and Jacob Wipf would have had little reason to speak with fellow inmates like Howard Moore—or his good friend Evan Thomas. Thomas came from a prominent family that itself had been divided by war. His oldest brother,

Norman, had used his formidable connections and eloquence to oppose the war from the outset; another brother, Ralph, became a captain in the Army Corps of Engineers; the youngest brother, Arthur, trained as a fighter pilot.

Evan, who stood above his brothers at six feet five, went his own way. After graduating from Princeton, he studied at Union Theological Seminary and then went to Scotland to serve as an assistant pastor in the Presbyterian Church. He came to embrace conscientious objection, but without the religious foundation and communal history on which the Hutterites based their stance. He was very much a singular objector. An individual's duty, he believed, was to "live life according to his highest ethical ideals and hope that the people would see the truth of his actions."[41]

When Evan Thomas appeared before the Board of Inquiry on July 19 at Fort Leavenworth, he said that the most effective way to counteract the Prussian model, in which the state dominates the individual, is to reject the principle of conscription. He stood by his conviction: "Every man must be true to himself."[42] The board found him to be sincere and offered him a place on a civilian farm. Thomas declined to accept the assignment. Accepting a furlough would still be following a military order and acceding to the principle that the American government has a right to conscript its citizens.

Thomas was transferred a hundred miles west, to Fort Riley. Before long Thomas and several friends went on a hunger strike. Moore was the first to strike, taking a stand against the "principle of conscription." Together with Evan Thomas, Harold Gray, a Harvard student and friend of Evan's, and Erling Lunde, a University of Chicago graduate, joined for the same principle. More than a week into the strike, Evan, who was thin to begin with, was weak and showing an irregular pulse. He was hospitalized and fed a milk and egg mixture through a tube. One by one, the men gave up the hunger strike, with Moore the last one to begin accepting meals.

Evan Thomas appeared before a court-martial at Camp Funston on October 3, accused of refusing an order to eat. He was sentenced to life in prison, at hard labor. He was transferred from Funston to Fort Leavenworth on October 22, one month before the Hofer brothers and Jacob Wipf arrived. For several days he worked. But when he learned that the Molokans were being held in solitary confinement with their hands manacled to the bars for nine hours a day, he stopped working. He decided to seek a similar confinement, in solidarity with the Molokans. After his first fourteen days in solitary and just two days after the Hutterites had arrived at Leavenworth, he wrote to his mother, Emma: "America surely is big enough and the American people liberal enough to allow these men liberty to conduct their lives in accordance with their own conscience as long as they do not injure others."[43] In the November 21 letter, Evan assured his mother that she had no cause to worry. She would make sure of that. Before the month ended, she traveled by train to Kansas and to Washington, D.C., to take up Evan's case with the men in charge of his care.

Appeals for Inquiry and More Humane Treatment

Meanwhile, Jacob Wipf's father, John, was trying to win his son's release. He recounted the details of Joseph Hofer's death in a November 30 letter to the hometown U.S. senator, Edwin Johnson, urging him to intervene before any more lives were lost: "I can't stand it no longer. So for God sake, please help us and put a stop to it. Go and see Hon. Baker secr of war. He can stop it, I know. Please do your best at ones [*sic*]."[44] Johnson, who was chairman of the Senate Committee on Revolutionary Claims and a lawyer by training, wrote to General P.C. Harris, the adjutant general in the War Department, on December 3, asking that the cases of the four Hutterites be investigated. By this time, Michael Hofer was dead as well, though it is not clear whether Johnson knew this in asking for a communal release: "I hope they will be liberated at any early date."[45]

Three days later, Harris replied, saying that the letters from Johnson and Wipf in effect constituted a request for clemency on behalf of David Hofer and Jacob Wipf. "A complete investigation and review will be made," Harris said.[46] As a kind of postscript, Harris quoted Colonel Rice at the Disciplinary Barracks, who in a recent report had said: "In my opinion their belief is so firm that I do not think they will ever submit." Three days later, on December 9, Harris wrote to tell the senator that Joseph and Michael Hofer had died. "In order that the third brother might accompany the remains home, the unexecuted portion of his confinement has been remitted."[47] Clemency for Wipf, he said, remained pending.

Senator Johnson also forwarded to Harris a copy of a letter from his

brother, F.H. Johnson, a judge and a member of the Local Board of Menne-
haha County, South Dakota. In the December 7 letter, the judge recounted
the details of the Hutterites' treatment—being driven at the point of bayonet from the train station to Leavenworth, on a run; having their outer clothing removed and standing for two hours till prison garb was issued. "If this
is true," F.H. Johnson said, "the men who handled these boys should be
court-martialed."[48]

Judge Johnson noted that David Hofer had been released but that Jacob
Wipf remained captive, as did a couple of other South Dakota conscientious objectors at Camp Funston. "I am inclined to think that these boys
have been punished enough and I would ask and request that you make a
personal appeal to the proper authorities and see if you cannot have these
boys given their discharge. I hardly think the government expects to have
anyone in the army treated as I am told these boys were treated." The War
Department promised to investigate.

Chapter Eight

Outside Advocates

*What will you do with the world? World is world and will remain world
until the Lord will come and end it all.*
—"The Diary of Paul Tschetter"

Rights Group Accuses Government of Torture

Though government officials were determined to sideline the National
Civil Liberties Bureau, if not put it out of business entirely, the little
organization in New York City remained a tireless advocate for conscientious objectors. The year 1918 was especially challenging, beginning with
the War Department's blunt notice (around the time that the Hofer brothers
and Jacob Wipf arrived at Camp Lewis in May) that the government would
no longer cooperate with requests for information. Then on August 31, federal military intelligence agents filed into the bureau's offices off Union
Square and seized the organization's records. And on October 30, having
been drafted after the government raised the eligibility age for soldiers, the
organization's thirty-four-year-old director, Roger Baldwin, went on trial.

Baldwin was accused of violating the Selective Service Act after he refused to appear for a physical examination ("I am opposed to the use of
force to accomplish any end, however good," he said. "I am therefore opposed to participation in this or any other war.").[1] Before the trial, Baldwin
showed a copy of his prepared speech to his friend Norman Thomas, vice
chairman of the National Civil Liberties Bureau and brother of Evan, a de-

tainee at Leavenworth. Despite a moving courtroom speech in which he portrayed conscription as "a flat contradiction of all our cherished ideals," Baldwin could not alter the law on the books. The judge said the federal mandate was clear. He sentenced Baldwin to a year in prison.

Thomas and other friends of Baldwin, including John Nevin Sayre—the peace activist and Episcopal minister whose family ties led to President Wilson—did their best to intervene. Wilson generally preferred not to get involved with individual appeals, but in Baldwin's case he contacted Attorney General Thomas Watt Gregory directly. Gregory assured Wilson that Baldwin had received fair treatment. The Justice Department had determined that Baldwin was "very intelligent" and had "a very pleasing personality." Nevertheless, Gregory said, an assistant who prepared the report had concluded with a warning: "Baldwin is one of a very dangerous class of persons, most of whom are at large in this country and from whom I fear we may hear a good deal in the future. I consider the punishment visited on him exceptionally light."[2]

In the fall of 1918, Baldwin was headed to jail and the National Civil Liberties Bureau was under siege. Still, the office labored on, serving as a nexus for social activists, labor leaders, parents, pastors, and others from across the country who were trying to influence wartime policies. High on the agenda was improving the prison conditions of conscientious objectors like the Hofer brothers and Jacob Wipf and securing their early release. While the bureau had no formal authority, it exercised power by conducting research, petitioning government officials, and engaging in publicity campaigns.

That fall the National Civil Liberties Bureau investigated conditions for conscientious objectors imprisoned at Fort Leavenworth and Fort Jay in New York Harbor. Based on information gleaned from teams of interviewers sent to both of the disciplinary barracks, the organization issued a report in November, concluding that Fort Jay and Fort Leavenworth were "fairly well run as prisons go" (the bureau had no investigative report on the third federal prison, Alcatraz). But the agency cited what it called several glaring and unconscionable exceptions: the use of dark cells, the practice of manacling, and the diet of bread and water for those prisoners in solitary confinement.[3]

This treatment, the Civil Liberties Bureau said, constituted a form of torture. "Torture inflicted upon any prisoner for any reason," the organization said, "is as stupid as it is wicked and abhorrent to the American spirit." Even more objectionable, the bureau said, was that this brutal treatment was being carried out against men whose only offense was a "steadfast refusal, for conscientious reasons, to become part of the military machine or obey military orders." These men are in no sense criminals, the bureau argued.

At both Forts Leavenworth and Jay, prisoners who refused to work generally spent half their time in isolation and half in an alternative lock-up. For the first fourteen days, in isolation, they were shackled to cell bars during traditional working hours that prison authorities saw as roughly equivalent to a laborer's daytime shift. At Fort Jay they received two slices of bread three times a day and a pitcher of water three times a day. During the week they were given no water with which to wash; once a week, on Saturday night, they received a shower bath.

Then after fourteen days of that confinement, the prisoners at Fort Jay were released into the prison yard for the next two weeks. There they received raw food, an ax for chopping wood, cooking utensils, and shelter at night. They were like castaways on an island, having to fend for themselves. If, after fourteen days in the yard, they were still unwilling to work, they went back to solitary confinement, and so the cycle continued. At Leavenworth, the solitary cells were in the subbasement. There, too, prisoners were handcuffed and chained to the bars of the door for nine hours a day. There, too, they received only bread and water during the period of isolation. In some cases, though, the report said, prisoners had been kept in solitary for thirty, forty, or even fifty days in a row.

The government and the Civil Liberties Bureau saw the treatment quite differently. Baldwin, before his arrest and trial, visited Castle Williams, near Fort Jay on Governor's Island off of New York City, where objectors were being held. To Baldwin, it was an abomination to find men who were loyal to their conscience being shackled to their bars and fed bread and water. But to Colonel Hunt, the commandant at Castle Williams, the punishment was commensurate with the crime. The War Department should not lock up these men in drawing rooms and feed them delicacies of the season, he said. They are "self-styled conscientious objectors" who were found guilty of "being pretenders."[4] They were unwilling to do work of any kind. Beyond that, many of the objectors had insulted the flag and national anthem by refusing to stand at attention. "It was necessary to restrain the other prisoners from assaulting them for this intolerable show of disrespect," Hunt said.

"The situation is urgent," the National Civil Liberties Bureau contended. "This torture can have but one end—the utter breaking of the men in body, mind or spirit." The bureau released its report on November 21, two days after the four Hutterites had arrived at Leavenworth and a week before two of the Hofer brothers died (Joseph on November 29 and Michael on December 3). November 21 is also when Evan Thomas wrote to his mother, Emma, to tell her about his first two weeks spent shackled in solitary confinement at Leavenworth.

After receiving the letter, Emma Thomas traveled to Washington and there met at the War Department with Assistant Secretary Keppel and also with Secretary Baker, who was joined by the general inspector of prisons. Louisa Thomas describes the scene in *Conscience*, a wartime saga of her family. When her great-great-grandmother told the men about the manacling, the general inspector interrupted: "I don't believe that."[5] They assured her that the treatment was not a prison regulation. Given the fact that all three prisons were manacling men in solitary confinement, and that the National Civil Liberties Bureau and others were protesting the treatment, it's difficult to believe that Baker, Keppel, and the inspector general did not know about the harsh methods of incarceration.

The commandant at Leavenworth, Sedgwick Rice, was certainly frank in confirming to Emma Thomas that her son was indeed standing nine hours a day with his hands manacled to the bars. He added: "You may rest assured that if he breaks down in any way—and it is not anticipated that he will—he will be given proper medical care." Emma Thomas took an overnight train to Kansas to make sure that Evan was well cared for. She found him, professing to be in good health, in a six-by-eight-foot space with three boards fastened together to serve as his pull-down plank bed. But as Louisa Thomas points out, the lines in the letter that he wrote from solitary confinement suggested otherwise. In contrast with earlier letters, the lines in this letter "wavered up and down across the page, and his words were spiked with errors."

Emma Thomas forwarded Rice's letter, which proved that conscientious objectors were in fact being manacled, to her son Norman. On December 1, Norman called Sayre, who left immediately for Washington. President Wilson agreed to meet with Sayre over lunch. Along with pressing for amnesty for conscientious objectors and political prisoners, including Eugene Debs, Sayre described Evan Thomas's imprisonment. Though Wilson was generally not inclined to show much compassion for dissenters, he found this report especially disturbing. Thomas was a close friend of Sayre and a former student of Wilson, not to mention a Presbyterian seminarian. "No such treatment ought to be meted out to conscientious objectors or any other prisoners in America," Wilson said. He promised to meet with Secretary Baker that same afternoon. Afterward, the president described Baker as sympathetic and told Sayre that "nothing barbarous or mediaeval will be permitted to continue in any form."

Things were now moving quickly. Three days later, on December 4, Rice left Leavenworth to confer with Baker in Washington—on the very day that David Hofer was released to accompany the body of his brothers home.[6] One suspects that the recent deaths of the Hutterite brothers were also on the agenda, along with the manacling of prisoners. That same day, Secretary Baker ordered that prisoners no longer be fastened to the bars of cells. In giving the order, Baker made clear that this harsh punitive technique had a long history:

> This and milder devices have been effective in the past in breaking the wilful or stubborn opposition of prisoners of the usual military type, who would not submit to the work requirements of disciplinary barracks. Instead of being allowed to lie in bunks while others worked, they have been compelled to choose between working or standing in discomfort during working hours. Practically, under usual conditions, this has been more a threat than an actuality, and as such it has been effective. But during recent months, with the influx of political prisoners to disciplinary barracks, particularly at Fort Leavenworth, extremity of attitude on the part of this new type of prisoners has at times led to extremity of discipline, as provided by military regulations. These clearly were not formulated with the political type of prisoner

in mind and their effectiveness as deterrents has been questionable. Men have returned for repeated experiences of the severest forms of discipline.[7]

Given that many of the conscientious objectors were, like the Hutterites, clearly acting upon religious convictions, it is striking that Baker chose to highlight political motivations of objectors. That term—and the suggestion that these men were radicals, since they displayed "extremity of attitude"— left the military looking well-intentioned and measured in its response. Though he officially ended the use of manacling, Baker expressed no objections with solitary confinement. That practice would continue.

Darius Rejali, an expert in the history of torture (his authoritative work, *Torture and Democracy*, runs more than eight hundred pages), concluded that the harshest prisoner punishments during the war fell on conscientious objectors like the Hutterites from Rockport, who refused all service or work in the military. The standard punishment for such men, standing handcuffs, is one of the many coercive physical techniques that Rejali refers to as "clean tortures"—that is, techniques that leave few marks.[8] For most prisoners subjected to handcuffing during the war, the punishment meant standing eight or nine hours while chained to their cell door, their arms extended forward.

A variation, known as "high cuffing," forced prisoners to hold their hands high above their heads, sometimes with their backs to the iron bars. The Hutterites experienced this treatment on at least one occasion: when they arrived at Alcatraz. Rejali wrote: "Prisoners described high cuffing as excruciatingly painful, and even the general public, otherwise unsympathetic with these prisoners, found the practice appalling. The practice ceased almost immediately after World War I." (In other parts of the world, the practice has continued, with recent accounts from Mexico, China, Russia, and American-occupied Iraq.)

In an appendix, Rejali lists scores of other "clean tortures," some of which were commonly used to coerce objectors during World War I, including: beating till eardrums burst, chilled in ice-cold baths or showers, dragged by rope, dunked headfirst in latrines, and exhaustion exercises (such as standing on one foot for an hour with the other foot tied to the hip). But Rejali argues that torture is not defined by its methods: "No particular practice is 'torture' in itself."[9] A doctor who pierces a patient's ear may be responsible for pain but not torture. Torture, he writes, occurs at that moment when public authorities use techniques of physical torment on restrained individuals for a public purpose (to intimidate, draw false confessions, or get information). By this definition, the Hutterites (who were restrained) indeed met with torture (in the form of standing handcuffs) during their imprisonment (by military officials) for failing to follow orders (in the public duty of going to war).

After Armistice, Requests for Release or Furlough

The National Civil Liberties Bureau repeatedly urged the army in the closing months of 1918 to allow men like Jacob Wipf to mount an appeal rather than simply to languish in prison. Wipf had been tried shortly before the Board of Inquiry, which Baker established to evaluate the suitability of conscientious objectors for farm furloughs or other assignments, began its work. The bureau said that justice required treating all men alike and making amends when there was discrimination: "These men are evidently entitled to precisely the same treatment as other objectors who were not tried, but who were brought before the Board of Inquiry and given the opportunity to perform nonmilitary service on furlough."[10] All of these imprisoned objectors—which included forty-five Mennonites from Camp Travis in Texas who had been sentenced to twenty-five years each in June 1918 and transferred to Leavenworth—should be given an opportunity to appear before the board, "just as if there had been no trials at all."

The bureau also had issues with the treatment of men whom the Board of Inquiry had looked favorably upon. Not all of the conscientious objectors accepted by the board for farm furloughs were actually released by camp commanders, even after the armistice on November 11. Some officers apparently wanted to test the men. Now that the threat of being sent to fight was removed, the officers wondered, would the objectors still refuse to work in a military camp? Or would they cross the Rubicon line and accept an assignment with the military, showing themselves to be hypocrites?

On November 19, the authorities at Camp Funston in Kansas had ordered conscientious objectors to pave a road, called Avenue B, which ran from the men's tents to the kitchen; officers said the existing dirt road fell short of sanitary standards. Some of the conscientious objectors began laying stone on the road, but others held out. Eight men who did not work were court-martialed for disobeying a lawful order and threatening military discipline. The eight, who ranged in age from twenty-four to twenty-seven, a mix of Hutterites and Mennonites, had all been drafted in the late summer of 1918 and granted farm furloughs by the Board of Inquiry. Their military commanders, however, had not released the men to farm work; in the case of one man, Joe Walter, the furlough denial came because he refused to fire a rifle on a practice range.

At the court-martial in December, the lawyer for the men, a civilian, F.D. Wicks, from Scotland, South Dakota, argued that the work was unnecessary, since a suitable path from the men's tents to the kitchen already was in place. Beyond that, the men had been approved for a furlough outside of the military training camp. The judge advocate expressed impatience with the men's unwillingness to build the roadway and, even more so, their long-standing refusal to help defend the nation against Germany. If everyone took such a position, the judge advocate said, the United States would become the stomping ground of the "Turks, the Bulgarians, the Bolsheviki of Russia, and the German Huns," and American children by the hundreds of thousands would be walking around "with both hands cut off."[11] The men were sentenced to life imprisonment, but the terms were reduced to five to twenty-five years. One man was soon discharged because of a technicality; the other seven were released within a year.

Even as the objectors at Camp Funston went on trial that December, several army officers faced dismissal over the mistreatment of men at the camp, in a high-profile case known as the "Funston Outrages."[12] Major Frank S. White, the judge advocate at the camp and the son of a former U.S. senator from Alabama, was censured and then discharged. Major G.O. Taussig, the head of the military police there, also received an honorable discharge. The officers denied any wrongdoing, but they were found to have at the least permitted mistreatment under their watch even though Secretary Baker had ordered that objectors should be "handled with tact and consideration" and not be treated as if they were violating military laws. This was the same directive that said of objectors: "their attitude in this respect will be quietly ignored, and they will be treated with kindly consideration." White would not go quietly. With the support of the American Legion, he launched a campaign that accused Baker of pampering objectors. The Kansas Legislature joined the cause, saying that Baker had "placed a premium on slackerism, cowardice, and mawkish sentimentality."

Leveraging Publicity and the Press

The deaths of the Hofer brothers at Leavenworth might have remained quietly remembered only within Hutterite circles had it not been for an unlikely partnership that emerged in late 1918 between the owner of a piano hardware company in Chicago and a Mennonite journalist and professor from Kansas. Both were active members of the National Civil Liberties Bureau's network of advocates. The business owner, Theodore H. Lunde, carried the most personal of ties to the plight of conscientious objectors; his son, Erling, had been court-martialed as an objector earlier in the year and was imprisoned at Fort Leavenworth, where his detention overlapped with that of the Hutterites.

Under the name of his business, the American Industrial Company, Theodore Lunde published several pamphlets related to events at Fort Leavenworth, including the deaths of Joseph and Michael Hofer. The National Civil Liberties Bureau described him as a "peppery individual" who "sometimes bombards the officials of the government with messages which are not polite"—but "we have never known his facts to be inaccurate."[13] President Woodrow Wilson would no doubt have begged to disagree. A year earlier, in September 1917, just as the military camps were beginning to train soldiers, Wilson urged Attorney General Gregory to consider charging Lunde with treason for publishing criticisms of the government ("There are many instances of this sort and one conviction would probably scotch a great many snakes," the president said).[14]

Meanwhile, the journalist and professor, Jacob Ewert, had also drawn scrutiny for his German-language newspaper, *Vorwaerts*, and his critical views of the war.[15] Representative Dudley Doolittle of Kansas appealed to

Gregory to launch "a real investigation" of Ewert, whom he regarded as "a real menace."[16] A visitor to Ewert's home would no doubt have regarded him as less of a menace than a paralytic man deserving of sympathy, if not pity. Though Ewert produced letters, tracts, and articles throughout the war, each piece represented a form of taxing labor. From his bed, he relied on one thumb to type.[17] Even then, he would have been unable to type any letters were it not for his brother, David, himself an invalid who could barely walk. David was able to feed paper into the machine. Then Jacob would peck out a typewritten line. When the line was complete, David would pull a string attached to the cylinder of the machine to shift down to a new line. In that way the brothers proceeded from line to line until the letter was finished.

Neither Jacob Ewert nor Theodore Lunde was brought up on charges, but both remained under watch throughout the war. As a Mennonite himself, Ewert was especially interested in the welfare of young men from the Anabaptist churches, like the four Hutterites from Rockport. He sent his blessing when Lunde traveled to Washington the day before Christmas in 1918 to seek the release of conscientious objectors at Fort Leavenworth. Lunde was among a group of twenty-three people who had collected fifteen thousand signatures on behalf of the objectors. The petition, presented to Secretary Baker, asked that the three hundred or so men serving sentences of ten to thirty years be released.[18] And if the men could not be immediately discharged, then they should at least be taken out of solitary confinement, the group said.

The group described the objectors as a sampling of America's finest, including Howard Moore, who before his imprisonment had received a medal from the Carnegie Hero Fund Commission for saving a girl's life at a Connecticut beach; George Wiershausen, whose scientific skills were said to have helped cure a crippled boy; and Evan Thomas, the Princeton graduate and seminarian. The petitioners reminded Baker that two of the objectors—Joseph and Michael Hofer—had died of pneumonia hastened by bad treatment. Responding to this appeal to release the objectors, Baker deflected responsibility. He said the discharge of men from the service was outside of his jurisdiction—that would be up to President Wilson. Within two weeks, though, Evan Thomas would be released; the Judge Advocate General's office had reviewed his court-martial record, found errors, and recommended that charges be dropped.

If petitions from outside advocates would not get the desired results for the remaining prisoners, then personal testimonies from the men themselves might force the hand of government officials. Lunde turned to the power of the printing press, in this case his own. In a self-published report that he titled "Examples of Brutalities, Tortures and Deaths to Political Prisoners under Military Regime," Lunde presented Wipf and the three Hofer brothers as exhibit A in listing atrocities committed at military camps and prisons.[19]

The report recounted their travails at Camp Lewis and Alcatraz, leading up to the death of Joseph and Michael Hofer at Fort Leavenworth, and said that Wipf remained in solitary confinement, on a diet of bread and water, "strung up" by chains nine hours a day, seven days a week. In January, Lunde sent the report to Alabama Representative S. Hubert Dent, chairman of the House Committee on Military Affairs. Lunde told the congressman: "Many of these young men I have met and spoken with in Camp and hospital, and I pronounce them as fine and noble human material as a government has ever exposed to abuse and destruction."[20]

The first published account of the experiences of Jacob Wipf and the Hofer brothers came in a pamphlet called "'Crucifixions' in the Twentieth Century," which was also issued by Lunde's American Industrial Company, within weeks of the "Brutalities, Tortures and Deaths" report. The article, about two and a half typewritten pages in length, conveys a "nearly unbelievable tale of religious persecution" experienced by the Hutterites at Alcatraz and at Fort Leavenworth. The account tells of the deaths of Joseph and Michael Hofer and of David Hofer's having been released. The source for the report is Jacob Wipf, who was confined to a hospital cot at Fort Leavenworth at the time when he told the story to an army officer.[21] The unnamed army officer in turn shared the account with Lunde.

Lunde also published "Desecration of the Dead by American 'Huns,'" which was based on Ewert's contacts with the Hofer family. Ewert secured a copy of David Hofer's report on his time in the prison system, as written down in German by David's father. Ewert translated the testimony and sent a copy to Lunde. A preface to the article states: "A narrative by David Hofer, which corroborates and amplifies '"Crucifixions" in the Twentieth Century,' though rendered without knowledge of the story told by Jacob Wipf." David Hofer's account, of a similar length, adds details from the assault that took place on the train to Camp Lewis and from their confinement at the camp.[22]

In a far bolder move, Lunde now approached the National Civil Liberties Bureau with a plan for prosecuting Secretary Baker himself.[23] Lunde envisioned filing an injunction against Baker in federal court in Washington, arguing that as the official invested with power to set rules and regulations in the disciplinary barracks he had permitted conditions that allowed for the "cruel and unusual punishment" of conscientious objectors, in violation of constitutional safeguards found in the Eighth Amendment. A similar injunction would be sought in the federal court that had jurisdiction over Fort Leavenworth, in this case making prison officers the respondents. Lunde anticipated that the testimony of conscientious objectors would "lift the roof off the courtroom." The nation would be shocked by the treatment accorded objectors, he believed, and government officials shamed into action. "Even if unsuccessful," Lunde wrote, "the publicity etc. might act as a deterrent."

Early in February 1919, Lunde outlined the legal strategy to officials at the National Civil Liberties Bureau, who immediately raised reservations. The bureau favored using straight-out publicity rather than lawsuits as leverage to win the release of objectors. As the bureau's Albert DeSilver told one supporter, "We believe that the most important thing to do at present is to create public opinion which will insure thousands of letters being written to President Wilson asking for an amnesty" for the prisoners.[24] The advocates were helped along the way by officials like Representative William E. Mason of Illinois, who entered the case of the Hofer brothers and Jacob Wipf into the *Congressional Record.*[25]

Lunde met with Baker and Keppel in Washington, a meeting that left him "despaired of obtaining any voluntary release for our political prisoners." Baker and Keppel impressed on Lunde the challenges of the political climate. The recent dismissal of Taussig and White had stirred up more public sympathy in favor of stern commanders like Wood and more antipathy for objectors. Lunde came to agree with the National Civil Liberties Bureau's assessment: "It becomes our task to create a public opinion in favor of the political prisoners sufficiently strong to compel favorable action."

Long after the war ended, Baker felt conflicted about how best to handle conscientious objectors, but in no way did he want to be accused of coddling these men. To those who called for an immediate release of objectors, he had this reply, which suggests how he responded to Lunde's appeal:

> I regret that this question, which seems so simple to you, has seemed difficult and complicated to me. The questions involved touch not only the rights of conscience, which I have sought earnestly to protect, but the obligations of citizenship, which I have felt it my duty to enforce. Meantime, the group of young men to whom you refer ought not to forget that the torch of idealism which they sought to hold aloft was threatened with extinction by the most menacing materialistic force the world has ever seen. The abolishment of future wars, for which I share your fervent hope, was immeasurably more advanced by the conscience which led young men to give up their lives for it than by the conscience which in the presence of vast and crushing destructive force found itself limited to protest.[26]

Release of Objectors Provokes Outcry

As the outset of 1919, Lunde was seeking the release of men like John Neufeld, a Mennonite from Inman, Kansas, where his family's fields turned amber with wheat every summer, who was imprisoned at Fort Leavenworth alongside Jacob Wipf, Erling Lunde, and the others. Neufeld's grandfather Heinrich Toews had immigrated to the United States from Russia, like the Hofers and the Wipfs, in the late nineteenth century. Reverend Toews had served as pastor of Inman's Bethel Mennonite Church, as did Neufeld's father. At the time of the draft in 1917, John Neufeld was working with the General Conference Mennonite Church in Oklahoma, constructing buildings for Native American missions.

The army pulled him off that job and assigned him to Camp Cody in New Mexico in the summer of 1918. Unlike the Hutterites at Camp Lewis, he agreed to work at camp, chopping wood and doing other chores. But, when he received a rifle with which to drill, he decided he could no longer take up noncombatant work. The day he stepped out of the marching platoon, a drill sergeant grabbed him around the neck and threw him to the ground. When Neufeld refused to resume his place in line, the sergeant punched him in the face and kicked him repeatedly.

Two weeks later, Neufeld was court-martialed. The prosecution called as a witness First Lieutenant Ben Wood, a military psychologist who had conducted an earlier psychological exam of Neufeld and who had been a witness at twenty-three similar trials, each time finding the defendant insincere. Having spoken with Neufeld for two hours, Wood said that he could confidently take a measure of his sincerity. Neufeld, he said, was simply using conscientious objection to shirk his civic duty. He was sentenced to fifteen years of hard labor.

When he arrived at Leavenworth on July 25, Neufeld agreed to resume working. He joined a group of nearly fifty objectors, known as the fifth gang, who labored in fields outside the prison walls, under guard, threshing and filling grain silos. The workday began with breakfast before six and then a drill. Both the drill and the work were acceptable now, Neufeld said, because he was "free from the army."[27]

A few months later, Neufeld experienced real freedom. On January 22, Secretary Baker ordered the immediate release of 113 conscientious objectors being held at Fort Leavenworth, Neufeld among them. On the day of his release, dressed in raggedy civilian clothes and still feeling feverish from a recent mild case of diphtheria, he marched through the iron gates under the chill noon sun. The men left in groups of ten, and Neufeld was in the last group out that day. They marched through one gate attended by a single sentry and then to the outside gates. The order came for "forward march." With that permission, the men walked to freedom and boarded trains for their respective hometowns. Neufeld said that the other prisoners left behind at Leavenworth had wished him well, showing no sense of ill will toward these fortunate conscientious objectors.

In announcing the release of the objectors, Baker spoke of their "honorable restoration to duty" and their immediate discharge from the army.[28] The men who walked to freedom had all been eligible for, or would have been eligible for, farm furloughs, but they had not yet been given that opportunity. The furlough program had worked well, Baker said, but now that the armistice had been signed, it made sense to return the men to productive work in civil life as soon as possible. The order, Baker assured, did not affect those objectors who were found to be insincere—they must serve out the remainder of their terms.

Although 113 families rejoiced over the decision, the outcry in other quarters was swift and fierce. The *Kansas City Star* expressed the sense of popular outrage, likening the release of the men to an "insult to the uniform."[29] The Kansas House of Representatives chastised Baker for releasing "slackers, cowards, and traitors, and dangerous civic nondescripts."[30] The legislatures of Nebraska, Oregon, and Idaho also approved resolutions of protest against the release of the men. Congressman Thomas A. Chandler of Oklahoma took up the attack in Washington:

> I think the release of these 113 conscientious objectors was an outrage. I cannot use any gentler term than that. Why should those men who refused to do a soldier's duty be discharged, in full standing and with full pay, while there remained at the same prison 3,500 men, some of whom had seen service on the battleline in France and many of them there for some trivial offense? . . . Any one who reads the list of names of those discharged from Fort Leavenworth will observe what a large percentage of German names it contained.[31]

Chandler warned that "German propagandists and sympathizers" might be trying to take advantage of Baker's misplaced generosity.

Throughout the war Baker had faced repeated questions about whether he was equipped to deal sternly with conscientious objectors. George Harvey, the editor of the *North American Review* and of *Harper's Weekly*, sought to denigrate Baker as a "pacifist Secretary of War." But Baker didn't regard himself as an appeaser of conscientious objectors, and he didn't want to give that appearance. For example, when the Nebraska State Senate adopted a resolution urging Congress to condemn Baker's decision to give an "honorable" discharge to "unpatriotic slackers," complete with an outfit of civilian clothing and full pay, he promptly replied.[32] Baker assured state lawmakers that the conscientious objectors had not received an honorable discharge. The discharge papers in each case, he said, made clear their record: "This is a conscientious objector who has done no military duty whatsoever, and who refused to wear the uniform."[33]

Wipf Appears before Board of Inquiry

Two weeks before Baker ordered the release of the 113 conscientious objectors, on January 5, Jacob Wipf had finally had a chance to state his case before the Board of Inquiry. In the best of all possible worlds, he had hoped to be released immediately. Short of that, he wanted to be found sincere in his convictions and offered a farm furlough, free finally of the prison at Leavenworth. Weeks went by, and Wipf heard nothing. Enoch Crowder, the judge advocate general, issued his findings on Wipf privately to military officials on January 22, the same day that Baker directed the release of 113 other objectors. Crowder noted that Wipf had served slightly more than seven months of his sentence, which was hard labor for twenty years. Unbeknownst to Wipf, Crowder wrote: "The record of trial in this case was carefully reviewed in this office and found legally sufficient to sustain the findings and sentence of the court."[34]

The record was clear, Crowder wrote, that Wipf, and by association the Hofer brothers, had disobeyed several orders to fall in and to sign the enlistment and assignment card while at Camp Lewis. These were commands that he had to obey, showing a minimal level of cooperation, even as a conscientious objector. And at Leavenworth, Crowder noted, Wipf had been in solitary confinement since he arrived in November and again refused to work. Crowder concluded: "The sentence imposed upon the prisoner was severe, but he was clearly guilty of the serious offense with which he was charged and found guilty. Certainly, until he has served a more substantial portion of his sentence, clemency should not be extended."

Crowder's ruling was apparently in keeping with his standard practice. In one case in which officers in his department challenged him, Crowder reportedly said that "military justice was a kind of justice that had to be administered in the camp by the camp commander without legal supervision."[35] Nevertheless, the officers knew that in cases of the "grossest injustice" an appeal could be discreetly made to Secretary Baker, who could, if he chose, take remedial action.

Then a few weeks later another army official, R.P. Truitt, prepared a memorandum that should have bolstered Wipf's case:

> This man was born and brought up in South Dakota. His father was a member of the church of the Huttrischen Brethren, and he was brought up in this faith. He was given ordinary early advantages, securing a small portion of a grammar school education. After leaving school he was employed regularly as a farmer at the colony of the Huttrischen Brethren. He is temperate and has never been arrested. He refused to perform the duties of a soldier on the grounds that his belief in this Huttrischen faith would not permit it.[36]

Meanwhile, the commandant at Leavenworth, Colonel Rice, said that "there appears to be no military reason why clemency should be extended" to Wipf.[37] In South Dakota and in Washington, Senator Johnson continued to pursue the case with General P.C. Harris, the adjutant general in the War Department.

In February, Harris reported that the Secretary Baker, like Crowder, had determined that no reduction in Wipf's sentence was in order.[38] Harris added that Wipf might be able to secure a release on parole after he had served one half of the twenty-year sentence, and the authorities might reduce that ten-year term even further because of good conduct (five days a month during the first year, and then ten days a month thereafter). That meant Wipf should count on more than seven years in prison, even in the best scenario.

Jacob's father, John Wipf, appealed to Frederick Keppel, the assistant secretary of war in charge of objectors, in a telegram. The words of a distraught parent spilled out:

> My son is married and has three children. He is a member of the Hutterish Brotherhood by birth and a full member of the Church from long before the war so that he could not accept either combatant or non-combatant military service but he was quite willing to accept the farm furlough and repeatedly asked for the same while yet in camp but since the board of inquiry did not mention the farm furlough at his examination it is possible there is some misunderstanding on this point as the services of my son are very urgently

needed at home in the family and for the spring work on the farm and since he has already suffered so much on account of his uncompromising attitude according to our religion I would hereby humbly beg of you to kindly investigate what recommendation was made by the board of inquiry in the case of my son and then to take pity on us and use your valued influence that he may also get his release at the next opportunity.[39]

Whatever the particulars of his case, Jacob Wipf belonged to a group of prisoners that many officers found objectionable at best. The Office of the Inspector General in the War Department responded to mounting criticism of the treatment of conscientious objectors, especially at Fort Leavenworth, with a blistering counterattack. The author of the report, Colonel A.L. Dade, said that the charges brought by Lunde and others were "part of the propaganda being put forth by conscientious objectors and their friends for the purpose of discrediting the Military Service and for securing release from custody of those objectors who are under sentence of Court Martial."[40]

Dade painted his portrait of life inside the barracks with a broad brush: "Depraved characters of many kinds find their way into the Disciplinary Barracks. This is inevitable. The Disciplinary Barracks is a penal institution and contains, as stated, 'the dregs of the Army' but the documents indicate or show plainly the fact that the prison authorities are fully aware of the character of the inmates." He went on: "The atmosphere of the place is surcharged with discontent, resentment, suspicion, and there is a seething undercurrent of schemeing [*sic*] and plotting, among the whole body of prisoners looking to escape or release from dustody [*sic*]."

Conscientious Objectors as Research Subjects

Though they were relatively few in number, conscientious objectors were of research interest to the federal government both during the war and afterward. One question looming in the forefront was whether men who resisted service in the army were held back by their inferior intelligence, as influential officials like Walter Kellogg and Harlan Stone of the Board of Inquiry suspected. Perhaps from having spent so much time together interviewing objectors, Kellogg and Stone offered a remarkably similar assessment of the men. Kellogg described a typical representative of the Mennonites (a broad category in which he also placed the Amish and Hutterites): "He shuffles awkwardly into the room—he seems only half awake. His features are heavy, dull and almost bovine."[41]

Stone lamented the "long lines of stolid, bovine-faced Dunkards, Mennonites, Hutterites, and the like, each one supremely interested in the salvation of his own soul even though the world perish."[42] Stone said they presented a "depressing example of dense ignorance of what was going on in the world."[43]

During his months spent interviewing more than eight hundred objectors in twenty camps, beginning in the summer of 1918, Kellogg said, he began to test their knowledge of events. When he asked the Mennonites whether they knew what the *Lusitania* was, they invariably did not, confirming their ignorance. He went on:

> It is difficult to realize that we have among our citizenry a class of men who are so intellectually inferior and so unworthy to assume its burdens and its responsibilities. I doubt if fifty per cent of the Mennonites examined, because of their ignorance and stupidity, ever should have been admitted to the Army at all; I am certain that ninety per cent of them need a far better preparation for citizenship than they have ever received. They are good tillers of the soil; they are, doubtless, according to their lights, good Christians, but they are essentially a type of Americans of which America cannot be proud.[44]

Kellogg did allow that Mennonites possessed a formidable knowledge of the Bible. Ask for justification, he said, and they can cite chapter and verse.

Kellogg and Stone clearly favored members of the Society of Friends. Though Quakers also balked at fighting, they knew their current events and expressed themselves with the polish of formal schooling. C. Henry Smith, a Mennonite history professor, offered a gentle rebuttal to the critique framed by Kellogg and Stone. For many Mennonites, Amish, and Hutterites, news of the world, at least prior to the war, was not of a high value, Smith said. "Each lived in a slightly different world," he said, "and showed greatest intelligence in the world in which his chief interests lay."[45]

At any rate, Smith noted, articulate speech about current events was an incomplete, if not biased, measure of sincerity.

Army officers also suspected that many objectors were mentally ill. The simple reasoning was that such men must be crazy to be objectors. Perhaps the saddest case in this regard was that of Edward Johnson, a thirty-six-year-old farmer from Barronet, Wisconsin. Though he had a wife and seven children dependent on him, he did not claim an exemption. He also did not report for duty. He was arrested for draft evasion on May 14, 1918, shortly before the Hofer brothers and Jacob Wipf left home, and sentenced to one year in prison at Fort Leavenworth. The judge noted that Johnson had a "very enviable reputation" but that he had become "obsessed" with religion and was "teaching and preaching that it is unlawful to kill."[46]

Johnson's wife wrote to William Morgan, a warden at Leavenworth, to express concerns about her husband's treatment, including being placed in solitary confinement and put on a diet of bread and water. His mental health apparently declined rapidly. The warden reported worrisome signs that Johnson was not of sound mind. Johnson's wife wrote back to say that her husband had always been well. But around the time that Baker ordered the release of 113 objectors, Johnson was sent to St. Elizabeth's Government Hospital for the Insane in Washington, D.C. It's not known whether he was reunited with his family.

Colonel Rice was also keenly interested in the mental condition of the prisoners in his care, suspecting that many were simply not bright enough to follow the army's direction. Among the conscientious objectors, especially those who were taking a political stance, he said, "some are well educated, smooth-talking, egocentric individuals." Others are "slackers who are trying to preserve themselves by following high ideals." He believed that many of the religious objectors might fall into a different camp: "Quite a few of these objectors are suffering from mental disease and are refusing to go into the Army because of delusional ideas."

In his annual report that covered the closing months of the war, Rice said that as "concerns the mental status of the so-called Conscientious Objector, it has not been possible, due to pressing work, to make a complete study of the records in these cases." He did note that of 110 cases examined, eight

were classified as mental deficiency—"intellectual but not legally irrespon-
sible—what one might call dullards or Constitutionally inferior individuals."[47]

But like Kellogg and Stone, Rice also conveyed a measure of respect for
Amish, Mennonites, and Hutterites. While some of the sects had "very peculiar customs," including never wearing jewelry and never shaving, they
knew how to work, at least at home.

> They are industrious and thrifty and confine themselves to rural regions
> entirely. Practically all of them speak German and for the most part it is be-
> lieved that this is the language used in their homes. . . . They object to the
> war because the Bible says, "Thou shalt not kill." They firmly believe that if
> they break this commandment that their soul would be lost and that they
> would be submitted to eternal persecution. They seem to be extremely sin-
> cere in their beliefs.[48]

During the war, the government wanted to systematically evaluate the intelligence, education, grounds of objection, and social and political history
of this cohort. Well before the Board of Inquiry began its examination of
men in the summer of 1918, Baker had ordered psychological examinations
for all objectors. Given the popular portrayal of objectors as lazy, dimwitted,
and crazy, the scientific studies showed surprising results. Conscientious
objectors were actually more intelligent than soldiers in general—at least
according to army mental tests. Tests showed that 46.5 percent of the conscientious objectors received a grade of A, B, or C+ (very superior, superior,
and high average), compared with 27.3 percent for soldiers as a whole.[49]

Report Finds That Objectors Are Mentally Fit

Mark A. May—a researcher at Syracuse University who prepared a summary of the data for the surgeon general a month after the war ended in
December 1918 and subsequently published an article in the *American Journal of Psychology*—concluded: "There is absolutely nothing in these data to
justify the hasty conclusion that objection to war is due to the low mentality
of the objector. It may be true that some objectors can be classed as fanat-

ics, others may be said to be stupid, but it can safely be said that at least 97 percent of the conscientious objectors reported here have sufficient intelligence to know what they are doing."[50]

May's report drew on samples of a thousand conscientious objectors and 94,000 other soldiers. Of the conscientious objectors, about half, or 554, were classified as Mennonites (this group apparently included Amish and Hutterites). The next-largest subgroups were members of the Society of Friends (80), Church of the Brethren (67), International Bible Students or Russellites (60), Dunkards (37), Israelites of the House of David (39), and the Church of Christ (31). Mennonites were clearly among the less well-educated objectors; fewer than 10 percent of Mennonites went to school beyond the eighth grade. The 12 percent of objectors overall who reached college were most often classified as socialists, Dunkards, or Quakers.

While the thousand men objected to war on religious, social, and political grounds, the vast majority, 90 percent, did so because of their religion, appealing to the Bible and church creed. Records showed that frequent objections included the following:

War is forbidden by church and creed.
War is forbidden in the Scriptures in general.
War is forbidden by Christ.
War is forbidden by the commandment.

The social objector, representing 5 percent of cases, appealed to individual freedom. The political objector, 3 percent, usually cited alien citizenship. Although objectors reported having ninety different occupations, including clerks, carpenters, and even a saloon keeper, most were farmers (90 percent of the Mennonites came from farms).

Objectors True to Heredity and Environment

May's report cast further doubts on the appropriateness of the court-martial of the Hofer brothers and Jacob Wipf. "The degree of sincerity of a conscientious objector is a thing almost impossible to determine," May concluded.[51] It is doubtful, he said, that ancestry or birthplace has anything to do with it. "Conscientious objectors cannot be intelligently disposed of by simply call-

ing them pro-German." In evaluating these men, tricky hypothetical questions serve no point, he said. Especially to be avoided are questions like
"What would you do if a German should attack your Grandmother?" (which
recalled the question put to Jacob Wipf at the court-martial: "If a man was
attacking or assaulting your sister, would you fight?"). Questions like this,
May said, which fail to distinguish between indiscriminate mass warfare
and individual self-defense, are not true tests of sincerity and "show poor
judgment on the part of the examiner."

The bulk of the Mennonites, including Hutterites and Amish, can be
classified as religious-literalist objectors. May characterized them this way:

> He is a Mennonite, born on a farm in a middle Western community. His par-
> ents together with others of their faith settled there many generations ago.
> He went to the country church school. There he was taught the Bible and
> some simple rules of living. He quit school at 8th grade and went to work
> on the farm. He attended church more or less regularly. He was taught to
> respect his minister and his views of life. He perhaps read the county news-
> paper and the Bible, outside of this he has done little reading. His informa-
> tion is limited to the happenings of his own community. He knows that we
> are at war with Germany but has no idea why.[52]

May then challenged the army's fierce determination to redirect men like
the Hofer brothers and Jacob Wipf into conformity. "So when creed, minister, parents and friends tell him that war is wrong and that he must not
fight, what could be expected of him? For a man like this not to be a conscientious objector would violate all the laws of heredity and environment that
operate to make men pursue certain courses of action."[53]

While the army may not have induced the four Hutterites to fight, the
vast majority of objectors changed course once they were in the system. In
less than two years, nearly three million American men entered the army
and received training. Of the approximately 64,700 men who filed claims
for conscientious objector status, about 21,000 men were inducted into
the army. After spending time in camps, some 80 percent of these men
(about 16,000) agreed to take up arms. In the end, only 3,989 men held
fast to their convictions against war and the military. Of that number, about

1,300 agreed to serve in the Medical Corps or another noncombatant service; 1,200 received furloughs; 99 joined Friends' reconstruction work; 504 were court-martialed and all but one convicted; 225 remained in camps, objecting to combat service; 715 remained in camps, objecting to combat or noncombatant service. Secretary Baker put the number in perspective: the ratio of men professing conscientious objection in the camps to total inductions was 3,989 to 2,810,296, or 0.14 percent.[54] The majority of the resisters were native born and belonged to historic pacifist denominations.

As Christopher Capozzola, a history professor at the Massachusetts Institute of Technology, concluded, testing the sincerity of objectors thinned their ranks. It is doubtful that any of those who remained among the 3,989 were insincere. But many sincere men were redirected into regular service. Capozzola wrote: "The policy's success came at a cost—namely, that numerous citizens with sincere objections to organized killing found it impossible to claim a legal right that had been designed precisely for them."[55]

Norman Thomas, the socialist and civil rights leader whose brother Evan was placed in solitary for refusing to work, put it this way: "When four-fifths of those entitled to noncombatant service do not accept it, it is obvious that not the threat of punishment but the pressure of community feeling is the primary cause of wholesale conversions."[56] More important than physical punishment was the "overwhelming weight of social pressure and the almost universal feeling in America that this war is a holy crusade."[57]

One of the most compelling testimonials for conscientious objectors came at the close of the war in a letter written by Sergeant Albert P. Brown to Secretary Baker after Brown's honorable discharge. Sergeant Brown had worked as a draftsman for fifteen months at Leavenworth. He commented on the "extreme conscientiousness of the work" of the conscientious objectors assigned as draftsmen, stenographers, and clerks. If the books they read provided a "fair index to these men's minds," he said, they were "wide awake," drawing from the likes of Ralph Waldo Emerson and Walt Whitman.

> But these men are suspected by the outside world of cowardice, so allow me to deal with that point. It requires great courage to live the daily life of a prisoner. . . . What many of these men endured at different camps throughout the

country, beatings, partial starvation, prods with bayonets, being strung up with ropes until they were nearly strangled, should have been sufficient to have vindicated their courage, when they might have put an end to their sufferings by accepting non-combatant service.[58]

Brown does not mention particular men by name nor indicate whether he had contact with the Hutterites (who, of course, would not have joined him at the drawing table). He urged their speedy release.

Wipf Goes Home

Secretary Baker had said that all prisoners would receive "considerate and intelligent treatment"—but not special consideration. He made it clear that two types of conscientious objectors should not expect release any time soon: those who were opposed to this particular war but not warfare in general, and those who were offered farm work or other service under civilian direction but refused such work.[59] It's not clear why Jacob Wipf would have remained imprisoned so late in the spring given that he did not fall into either one of these categories. He certainly was opposed to war of all kinds; and he was never given a chance to conduct work under civilian direction.

Ewert continued to lobby on behalf of Jacob Wipf, sending a telegram to Keppel on March 15. He first made the case for the young man's value at home: "[Wipf] is married and has three children and is greatly needed at home on the farm."[60] Ewert noted that Wipf had never been given the opportunity to apply for a farm furlough, work that he would have welcomed. He continued: "We would be inexpressibly thankful if you could use your influence either to get the case of Jacob J. Wipf included with the next bunch that is to be released or to be granted a special partion [sic] letter."

In a letter sent the same day, Ewert went into more detail in making a case for Wipf's release. Wipf appeared before the Board of Inquiry at Fort Leavenworth on January 5, Ewert said, but as of this date in March he still had not been able to find out what the board recommended. Meanwhile, Wipf was not among the 113 objectors whose release was announced on January 22. According to Ewert, Colonel Rice had expected Wipf to be released with the other objectors.

Ewert wrote: "Jacob J. Wipf has been a member of the Hutterish Mennonite Church since long before the war and in harmony with the teachings
of his Church has absolutely refused all participation in combatant or noncombatant military service, but he has never refused to accept agricultural
service on farm furlough."[61] "Most of the other members of the [Hutterish
Mennonite] Church were fortunate to get farm furlough, but this has not
been the case with Jacob J. Wipf and with a few other Hutterish Mennonites."

An assistant to Keppel, Major Jason S. Joy, immediately sent a memorandum to the office of the judge advocate general in which he made a
powerful disclosure. For the first time, the military acknowledged that it
had mishandled Wipf's appeal for a farm furlough. Joy wrote:

> The case of conscientious objector, Jacob J. Wipf, referred to in the attached
> appeals for clemency, seems to me of a character to merit early action by the
> Board. On his first examination by the Board of Inquiry [on Jan. 5] he was
> adjudged sincere in his scruples to combatant and non-combatant service as
> well. He should then have been offered a farm furlough, which seems not
> to have been granted. The special representative of the Secretary, appointed
> to personally interrogate men professing conscientious scruples, which re-
> cently examined Wipf at Fort Leavenworth, has recommended him for spe-
> cial consideration in view of the unfortunate circumstances of his case. In
> the absence of Assistant Secretary Keppel, I take the liberty of bringing his
> case to your attention especially.[62]

Joy acknowledged that Wipf was found to be sincere in his beliefs when he
had the first opportunity to be evaluated by the Board of Inquiry in January. By then, Joseph and Michael Hofer were dead, and David Hofer was
back home in the colony. If Jacob Wipf was sincere in January, he was in
all likelihood sincere in May 1918, when he arrived at Camp Lewis, and in
June, when he was court-martialed and sentenced to twenty years of hard
labor. And by implication, the Hofer brothers, who faced the same set of
charges and responded in kind during the trial and detention, were sincere
as well and deserving of a farm furlough instead of having been placed in
the dungeon.

On March 22, 1919, the Office of the Judge Advocate General of the Army issued a clemency memorandum for Jacob Wipf. The document noted that an earlier report, on February 24, had taken ten years off of his sentence. And now the army ordered that the remaining years also be remitted and that he be discharged. The document noted that he had been confined for nine months and summarized his case. Under physical ailments, the report cited small hemorrhoids. His education was listed as "fair" (rather than "good" or "none," the other two options). His civil life record was "good" (rather than "bad" or "no record"), and his conduct in confinement was "fair" (rather than "excellent" or "bad"). Offenses for which he had been previously convicted: none. Age: thirty-one. In the section for noting circumstances attending offense, the document mentioned that he was of Russian parentage and spoke the German language. Up until the end, this biographical detail remains underscored. The document was signed by E.A. Kreger, acting judge advocate general.

On April 13, 1919, nearly eleven months after his arrest, Jacob Wipf reversed his walk through the iron gates of Leavenworth, free to return to South Dakota in time for spring planting.

Chapter Nine

Official Misjudgment

Ye shall be brought before rulers and kings for my sake,
for a testimony against them.
—Mark 13:9

Hutterite Colonies Pack for Canada

When he finally returned to South Dakota, Jacob Wipf found a Hutterite homeland transformed. Many of the colonies had abandoned their farms and moved to Canada, having purchased land in Manitoba and Alberta where they looked forward to a warmer reception. While the treatment of the Hofer brothers and Jacob Wipf confirmed the rightness of the decision to move, the Hutterites had begun exploring land options in Canada well before the men left home to report to Camp Lewis, as the war fever began to spread.[1] When the United States sent men to war in 1918, the Hutterites counted eighteen colonies in the country, two of them in Montana and the rest in South Dakota. By the spring of 1919, only seven colonies remained, including Rockport, where Joseph and Michael Hofer had just been buried.

Meanwhile, the troubles continued in South Dakota, even after the war. The South Dakota Council of Defense was pressing to disband the remaining colonies, arguing that they were leveraging their religion for an unfair economic advantage over neighboring farmers (not to mention, the council said, being an unpatriotic menace to society). The state took up the cause.

In round one, the Beadle County Circuit Court decided against the Hutterites, recommending that their communal corporations cease all farming.
The South Dakota Supreme Court in the end did not require the dissolution
of colonies but did suggest that its judicial sympathies lay with critics of the
Hutterites.[2]

When they reunited that spring, Jacob Wipf and David Hofer may have
taken a short walk up the Rockport hillside to the cemetery to pay their
respects to Joseph and Michael. One pictures them bending low to read the
grave markers, sharing tears if not words as they remembered all that they
had been through. In the years after their release from Fort Leavenworth,
David Hofer and Jacob Wipf spoke only rarely with others about their imprisonment, family members said. A daughter of David Hofer, Katie Hofer
Waldner, who welcomed the author to her home at the Miller Colony in
Montana, said that the subject remained forever emotional for her grandfather.[3]

Waldner, who was eighty-three at the time of the interview in 2009, sat
in a rocker, a "Love One Another" cross-stitching on the wall behind her.
She said, "You could see when he started telling us about what happened,
the tears came. We didn't talk about it much." Work in the fields offered a
welcome respite for her grandfather, she said. She could still see him cul-
tivating with a team of white horses, readying the land for another crop of
wheat. As he got older, she said, David Hofer talked about pain in his hips,
which he attributed to the time he had spent hanging in chains at Alcatraz.

Joe Hofer, bonded by name to the grandfather who died at Leavenworth,
learned to know Jacob Wipf after the war when they lived on the same
colony in Canada. At the time of an interview in 2009, at Hofer's home
on the Kyle Colony in Saskatchewan, he was seventy-two and was assigned
to the care of calves in the dairy barn. He said that Wipf was a blacksmith
both before and after the war: "He had arms like an ox. He was strong. Time
[spent working] was nothing to him."[4]

In the 1950s, the two men worked together, sometimes in the fields,
sometimes in construction. Hofer recalled: "We would drive a couple of
miles to get a soil and gravel mix. Then he would build sidewalks seven or
eight inches high that would pack hard as a rock. He loved every minute of
it. He loved working with soil." He said Wipf occasionally spoke about his

ordeal: "He said it was hard to come back to the colony after the war and start over. While he was away, he was sure that he was going to die."

Though the story of the Hofer brothers and Jacob Wipf is known to every Hutterite, care is taken not to glorify the men in a way that would lift them up above others in the community. "We don't try to make heroes out of our ancestors," said Jacob P. Wipf, who is a nephew of the imprisoned Jacob Wipf and the senior minister at the Miller Colony in Montana, where several of Michael Hofer's grandchildren still live.[5] "We teach the New Testament and the Bible," said Wipf, who is regarded as a leading historian for the Lehrerleut branch of the Hutterites, to which the Hofer brothers and Jacob Wipf belonged.[6]

The Rockport cemetery where the Hofer brothers are buried, there on a bluff on the west bank of the James River, conveys that sense of each person being equal in the eyes of the Lord. The ankle-high metal grave markers for Joseph and Michael Hofer are indistinguishable from those of their neighbors until one kneels down close enough to see a single appended word: martyr. Joseph J. Wipf, the present minister at Rockport, said: "We didn't want anybody to think they were better than the rest of us are. A few of them went through the same treatment and came back alive."[7]

Ascribing Best of Intentions to Washington

The United States government never apologized to the families or to the Hutterite church after the war. While the Hutterites are certain that the Hofer brothers died because of mistreatment, becoming martyrs for the faith, they fault only faceless, unnamed officers or soldiers for that abuse, certainly not the leaders in Washington, D.C. Neither the family members nor the ministers that the author spoke with hold the government as a whole responsible for the mistreatment of the men or expect a formal apology. "I don't think the government knew what was going on," Jacob Wipf, the minister, said. "As soon as the authorities found out what was going on, Jacob Wipf was released right away."[8] Joe Kleinsasser, a junior minister at the Kingsbury Colony in Montana and a grandson of Michael Hofer, said, "Those generals in the army camps did this on their own."

The Hutterites are not alone in ascribing honorable intentions to lead-

The grave marker for Michael Hofer at the Rockport Colony, South Dakota.

The grave marker for Joseph Hofer at the Rockport Colony, South Dakota.

Family members stand by Mary Hofer Kleinsasser, daughter of Michael Hofer, at her home in the Miller Colony in Choteau, Montana.

ers in Washington, including the point man for the war, Secretary Newton Baker. Church leaders at the time thought that he treated objectors more sympathetically than did most military leaders. Writing in the decade after the war, C. Henry Smith, a Mennonite historian, concluded that the Hofer brothers "died as a result of exposure and torture received at the hands of prison guards."[9] But Smith was quick to free President Wilson and Secretary Baker of any culpability in the case; rather, he wrote, they "displayed the greatest consideration for the scruples of the sincere objectors."[10] As with the Hutterites, he distinguished between a well-meaning federal government and aberrant military officers or guards at camps and prisons.

Not every war analyst was so forgiving. In a memoir written nearly a half century after the war, Frank Harris, editor of the *Saturday Review*, sought to hold Secretary Baker personally culpable: "The story of the martyrdom of the three Hofer brothers, who belonged to the religious sect of the Men-

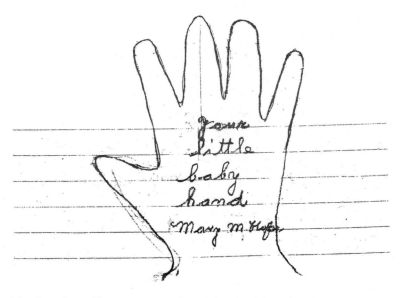

Michael Hofer's wife, Mary, sent a hand sketch of their daughter, "Baby Mary,"
to her husband in prison.
Mary Hofer Kleinsasser

nonites, will always in my mind be associated with Mr. Secretary Baker."[11] Harris asserted that the mistreatment of the four Hutterites and of other objectors was revealed to Baker "again and again, month after month, day after day," before he was moved to action. On December 6, 1918, he "found time to issue an order prohibiting cruel corporal punishment"—handcuffing prisoners in standing position to the bars of their cells. Even so, Harris said, several days later Jacob Wipf was still being handcuffed at Fort Leavenworth. Harris concluded: "Secretary Baker then knew such torturing was being practiced, knew too that it was illegal."

Donald Johnson, in his study of wartime civil liberties and the emergence of the American Civil Liberties Union, took the more favorable, and common, view of government intentions. Baker, he said, was "most sympathetic and generous."[12] Johnson was especially aware of the challenges in pleasing both military associates and conscientious objectors, not to mention a restive public. He noted that Baker created a Board of Inquiry to review court-martial sentences and to select "sincere" objectors for summer farm work. He described Baker's readiness to discharge objectors as quickly as he could after Armistice Day—even though the firestorm over the announced release of 113 men on January 22 set back those plans. Though most of Wilson's cabinet members were "narrow, legalistic, and antisocialist," Johnson said Baker was "always generous and tolerant."[13]

On paper, certainly, Baker tried to prevent abuses. His directive that conscientious objectors be treated with "tact and consideration" and be segregated in the training camps, for example, suggested a benevolent leader. But his willingness to compromise on matters of conscience went only so far. Baker was unflinching in his commitment to shared sacrifice during wartime. He also would not chance any threat to the effectiveness of the army. While the Hutterites were imprisoned at Alcatraz he reflected on his priorities:

> The thing I must do at all costs is to get an efficient Army, and to embrace no other thing at the expense of the Army's efficiency. Incidentally, whenever I can find things which can be done to help collateral causes without prejudice to the efficiency of the Army I am glad to do them, but my point of view requires me to ask in each instance the question: "Will this help the Army?", then "Will it hurt the Army?" If it will hurt, I have to abandon it.[14]

If he thought the military was being unreasonable, Baker was willing to say so. For example, he went against General John J. Pershing in May 1918 in extending clemency to two American soldiers who had been sentenced to death for falling asleep while on night watch.[15] But leniency with men who faltered in their service in the army was not the same as leniency with men who refused such service.

Baker and Wilson Underestimate Depth of Convictions

Perhaps his most glaring misjudgment with regard to objectors—one that was certainly shared by President Wilson and many in the military—was the failure to appreciate the depth and sincerity of their pacifist convictions. Wilson, Baker, and the commanders and soldiers under their leadership

believed that these men could be persuaded to put on the uniform and
shoulder their load, as fighters or at least as laborers, putting aside their
pacifist scruples to become members in good standing of the armed forces.
Through their imprisonment, hundreds of men put the lie to that assumption. They would not serve as long as their service was required within the
military.

Baker showed little patience with the conscientious objectors when they
did not come around to his way of thinking. After the war he continued to
harbor a borderline disgust with these men who would not fight:

> I knew the horror of [war], the tragedy of it; and I have no sympathy what-
> ever, intellectually or sentimentally, with conscientious or any other kind of
> objection of people who stayed on this side and preferred places of safety
> and of profit to the places of peril and obligation which the situation of their
> fellow-citizens required of them, whatever they might think about the pur-
> pose of war.[16]

He portrayed objectors as isolated and ignorant, living "on the tops of lonely
mountains, remote from civilization." When he visited with a couple of
dozen objectors at Camp Meade in the fall of 1917, he said that "only two
of those with whom I talked seemed quite normal mentally."[17] When he
envisioned the 504 court-martialed objectors who held out to the end, he
scarcely allowed room for legitimate religious convictions against the war:
"Some were anarchists, professedly hostile by force to any form of social
organization; some were slackers; some cowards; some were sincere religious objectors; some were objectors on social or personal grounds and
were perfectly sincere."

Despite having a mind well-versed in the nuance of law, Baker also failed
to appreciate what to conscientious objectors was a fundamental and essential distinction between noncombatant service under army command and
civilian control. In commenting on the courts-martial, he said:

> Even of this number of 504, a substantial group came from camps where it
> would appear that they had not been considerately or sympathetically treated
> and, for one reason or another, not offered the opportunity of noncombat-

ant service, so that a number of them were court-martialed who, upon later study, it appears clear would have been saved from that had a uniform course been consistently followed.[18]

The Hofer brothers and Jacob Wipf were offered noncombatant service, but that made no difference. What they needed was a chance to serve without having to sign up as soldiers, put on a uniform, or feel themselves a part of the army.

President Wilson and Secretary Baker believed that the United States was fighting a war for freedom, if not a war to end all wars. The common good, they argued, required a common sacrifice, including the setting aside of unorthodox religious scruples. The Hofer brothers and Jacob Wipf believed just as deeply that they were required to follow a Christian path of nonviolence and that people whose convictions stood so firmly against war should not be required to serve in the army.

In that standoff in 1918, one side had to give, and as it did the nation witnessed a miscarriage of justice. The war overwhelmed constitutional guarantees of freedom to practice religion and to safeguard citizens from torture and cruel punishment. If the Hofer brothers and Jacob Wipf were drafted today, they most assuredly would not end up standing in chains in a dungeon. Though conscientious objectors would have had every reason to predict otherwise, the arc of the Constitution and even the good graces of the military would bend their way in the decades after the Great War.

Epilogue

Washington Adds Civilian Option in World War II

At the onset of World War II, it appeared as if the United States had failed to learn from its mishandling of conscientious objectors in World War I. When the Germans invaded Paris on June 20, 1940, Congress began deliberating a draft measure. Lawmakers assumed that pacifists would serve in the military as noncombatant soldiers. But the pacifist denominations lobbied with a more unified voice than they had managed in the previous war, determined to remind officials of the flaws in that earlier conscription system. Apart from any moral considerations, the government had practical reasons to strike a compromise with the church leaders this time around. From the military's perspective, conscientious objectors had created problems far out of proportion with their numbers in World War I.

In a far-reaching concession, the draft measure approved by Congress in September 1940 allowed for conscientious objectors to be assigned to "work of national importance" under civilian direction.[1] Civilian Public Service emerged as an alternative to military camps, financed in part by the participating churches. During the war, CPS men built dams, fought forest fires, planted trees, constructed roads, served as guinea pigs for medical research, and cared for the mentally ill. More than twelve thousand men served in the civilian programs (even so, about five thousand objectors went to prison during the war, the majority of whom were Jehovah's Witnesses who had declined to seek conscientious objector status).

The number of objectors grew during the Korean War and then the Vietnam War, including one remarkable year, 1972, when more registrants were classified as conscientious objectors than were inducted into the army.[2] The nation's military draft ended in 1973, a year after the United States and South Vietnam signed a cease-fire with North Vietnam and the Vietcong.

Every Man Must Register

In 2013, federal law still requires nearly every male residing in the United States to register with the Selective Service System when he turns eighteen.[3] Registrant information goes into a database of eligible men, cataloged in case a draft should be ordered to supplement the current all-volunteer armed forces (now fighting a single war, in Afghanistan). Men remain in the active registry until age twenty-six.

If a draft were to follow the procedure in place during the Vietnam War, men would be conscripted according to a lottery pegged to their date of birth; they would undergo a medical screening; and then they would report to a local Selective Service board, or draft board, which would decide whether the men qualify for an exemption or deferment of military service or whether they should be inducted into the armed forces. One question certain to arise in a new draft is whether women, who until recently were barred from front-line combat positions, should be forced to serve as well.

Representative Charles Rangel, a Democrat from New York, has repeatedly called for a reinstatement of the military draft as a way to make the armed services representative of the American public at large, drawing more evenly across racial and economic lines. With little public support for a draft, let alone the latest wars in Afghanistan and Iraq, the prospects of reinstating it appear dim at best (the House rejected one measure 402–2 in 2003).

Conscientious objectors must also register with Selective Service at age eighteen. If a draft begins and they are called to serve, they would have the opportunity to file a claim for exemption from military service (there is no "check box" for conscientious objectors on the registration enrollment

form). The government defines a conscientious objector as "one who is opposed to serving in the armed forces and/or bearing arms on the grounds
of moral or religious principles."

Unlike the policy in place through much of World War I, objectors do
not have to belong to a religious group to qualify for alternative service. A
registrant would have to appear before a local draft board to explain his or
her beliefs, which could be supplemented by a personal written statement
and testimonials from people who can attest to an applicant's sincerity. The
local board would then decide whether to grant conscientious objector clas-
sification.

The military has in place a dual-track form of service. As in World War I,
men can choose to serve in the military but not carry a gun, in a noncombatant capacity; those who are opposed to any form of military contribution
would be assigned to alternative service under civilian direction, perhaps in
conservation, health care, or education. In 2010, after years of negotiations,
Mennonite Voluntary Service signed an agreement with Selective Service
designating MVS as an employer for conscientious objectors, the first faith-
based organization to be so recognized.[4] However remote the prospects for
a return to conscription now appear, should that happen, conscientious objectors would enjoy civilian service options that were unthinkable in World
War I.

Conscientious Objector Status Assured for Hutterites Today

If the Hofer brothers and Jacob Wipf were drafted today, they would clearly
qualify as conscientious objectors, according to military regulations. The
way regulations stand now, if you have a sincere religious objection to participation in any form (or you hold nontraditional views that occupy the
same position as religion and lead to the same conclusion), then you need
not serve in the military in any capacity, said Daniel Mach, director of the
American Civil Liberties Union's Program on Freedom of Religion and
Belief.[5] The military's regulations for conscientious objectors, Mach said,
were "in their infancy" during World War I. Given how the regulations have
evolved, the Hutterites "would never have had to go through this experience
in the first place."

That apparent automatic granting of conscientious objector status to the Hutterites today rests not with the free-exercise-of-religion clause in the First Amendment, however, but with the military itself. Exemption from military service remains a privilege that is extended by military regulation, not a constitutional guarantee. Conscience does not stand above the law. The Supreme Court issued a stern reminder of that in a 1990 decision, *Employment Division v. Smith.*

Two members of the Native American Church, Alfred Smith and Galen Black, were fired from their state jobs in Oregon because they used the illegal hallucinogen peyote in a religious ceremony. They were also denied unemployment compensation because of the conduct that led to the firing. Smith and Black argued that the state's unemployment law had, in effect, taken away their right to free exercise of religion. The high court disagreed. When the government issues a "valid and neutral law of general applicability," a religious believer, no matter how sincere, cannot automatically claim an exemption.[6] The court said that the believer would have to establish some special circumstance, like government targeting of a particular religious group.

Backed by conservative and progressive religious groups, lawmakers sought to recalibrate the balance between the right to live out religious convictions and the right to regulate conduct.[7] In 1993, Congress approved the Religious Freedom Restoration Act, a bid to outflank the *Smith* ruling. The Religious Freedom Restoration Act holds that if a law burdens someone's religious practice—even if that law applies to all and does not target one particular religion—then the government must still make a compelling case as to why the law should be applied to that person whose religious freedom is at risk. In a zoning case that involved a Catholic church in Texas, the Supreme Court ruled that the act was unconstitutional as applied to states; at the federal level, the law remains in effect. "The First Amendment as now interpreted does not give conscientious objectors a right to opt out of military service, but R.F.R.A. likely would," Mach said.

Even if they were drafted and forced to serve under military command, the Hutterites today would also find robust constitutional safeguards against being put on a bread and water diet or being chained in their cells. For example, in *Hope v. Pelzer*, which was heard by the Supreme Court in

2002, justices considered a case with some striking similarities to Alcatraz in 1918.[8] A prisoner in Alabama, Larry Hope, was twice chained to a bar known as a hitching post and left to stand in the summer sun, once for seven hours, because he refused to work. He was only slightly taller than the post, so his arms were fastened above shoulder height, cutting off his circulation.

In this case, the court ruled that not only was this a violation of the Eighth Amendment ban on cruel and unusual punishment but it was so clearly a violation—an "obvious" call, the justices said—that the prisoner should be entitled to sue for damages. In a related matter, the court has also ruled that prisoners are protected from inadequate nutrition and vermin infestation under the Eighth Amendment. Speaking of the Hutterites, Mach said: "I have no doubt that what happened to them was a violation of the Eighth Amendment under our present conception."

Hutterites Thrive in Canada and the United States

Meanwhile, the Hutterites are enjoying what some scholars regard as a "Second Golden Age."[9] In the 1990s, for the first time since the sixteenth century, when they flourished in Eastern Europe, the Hutterites numbered more than forty thousand. When the Hutterites immigrated to the United States from Russia in the 1870s, they counted 425 members living in three small communities. Today, the Hutterite population approaches fifty thousand, spread across hundreds of colonies in the northern plains states of the United States (130 colonies) and the prairie provinces of Canada (351 colonies).[10]

Just as many Hutterites worked in shops and trades in the first Golden Age, they are doing so today as well, displaying some of the most advanced industrial processes. Colonies build (and often patent) commercial feeders, heat pumps, barn ventilation systems, kitchen equipment, furniture. Farming continues to be the dominant industry on the colonies.

By their migrations in the years after World War I, the Hutterites have confirmed that they hold no ill will toward authorities in the United States. The Hutterite presence in the United States reached a low point by the Great

Depression, when only two colonies permanently remained, one in South Dakota (Bon Homme, the first colony established by immigrants from Russia) and one in Montana (the Spring Creek Colony). The family members of the Hofer brothers and Jacob Wipf went to Alberta; a separate branch of the Hutterite church would take ownership of the Rockport Colony.

Then the migration switched directions. In 1935, South Dakota, in an effort to stem the departure of successful farmers and reverse its economic decline, passed the Communal Societies Act. That measure allowed Hutterites to incorporate as communal organizations and to operate with favorable tax rates. At the same time, Canada appeared to be less welcoming. Alberta approved the Communal Land Sales Prohibition Act, which beginning in 1942 prohibited Hutterites from building colonies within forty miles of each other and limited the size of their farms. Hutterites reversed their trek across the border, including members of the original Rockport Colony, who settled near Choteau, Montana, in 1949, organizing under the name Miller Colony.

Blurring the Lines between the Church and the World

The threats to the Hutterites, as well as to other Anabaptist churches like the Mennonites, are arguably more stealthy today than those they faced during World War I, when mobs painted churches yellow and burned books and beat conscientious objectors. It's more difficult to track the encroaching influence of materialism, individualism, and nationalism.[11] Hutterite business and personal relationships with outsiders are increasing, making it ever more of a challenge to maintain a distinct identity; new technology and media also offer channels for ideas that threaten traditional communal understandings. Hutterites view many Mennonites as having fallen away in the past century, becoming increasingly like their neighbors in lifestyle and convictions.

A recent national survey of Mennonites supports that perception, showing a weakening of traditional convictions.[12] In 1972, 11 percent of Mennonites said that if drafted, they would enter the military rather than become a conscientious objector; in 1989, 16 percent said they would opt for the military; in 2006, 21 percent conveyed their readiness to don a uniform. More than half of the members surveyed in 2006—56 percent—believed it was "all right for Christians to be in non-combatant service in the armed forces." In yet another indicator of Mennonites' readiness to embrace a national identity, and serve when the government calls, 48 percent believed that America is a Christian nation. There are no comparable surveys for the Hutterites.

Of course, the survey results reflect essentially peacetime realities. Should the United States find itself under a threat grave enough to warrant a national call to arms, the pressures to conform would be of a frighteningly different order. The response to the terrorist attacks of September 11 served as the most recent reminder that in war, the world quickly divides into good and evil, ally and enemy, loyal and disloyal. When confronted with jihadism, the United States swept up suspects, the innocent and true warriors alike.

With suspects in captivity, the United States descended into the ranks of nations that systematically torture prisoners. Well-established torture techniques like waterboarding became acceptable practice, though under the cover of terms like "enhanced interrogation techniques." Government officials twisted the Constitution and the Geneva Conventions to condone this torture, in doing so denying the foundational principle that all prisoners are human beings with inherent human rights. Though President Barack Obama acknowledged that waterboarding is an act of torture banned by international law, his administration brought no charges against the Bush administration officials who approved the torture. Washington appeared eager to close a tragic chapter, as in World War I, without apology.

By now, the World War I chapter is distant history. Frank Buckles, the longest surviving American World War I veteran, died in February 2011 at the age of 110. His death in West Virginia laid to rest the "last living link" to the men who served in France (where Buckles drove an ambulance).[13] Buckles, a corporal in the U.S. Army, was buried with full military honors at Arlington National Cemetery.

At the time of their deaths, no tributes were paid to Joseph and Michael Hofer, who died in prison at Fort Leavenworth, or to David Hofer or Jacob

Wipf, who died years later on communal farms. But in holding fast to their religious convictions, they joined a growing stream of Americans who insisted, during the war and in the decades that followed, that the United States would only be as free as the Hutterites, the Mennonites, the Amish, the Brethren, the Quakers, the Molokans, the Seventh-day Adventists, the Jehovah's Witnesses, and the socialists among us.

Notes

Preface

1. Michael Hofer to Maria Hofer, August 7, 1918.
2. David Hofer to Anna Hofer, August 18, 1918.
3. Joseph Hofer to Maria Hofer, August. 7, 1918.
4. Keim and Stoltzfus, *Politics of Conscience*, 40.
5. Joseph Hofer to Maria Hofer, November 17, 1918.
6. Michael Hofer to Maria Hofer, November 17, 1918.

Chapter 1. Called to Duty

1. Biblical references are drawn from the King James Version, in this case, Luke 6:27.
2. Mike Kleinsasser, a minister at the Kingsbury Colony in Montana and a grandson of Michael Hofer, said of beards: "In the Hutterite custom, a beard means a lot. It's basically your wedding ring. When you get married, you grow a beard." Mike Kleinsasser, conversation with author, February 21, 2009.
3. *Parkston Advance*, May 3, 1918.
4. *Alexandria Herald*, April 19, 1918.
5. Ibid.
6. *Daily Argus-Leader*, May 25, 1918.
7. *Freeman Courier*, April 26, 1917.
8. The details and quotations in this paragraph and the subsequent two can be found in the *Daily Argus-Leader*, May 21, May 24, and May 25, 1918.

9. Joe Hofer, conversation with author, June 4, 2009. As a young man, in his twenties and thirties, he worked alongside Jacob Wipf, who recounted his experiences in the war.

10. *Hutterite CO's in World War I.*

11. Kellogg, *Conscientious Objector,* 40–41.

12. Friesen, *Peter Riedemann's Hutterite Confession,* 119–120.

13. *Chronicle of the Hutterian Brethren,* 139.

14. This doctrine is anchored in the New Testament, particularly Matthew 5:38–44.

15. *Parkston Advance,* May 18, 1918.

16. Report of Selective Service Local Board, Elkhart County, Indiana, December 30, 1918.

17. Capozzola, *Uncle Sam,* 39. About fifty-four Hutterites, many of them married and with children, were drafted during the war.

18. Enoch H. Crowder to the Adjutant General of Michigan, July 30, 1918.

19. Unruh, "Century of Mennonites in Dakota," 116; Homan, *American Mennonites and the Great War,* 50. The American Union Against Militarism also advised all conscientious objectors to register.

20. *Alexandria Herald,* May 31, 1918.

21. The Yankton quotations in this paragraph and the subsequent one are from the *Yankton Press and Dakotan,* May 9 and June 6, 1918.

22. *Alexandria Herald,* May 31, 1918.

23. *Sioux Falls Argus Leader,* March 22, 1918.

24. Richter, "Dakota-Germans and World War I."

25. Sawyer, "Anti-German Sentiment," 490.

26. McAdoo, *Crowded Years,* 278–279.

27. *Fulton Advocate,* April 25, 1918.

28. Sawyer, "Anti-German Sentiment," 472–473.

29. N. Thomas, "The Hutterian Brethren."

30. *Sioux Falls Press,* May 10, 1918.

31. "Hutterite Brethren and War," 354–355. The petition was signed by David Hofer, Elias Walter, and Joseph Kleinsasser and sent to President Woodrow Wilson.

32. The sources for the historical overview include Hostetler, *Hutterite Society;* R. Janzen and Stanton, *Hutterites in North America;* Kraybill and Bowman, *On the Backroad to Heaven;* Packull, *Hutterite Beginnings;* Rhodes, *Nightwatch: An Inquiry into Solitude;* Roth, *Stories;* and Smith, *Coming of the Russian Mennonites.*

33. *Chronicle of the Hutterian Brethren; The Bloody Theater or Martyrs Mirror of the Defenseless Christians.* The *Chronicle of the Hutterian Brethren* consists of two volumes, the *Grosse-Geschichtsbuch,* or *Great Chronicle,* and the *Kleine-Geschichtsbuch,*

or *Small Chronicle*. This edition of the *Martyrs Mirror*, a fixture in Mennonite homes, was translated from the 1660 work compiled by the Dutch chronicler Thieleman J. van Braght. The first English translation, in 1748–1749, was, at 1,500 pages, the largest book published in colonial America.

34. *Chronicle*, vol. 1, 360.

35. *Mirror of the Martyrs*, 53.

36. Castelli, *Martyrdom and Memory*, 4.

37. The start of the Anabaptist movement is commonly placed in Zurich in 1525, scene of the first adult baptisms. Anabaptism soon spread into the Austrian territory of Tyrol, which was ruled by Archduke Ferdinand I. Ferdinand set out to extinguish the movement, which he perceived as a threat to political and church structures. He objected to the rejection of infant baptism and also the practice, in some quarters, of holding all goods in common. On August 20, 1527, he issued a battle plan. All those who taught the community of goods, he said, should be beheaded. More decrees followed. The state could seize the property of Anabaptists, according to a decree dated April 1, 1528. Then on May 18, 1529, he decreed death by fire for Anabaptists. The Hutterites were among those Anabaptists who fled to Moravia, where they were beyond the reach of Ferdinand and free to share what they owned.

38. Hutterites often cite Acts 2:44–47; the companion passage is Acts 4:32–35.

39. L. Gross, *Golden Years of the Hutterites*.

40. Janzen and Stanton note that the group also abandoned communal living from 1690 to 1757; membership dwindled to forty-nine people. For a combined period exceeding one hundred years, then, Hutterites lived as, at best, a semi-communal people. See R. Janzen and Stanton, *Hutterites in North America*, 25–29.

41. David Hofer to Anna Hofer, May 26, 1918.

42. Wurtz, "One Man's Encounter."

43. Michael Hofer to Maria Hofer, May 26, 1918.

44. David Hofer to Anna Hofer, May 27, 1918.

45. *Alexandria Herald*, June 21, 1918.

46. Michael A. Stahl, "Michael A. Stahl's Account," in *Hutterite CO's in World War I*.

47. Waltner, "A 'C.O.' in the First World War," 4–5. Waltner left for Fort Riley, then Funston, and finally Camp Cody in New Mexico. He arrived at Camp Cody either at the end of 1917 or in the beginning of 1918.

48. Leisy, "Martial Adventures of a Conscientious Objector," 3.

49. A two-page National Archives record of South Dakota men who boarded the train for Camp Lewis on May 25, 1918, the date of their induction, lists the Hofer brothers, Jacob Wipf, William Danforth, and James Montgomery.

50. Wurtz, "One Man's Encounter," 102.

51. David Hofer to Anna Hofer, May 26, 1918.

52. Ibid.

53. Ibid.

54. Michael Hofer to Maria Hofer, May 26, 1918.

Chapter 2. Forced Migrations

1. McNutt, "Camp Lewis as Eastern Magazine Writer Sees It."

2. Leighton, *Country about Camp Lewis.*

3. *Tacoma Ledger,* June 26, 1917.

4. Fortescue, "Training the New Armies of Liberty."

5. Estimates on per capita costs vary. The essay "Fort Lewis, Part I, 1917–1927" at www.historylink.org uses the figure $142; Huddleston, in *Fort Lewis,* cites $158.

6. Powell, "Making the Makers of Victory."

7. *Trench and Camp,* June 2, 1918.

8. Janzen, "My Experiences as a Young Man."

9. Michael Hofer to Maria Hofer, May 29, 1918.

10. Joseph Hofer to Maria Hofer, May 29, 1918.

11. "Record of the Trial of Recruits."

12. David Hofer to Anna Hofer, written between May 27 and June 8, 1918.

13. Michael Hofer to Maria Hofer, June 8, 1918.

14. Joseph Hofer to Maria Hofer, June [4–7], 1918.

15. "Record of the Trial of Recruits."

16. Michael Hofer to Maria Hofer, June 18, 1918.

17. *Post-Intelligencer,* June 16, 1918; Powell, "Making the Makers of Victory."

18. Mary Darling to Roger Baldwin, April 9, 1918.

19. Clyde Crobaugh to Roger Baldwin, February 25, 1918.

20. *Tacoma Daily News,* September 7, 1917.

21. Ibid.

22. *Post-Intelligencer,* June 16, 1918.

23. *Alexandria Herald,* June 21, 1918.

24. Powell, "Making the Makers of Victory."

25. Coffman, *War to End All Wars.*

26. Michael Hofer to Maria Hofer, June 8, 1918.

27. David Hofer to Anna Hofer, June 8, 1918.

28. *Sioux City Daily Tribune,* October 23, 1917.

29. Stahl, *Hutterite CO's in World War I.* Stahl refers to twelve Hutterites being mistreated; the Sioux City reporter refers to fifteen Hutterites but without providing names, so it's not possible to know for certain whether this is the same group

but with conflicting versions of the truth. Stahl was transferred to Camp Dodge and released in December 1918.

30. S.M. Williams to Governor Capper, October 3, 1918. Cited in Shields, "Treatment of Conscientious Objectors," 262.

31. Janzen, "My Experiences as a Young Man."

32. Schlabach, "Diary of a Conscientious Objector," 74.

33. Ibid., 84.

34. J.M. Hofer, "Diary of Paul Tschetter," 119.

35. Ibid., 120.

36. A. Hofer and Walter, *History of the Hutterite Mennonites*, 49.

37. Frazier, *Great Plains*.

38. J.M. Hofer, "Diary of Paul Tschetter," 198.

39. Ibid., 208.

40. Ibid., 209.

41. Correll, "President Grant and the Mennonite Immigration," 146.

42. R. Janzen, *Paul Tschetter*, 81.

43. Unruh, "Century of Mennonites in Dakota," 61. It's not clear why Tschetter allowed himself to be photographed; Hutterites would have taught against making graven images, which would include photographs.

44. Correll, "President Grant and the Mennonite Immigration," 147.

45. Jansen, *Memoirs of Peter Jansen*; and Correll, "President Grant and the Mennonite Immigration."

46. Jansen, *Memoirs of Peter Jansen*, 35.

47. Ibid.

48. J.M. Hofer, "Diary of Paul Tschetter," 217.

49. Ibid.

50. Correll, "President Grant and the Mennonite Immigration," 147

51. Ibid., 150.

52. The sense of gratefulness to President Ulysses S. Grant remains. In a centennial book on the Hutterite settlement in South Dakota, a tribute page reads: "We thank and praise God for President Ulysses S. Grant for extending hospitality and interest to a strange people with rather special requests." A. Hofer and Walter, *History of the Hutterite Mennonites*, 7.

53. Unruh, "Century of Mennonites in Dakota."

54. Government land could be purchased at $1.25 per acre through the Homestead Act of 1862; the railroads often sold their land for more, at $2.50 to $7.50 per acre.

55. Unruh, "Century of Mennonites in Dakota," 20.

56. Ibid., 51; R. Janzen, *Paul Tschetter*, 1.

57. One of the three longstanding Hutterite branches, the Schmiedeleut, divided in 1992, creating a fourth unit. The largest branch today is the Dariusleut, with 159 colonies; the Lehrerleut, 139 colonies; Schmiedeleut One, 61 colonies; Schmiedeleut Two, 118 colonies; and unaffiliated, six colonies. Hutterites number about 49,000 worldwide, with nearly all members living in Canada or in the United States. See R. Janzen and Stanton, *Hutterites*, 74.

58. Young, "Mennonites in South Dakota," 485.

59. Riley and Johnson, *South Dakota's Hutterite Colonies.*

60. Jansen, *Memoirs of Peter Jansen*, 39.

61. Kleinsasser, *Our Journey of Faith*, 1.

62. Beadle, *Autobiography of William Henry Harrison Beadle*, 8.

63. Schell, *History of South Dakota*, 159.

64. Eaton and Mayer, *Man's Capacity*, 3. The number is found in a federal census taken in June 1880, with trained enumerators, as they were called, fanning out across the plains of the Dakota Territory, which had been settled by Hutterites and pioneer immigrants in the 1870s. Along with noting names, ages, place of birth, and other standard data, the three census agents who visited the Hutterite colonies made special note of distinctive features, including language spoken: "This group speaks, reads and writes the original German language." John D. Unruh listed the census count as 321 Hutterian Brethren; he estimates that 275 Hutterites settled in the original three communal colonies, in "Century of Mennonites in Dakota," 115.

65. Riley, *Hutterites and Their Agriculture*, 5.

66. Eaton and Mayer, *Man's Capacity*, 26.

67. Ibid., 41.

68. Unruh describes the agricultural success of the colonies in "Century of Mennonites in South Dakota," 115.

69. Ibid., 116

70. Ibid.

Chapter 3. A Nation Rises Up

1. *Tacoma Daily News*, April 25, 1918.

2. The flag was finally flown on December 7, 1918, after two failed efforts earlier in the year. On the first try, the weight of the flag broke the pole; on the second, the flag eyes tore the halyard. The second pole rose 200 feet high. On the day of the flag's unveiling, the *News Tribune* reported that the flag was not of the largest dimensions in the world (or the highest off the ground), but it was the largest flag in the world to be put aloft. The flag is pictured in chapter 9.

3. *New York Times*, May 31, 1918.

4. *New York Times*, September 12, 2010.

5. Ford, *Americans All!*, 44.

6. American loans to the Allies during the war totaled around $9.6 billion; Britain alone borrowed $4.3 billion. The loans allowed the combatants to buy American goods, including armaments, and created a significant and early vested interest in an Allied victory. Ferguson, *Pity of War*, xxv.

7. Heaton, *Cobb of "The World,"* 270. Frank Cobb, an editorial writer for the *World*, quoted the president reflecting on the implications of war during their private talk in the White House at one in the morning. The next day Wilson asked Congress to declare war.

8. News references are from the *New York Times*, April 3, 1917.

9. Tryon, "Draft in World War I," 339.

10. Ibid., 340.

11. *Foundations for the Future; Encyclopedia of Cleveland History.* The other partner in the firm was Hostetler's law school classmate, Thomas L. Sidlo.

12. Joseph C. Hostetler to Newton D. Baker, January 16, 1918, and May 19, 1918.

13. *New York Times*, December 26, 1937.

14. Ibid.

15. Cramer, *Newton D. Baker*, 81–82.

16. Bowman, *Church of the Brethren and War*, 223.

17. Higham, *Strangers in the Land*; Vought, *Bully Pulpit*.

18. Baker, "Embattled Democracy," 198–199, cited in Beaver, *Newton D. Baker*, 219.

19. Kellogg, *Conscientious Objector*, xii–xiii.

20. *The Statutes at Large of the United States*, 65th Congress, 1st Session (Washington, 1919), vol. 40, part I, 78. The original draft said that no person shall be exempted from "military service." By removing that condition, the president had the option of defining noncombatant service along civilian lines.

21. Smith, *Coming of the Russian Mennonites*, 272.

22. Lehman and Nolt, *Mennonites, Amish, and the American Civil War*.

23. Hershberger, *War, Peace, and Nonresistance*, 98–106.

24. Keim and Stoltzfus, *Politics of Conscience*, 37.

25. John Nevin Sayre to Woodrow Wilson, April 27, 1917. Wilson, *Papers*, 44: 288–89.

26. Russo, "Conscientious Objector," 333.

27. Ibid.

28. Schultz Huxman, "Mennonite Rhetoric."

29. Keim and Stoltzfus, *Politics of Conscience*, 22.

30. Jones, *Service of Love*.

31. Keim and Stoltzfus, *Politics of Conscience*, 38.

32. Schultz Huxman, "Mennonite Rhetoric," 291.

33. Sawyer, "Anti-German Sentiment."

34. Capozzola, *Uncle Sam.*

35. Zieger, *America's Great War,* 60.

36. Estimates for the number of polling places vary. In Zieger's *America's Great War* and Coffman's *War to End All Wars,* the number is 4,648.

37. Chambers, *To Raise an Army,* 211.

38. *Hutterite CO's in World War 1,* 138–140.

39. Teichroew, "Mennonites and the Conscription Trap," 12.

40. Jones, *Service of Love,* 50.

41. Ibid., 52. Emphasis in the original.

42. Newton D. Baker to Woodrow Wilson, August 27, 1917. Wilson, *Papers,* 42: 74.

43. Stone, "Conscientious Objector," 253.

44. Capozzola, *Uncle Sam,* 57; L. Thomas, *Conscience,* 121.

45. Juhnke, *Vision, Doctrine, War,* 215.

46. Keim and Stoltzfus, *Politics of Conscience,* 40.

47. Newton D. Baker to Woodrow Wilson, October 1, 1917. Wilson, *Papers,* 44: 288–89.

48. Newton D. Baker to Woodrow Wilson, September 19, 1917. Wilson, *Papers,* 44: 221.

49. Cramer, *Newton D. Baker,* 105.

50. Kellogg, *Conscientious Objector.* Kellogg puts the figure at 3,900; Stone at 3,989. Capozzola suggests that four-fifths of the objectors were dissuaded from their position by coercion, cajoling, argument, or incentives. Capozzola, *Uncle Sam,* 60.

51. "Minute Book," 26.

52. Newton D. Baker to Woodrow Wilson, September 10, 1917. Wilson, *Papers,* 44: 225.

53. Ibid.

54. Bowman, *Church of the Brethren and War,* 172.

55. For example, the *Detroit News,* on November 20, 1917, told of objectors being thrown into the guardhouse.

56. Chambers, *To Raise an Army,* 78.

57. Homan, *American Mennonites,* 103.

58. The case ended in 1920 in Federal District Court, with Hofer and Wipf receiving hundred-dollar fines and with Entz being acquitted.

59. Chambers, *To Raise an Army,* 216.

60. "A CO in Camp Meade during World War I," unpublished, 1981, in Homan, *American Mennonites,* 105.

61. Samuel T. Ansell to Newton D. Baker, memorandum, September 18, 1917.

62. Henry P. McCain to Frederick P. Keppel, memorandum, May 20, 1918.

63. Homan, *American Mennonites,* 143.

Chapter 4. Standing Trial

1. Ulmer, *Military Justice*, 33. As revised by Congress in 1916, Article 17 of the code "reflected a greater concern with the right to counsel."

2. Even if a defense counsel assigned by the military sought to mount a vigorous case, time might dictate otherwise. Often there were only a few days between the assignment of counsel and the trial.

3. *New York Times*, August 25, 1919.

4. H.E. Foster to Roger Baldwin, March 16, 1918.

5. War Department memorandum, May 13, 1918.

6. In his *Diary*, Noah Leatherman, a Mennonite conscientious objector, recalled that one captain at Camp Funston simply crossed off the word "soldier" to persuade men to sign the card.

7. Homan, "CO on Trial," 9.

8. Ibid., 2.

9. Showalter's time at Fort Leavenworth would overlap with the stay of the Hofer brothers and Jacob Wipf. He arrived at the disciplinary barracks in the days after the October 23, 1918, court-martial. On December 10, Showalter was transferred to Camp Dodge, Iowa, and released in February.

10. David Hofer to Anna Hofer, June 12, 1918.

11. Michael Hofer to Maria Hofer, June 11, 1918.

12. Joseph Hofer to Maria Hofer, June 11, 1918.

13. *Alexandria Herald*, June 21, 1918.

14. Homan, "Military Justice," 372.

15. Homan, *American Mennonites*, 145. This number is an estimate.

16. Homan, "Mennonites and Military Justice," 370–371.

17. After review by commanding officers, many of the original sentences were markedly reduced. For example, seventeen of the 503 objectors convicted were originally sentenced to death, and 142 received life terms. In the end, the most severe sentence, issued to two men, was fifty years.

18. Roger Baldwin to Kenneth G. Darling, November 12, 1917.

19. Capozzola, *Uncle Sam*, 30.

20. Kohn, *American Political Prisoners*, 29.

21. Michael Hofer to Maria Hofer, June 18, 1918.

22. David Hofer to Anna Hofer, June 14, 1918.

23. Joseph Hofer to Maria Hofer, June 14, 1918.

24. Wurtz, "One Man's Encounter."

25. Joseph Kleinsasser to Frederick P. Keppel, March 28, 1918; April 18, 1918; July

14, 1918. Less than a week after Kleinsasser protested the treatment of Wurtz, officials in Washington sharply demanded an explanation: "You will investigate and report to this office immediately, case of Andrew Wurtz, reported to be conscientious objector at your camp," Henry P. McCain to Camp Lewis, telegram, July 19, 1918.

26. Joseph Hofer to Maria Hofer, June 18, 1918.

27. Anna Hofer to David Hofer, June 14, 1918.

28. Anna Hofer to David Hofer, June 22, 1918.

29. Susannah Hofer to David, Michael, and Joseph Hofer, June 17, 1918.

30. Kant, *Gentle People*, 6.

31. Joseph J. Wipf to David, Joseph, and Michael Hofer and Jacob Wipf, June 28, 1918.

32. Michael Hofer to Maria Hofer, June 24, 1918.

33. Michael Hofer to Maria Hofer, July 1, 1918.

34. Joseph Hofer to Maria Hofer, June 23, 1918.

35. Joseph Hofer to Maria Hofer, July 10, 1918.

36. War Department news release, June 25, 1918.

37. Thomas, "Justice to War's Heretics."

38. Board of Inquiry to Newton D. Baker, report on conscientious objectors at Camp Lewis, July 9, 1918.

39. Stone, "Conscientious Objector," 259.

40. These are Kellogg's figures. Stone offered slightly different numbers in some cases: 1,300 accepted noncombatant service; 1,300 received farm furloughs; and 99 left for reconstruction in France. Only 404 were subjected to court-martial, many before the board convened.

41. Kellogg, *Conscientious Objector*, 27–28.

42. Ibid., 27.

Chapter 5. The Dungeons of Alcatraz

1. Zieglschmid, *Das Klein-Geschichtsbuch der Hutterischen Bruder* (The Chronicle of the Hutterian Brethren), 482–483.

2. *Manual for Courts-Martial.*

3. Clauss, *Alcatraz*, 27.

4. Ibid. In the letter that David Hofer wrote to Jonas S. Hartzler after his release from prison on January 10, 1919, he quoted the guards as saying, "You'll die here. We took four out of here dead just yesterday."

5. "Discover Alcatraz: Escapes," a brochure (Golden Gate National Parks Conservancy, 1997).

6. Thompson, "The Rock," 289.

7. *The Rock*, vol. 3, no. 8, February 1918, 6.

8. Ibid.

9. Martini, *Fortress Alcatraz*, 112.

10. *The Rock*, vol. 3, no. 8, February 1918, 9.

11. *The Rock*, vol. 3, no. 1, July 1917, 4.

12. Ossewaarde, "Addresses on Patriotism."

13. *Examiner*, November 10, 1918.

14. Martini, *Alcatraz at War*, 52. The military no longer retains records of prisoners kept at Alcatraz during the war.

15. Ibid., 50.

16. Ibid., 52.

17. Ibid., 110–111.

18. *San Francisco Chronicle*, November 22, 1917.

19. Godwin, *Alcatraz*, 30–31.

20. Martini, *Alcatraz at War*, 52.

21. *San Francisco Chronicle*, October 5, 1919.

22. "'Crucifixions' in the Twentieth Century."

23. The author visited the basement twice, in 2006 and in 2010. Because of concerns about visitor safety and federal liability, the basement is unavailable for public tours, despite its historical significance.

24. Martini, *Alcatraz at War*, 78.

25. Howard W. Moore, who was held alongside Jacob Wipf at Leavenworth and later published a wartime memoir, for example, writes: "Sea water seeped through its walls and stood on the floor." Moore, *Plowing My Own Furrow*, 132.

26. J. Hofer, *History of the Hutterites*, 62.

27. David Hofer to J.S. Hartzler, January 10, 1919.

28. "'Crucifixions' in the Twentieth Century."

29. Michael Hofer to Maria Hofer, September 16, 1918.

30. Michael Hofer to Maria Hofer, August 7, 1918.

31. Michael Hofer to Maria Hofer, September 3, 1918.

32. Joseph Hofer to Maria Hofer, August 7, 1918.

33. Family members also visited the four men at both Alcatraz and at Fort Leavenworth.

34. David Hofer to Anna Hofer and children, August 18, 1918.

35. Grosser, *Alcatraz*, 10–11. Grosser's memoir was posthumously published; he was released from Alcatraz on December 2, 1920; he committed suicide in 1933. In the foreword to the book appears this tribute: "This is the story of a heretic. . . . His

heresy—in 1917 the heresy—consisted of a passionate belief that the common people of all lands were brothers, and that it was wrong to have any traffic with the
business of slaughtering them." See also, Kohn, *American Political Prisoners*, 59–62.

36. Letter from unknown conscientious objector to "George," likely George
Huddle, July 7, 1919. The letter is in the Philip Grosser collection maintained by his
granddaughter Jean Grosser.

37. *San Francisco Chronicle*, December 14, 1919.

38. Alice Park to the National Civil Liberties Bureau, December 16, 1919.

39. Martini, *Fortress Alcatraz*, 113.

40. Rideau, *In the Place of Justice*, 64–65.

41. Albert DeSilver to Newton Baker, February 5, 1919.

42. Ward, *Alcatraz*, 113–114.

43. Ibid., 115

44. Haney and Lynch, "Regulating Prisons of the Future"; Esslinger, *Alcatraz*.

45. Esslinger, *Alcatraz*, 98.

46. Medley, Petitioner, 134 U.S. 160.

47. Haney and Lynch, "Regulating Prisons of the Future."

48. Gibbons and Katzenbach, "Confronting Confinement," 59; Gawande, "Annals of Human Rights: Hellhole."

49. Psychologists for Social Responsibility to Robert M. Gates, January 3, 2011.
On July 30, 2013, Private Manning was convicted of six counts of violating the Espionage Act of 1917 and other crimes.

50. Samuel T. Ansell, acting judge advocate general, report, War Department,
September 30, 1918.

51. *New York Times*, February 14, 1919. Though Ansell was not speaking of conscientious objectors—he had in mind regular soldiers like a new recruit who was sentenced to forty years for refusing to turn over his cigarette—many of his criticisms
extended to any evaluation of justice served in the objector cases as well.

Chapter 6. Enemy on the Home Front

1. Joseph, "The United States," 14–15.

2. *New York Times*, September 15, 1918.

3. Teichroew, "Military Surveillance," "Note on the Mennonites."

4. "Note on the Mennonites, Subsection 4."

5. Ibid., 98.

6. Ibid.

7. Churchill to A.B. Bielaski, chief of the Bureau of Investigation, June 3, 1918, as
found in Teichroew, "Military Surveillance," 98.

8. Ibid., 127.

9. Ibid., 98.

10. Capozzola, *Uncle Sam*, 8.

11. *New York Times*, June 15, 1917.

12. Johnson, *Challenge to American Freedoms*, 65.

13. Kennedy, *Over Here*, 75.

14. Hilton, "Freedom of the Press," 349.

15. Kennedy, *Over Here*, 66.

16. Ibid., 68.

17. *Sioux Falls Press*, January 8, 1918, cited in "The Treatment of German Americans," April 24, 1975.

18. *New York Times*, May 3, 2006.

19. Work, *Darkest before Dawn*, 127, 260.

20. Ibid., 196.

21. Dick, "Noose for the Minister," 262.

22. *New York Times*, August 2, 1917.

23. Juhnke, "Mob Violence."

24. *Canton Pilot*, May 2, 1918.

25. Dick, "Noose for the Minister."

26. Juhnke, "John Schrag."

27. Gerlof D. Homan provides a detailed account in "The Burning."

28. Homan, "Americanism," 4.

29. Ewert, "Martyrs of Alcatraz."

Chapter 7. Midnight at Leavenworth

1. *Examiner*, November 12, 1918; *Tacoma News Tribune*, November 11, 1918.

2. *Examiner*, November 17, 1918.

3. Michael Hofer to Maria Hofer, November 17, 1918.

4. Joseph Hofer to Maria Hofer, November 17, 1918.

5. David Hofer to J.S. Hartzler, January 10, 1919. The details that follow are largely drawn from this letter.

6. "Desecration of the Dead" mentions bayonets, though the letter from Hofer to Hartzler does not. This version was picked up by, among others, A.J.F. Zieglschmid, *Das Klein-Geschichtsbuch der Hutterischen Bruder*, translated from the German by Franz Wiebe, 1974, as "The Martyrdom of Joseph and Michael Hofer," 482–486.

7. Report from Walton M. Modisette, major of U.S. Calvary, December 19, 1918.

8. Report from Sedgwick Rice, commandant, U.S. Disciplinary Barracks, Fort Leavenworth, KS, December 30, 1918.

9. Meyer, *"Hey! Yellowbacks!"* 133–134.

10. The enterprise is well documented in Price, "History of the United States Disciplinary Barracks."

11. Cottrell, *Roger Nash Baldwin*, 62.

12. Lane, "Strike at Fort Leavenworth."

13. *Kansas City Journal*, August 6, 1918.

14. Newton D. Baker to Sedgwick Rice, October 24, 1918.

15. Elmer Liechty to Liechty family, November 1918.

16. Showalter, *Nonresistance under Test*, 9–11.

17. Brock, *"These Strange Criminals,"* 151.

18. Ibid., 129.

19. National Civil Liberties Bureau to Newton D. Baker, November 19, 1918.

20. Interview with Noah Leatherman, June 30, 1970, Schowalter Oral History Project, Bethel College; Leatherman, *Diary*, 49. Leatherman was discharged on January 27, 1919.

21. Beachy, "From Persecution to Acclaim," 11–13.

22. Homan, *American Mennonites*, 154.

23. Preheim, "He Will Be with Us."

24. J.D. Mininger to J. Barnard Walton, December 4, 1918.

25. P.C. Harris to Edwin S. Johnson, January 14, 1919.

26. Taubenberger and Morens, "1918 Influenza"; *New York Times*, October 13, 2009.

27. Barry, *Great Influenza*, 238.

28. Taubenberger and Morens, "1918 Influenza," 17.

29. Barry, *Great Influenza*, 232.

30. Porter, *Pale Horse*, 201.

31. *Chronicle of the Hutterian Brethren*, 807.

32. Roger Baldwin to Robert P. Scripps, August 12, 1919; Robert Whitaker to Roger Baldwin, August 28, 1919.

33. David M. Morens, conversation with author, April 28, 2011.

34. "Wolf Creek," *Freeman Courier*, December 5, 1918.

35. "Wolf Creek," *Freeman Courier*, December 11, 1918.

36. "Mendel's Visit to Funston," *Freeman Courier*, October 25, 1917; Funk, "Divided Loyalties," 31.

37. Moore, *Plowing My Own Furrow*, 132.

38. Ibid., 133.

39. Ibid., 134.

40. Ibid., 135–136.

41. L. Thomas, *Conscience*, 122.

42. Ibid., 206.

43. Ibid., 242.

44. John J. Wipf to Edwin S. Johnson, November 30, 1918.

45. Edwin S. Johnson to P.C. Harris, December 3, 1918.

46. P.C. Harris to Edwin S. Johnson, December 6, 1918.

47. P.C. Harris to Edwin S. Johnson, December 9, 1918.

48. F.H. Johnson to Edwin S. Johnson, December 7, 1918.

Chapter 8. Outside Advocates

1. Transcript of the trial of Roger Baldwin, Federal Court, October 30, 1918.

2. Thomas W. Gregory to Woodrow Wilson, November 9, 1918. Wilson, *Papers*, 53: 12–13.

3. "Political Prisoners in Federal Military Prisons." National Civil Liberties Bureau to Newton Baker, memorandum, November 30, 1918.

4. *New York Times*, September 14, 1918.

5. L. Thomas, *Conscience*, 244–245.

6. Frederick P. Keppel to Theodore H. Lunde, December 4, 1918.

7. News release, War Department, December 6, 1918. In *For Peace and Justice*, Chatfield notes that Nevin Sayre may have helped end the practice by speaking with President Wilson in December, 58.

8. Rejali, *Torture and Democracy*, 309, 553.

9. Ibid., 559. The U.N. Convention Against Torture and Other Cruel, Inhuman or Degrading Treatment or Punishment, CAT, defines torture as

[A]ny act by which severe pain or suffering, whether physical or mental, is intentionally inflicted on a person for such purposes as obtaining from him or a third person information or a confession, punishing him for an act he or a third person has committed or is suspected of having committed, or intimidating or coercing him or a third person, or for any reason based on discrimination of any kind, when such pain or suffering is inflicted by or at the instigation of or with the consent or acquiescence of a public official or other person acting in an official capacity.

Once again, the defining elements of torture were present at Alcatraz: severe pain or suffering, public officials, coercion. The United States signed the CAT in 1988, but M. Cherif Bassiouni points out that torture "has long been prohibited under international humanitarian law," well before World War I. The 1899 Hague Convention on the Laws and Customs of War on Land and the 1907 Hague Convention on the Laws and Customs of War on Land outlaw torture, requiring that prisoners be humanely treated. That said, in an e-mail interview, he noted that the

1907 Hague Convention was "not very specific" in distinguishing between humane and inhumane treatment. Bassiouni, interview with author, May 16, 2011; Bassiouni, *Institutionalization*, 14–17.

10. National Civil Liberties Bureau, memorandum, October 15, 1918.

11. Homan, "Conscientious Objectors," 8.

12. *New York Times*, December 28, 1918.

13. Albert DeSilver to John D. Barry, May 7, 1919.

14. Woodrow Wilson to Thomas W. Gregory, September 25, 1917. Wilson, *Papers*, 44:247.

15. Jacob Ewert often spelled his surname "Evert." For example, the Tabor College letterhead on which he wrote to Newton D. Baker, the secretary of war, on January 8, 1919, identifies him as J.G. Evert. But his pamphlets in the WorldCat database are attributed to Jacob G. Ewert; *The Mennonite Encyclopedia* and *Global Anabaptist Mennonite Encyclopedia* likewise refer to Jacob Ewert. His paternal ancestors used the name Ewert, and so Evert appears to be an Anglicized version, according to the Mennonite Library and Archives in North Newton, KS.

16. Dudley Doolittle to Thomas W. Gregory, July 16, 1918.

17. Hiebert, *Feeding the Hungry*, 287–292.

18. *New York Times*, December 25, 1918.

19. Jonas S. Hartzler, a Mennonite advocate for conscientious objectors, also cited the case of the four Hutterites as the most extreme example of abuse. In a January 29, 1920, letter to W. Lee Ustick of *The World Tomorrow*, he wrote: "Do you have the experiences of the Hofer boys of Alexandria, S. Dak.? That is the most cruel that I have yet seen."

20. Theodore H. Lunde to S. Hubert Dent, January 13, 1919. That same month, Dent had the cases entered into the *Congressional Record*, beginning with the Hofer brothers and Jacob Wipf. On March 3, 1919, in the *Congressional Record*, Representative William E. Mason of Illinois also cited the Hutterites first in rebutting charges that conscientious objectors had been treated with leniency.

21. Lunde chose to conceal the identity of his source, likely to avoid repercussions for the officer. In his diary entry on December 19, 1918, Noah Leatherman refers to a "discharged sergeant" who became "acquainted and sympathetic with the C.O.'s" and intended to travel to see Lunde in Chicago and report on the four Hutterites, *Diary*, 56–57. The sergeant referred to may be Albert P. Brown, who after being honorably discharged sent a letter to Secretary Baker in praise of objectors he learned to know, December 20, 1918. Military records show that Jacob Wipf was admitted to the hospital on December 13, 1918, with acute tonsillitis, and, in the words of the authorities at Fort Leavenworth, was "returned to duty" on December 18.

22. The article "Desecration of the Dead by American 'Huns'" does not carry a

byline or other notation directly attributing it to an author. Jacob Ewert said that he prepared the article, translating it from a German account based on David Hofer's testimony as transcribed by his father. The article closely tracks "Vier Hutterische Mennoniten im Militärkerker," or "The Hutterite Mennonites in Military Prison," which was written by Ewert.

23. Theodore H. Lunde to the National Civil Liberties Bureau, October 22, 1918; February 3, 1919; February 13, 1919; February 26, 1919. National Civil Liberties Bureau to Theodore H. Lunde, October 27, 1918; February 11, 1919; February 17, 1919.

24. Albert DeSilver to Robert W. Ryan, March 13, 1919.

25. *Congressional Record*, March 3, 1919.

26. Newton Baker to Lenetta M. Cooper, June 30, 1919.

27. Mock, *Writing Peace*, 218.

28. *New York Times*, January 23, 1919.

29. *Kansas City Star*, January 23, 1919.

30. *Kansas City Star*, January 27, 1919.

31. *New York Times*, February 16, 1919.

32. Resolution of the State Senate of Nebraska, February 5, 1919.

33. Newton D. Baker to the secretary of state, Nebraska, February 26, 1919.

34. E.H. Crowder to Newton D. Baker, memorandum, January 22, 1919.

35. Memo entitled "Criticism of the Department," undated, in the personal correspondence of Newton D. Baker.

36. R.P. Truitt to Marine Corps, memorandum, February 21, 1919.

37. P.C. Harris to Edwin S. Johnson, January 14, 1919.

38. P.C. Harris to Edwin S. Johnson, February 15, 1919.

39. John J. Wipf to Frederick P. Keppel, telegram, March 17, 1919.

40. Memo from A.L. Dade, Office of the Inspector General, War Department, January 24, 1919.

41. Kellogg, *Conscientious Objector*, 38.

42. H. Stone, "Conscientious Objector," 262.

43. Ibid., 260.

44. Kellogg, *Conscientious Objector*, 41.

45. Smith, *Coming of Russian Mennonites*, 291.

46. Capozzola, *Uncle Sam*, 75; Kohn, *American Political Prisoners*, 45–48.

47. Sedgwick Rice, commandant, Fort Leavenworth, annual report for 1919.

48. Sedgwick Rice, commandant, Fort Leavenworth, annual report for 1918.

49. May, "Psychological Examination."

50. Ibid., 153.

51. Ibid., 159.

52. Ibid., 160–161.

53. Ibid., 161.

54. Kellogg, *Conscientious Objector*; Capozzola, *Uncle Sam*, 60; Baker, "Statement Concerning the Treatment."

55. Capozzola, *Uncle Sam*, 77.

56. N. Thomas, *Conscientious Objector*, 83–84.

57. N. Thomas, "Justice to War's Heretics."

58. Albert P. Brown to Newton D. Baker, December 20, 1918.

59. News release, War Department, February 13, 1919.

60. J.G. Evert to Frederick P. Keppel, telegram, March 15, 1919.

61. J.G. Evert to Frederick P. Keppel, March 15, 1919.

62. Jason S. Joy to the Judge Advocate General, memorandum, March 18, 1919.

Chapter 9. Official Misjudgment

1. *Parkston Advance*, May 3, 1918; J. Hofer, *History of the Hutterites*, 62.

2. Sawyer, "Anti-German Sentiment," 508–509.

3. Katie Hofer Waldner, conversation with author, February 23, 2009. Waldner died in 2016.

4. Joe Hofer, conversation with author, June 4, 2009.

5. Michael Hofer's daughter, Mary Hofer Kleinsasser, who lived at the Miller Colony, died in 2012 at the age of 94.

6. Jacob Wipf, conversation with author, February 21, 2009.

7. Preheim, "He Will Be with Us," 7.

8. Jacob Wipf and Joe Kleinsasser, conversation with author, February 21, 2009.

9. Smith, *Story of the Mennonites*, 800.

10. Ibid., 795.

11. Harris, *My Life and Loves*, 945–946.

12. Johnson, *Challenge to American Freedoms*, 26.

13. Ibid., 53.

14. Letter from Newton D. Baker to George F. Peabody, August 22, 1918.

15. Letter from Newton D. Baker to President Woodrow Wilson, May 1, 1918.

16. Reply from Newton D. Baker to socialist convention seeking release of conscientious objectors, Baker Papers, 1918–1919; no specific date listed.

17. Newton D. Baker to Woodrow Wilson, October 1, 1917. Wilson, *Papers*, 44: 288–89.

18. Newton D. Baker to Woodrow Wilson, July 1, 1919. Newton D. Baker papers, Library of Congress, Washington, D.C.

Epilogue

1. Keim, *CPS Story*, 24.

2. Moskos and Chambers, *New Conscientious Objection*, 42.

3. The Selective Service agency provides information about registration, including details about what would happen in the event of a draft, at www.sss.gov.

4. Resources on conscientious objection—including a "Peacemaker Registration Form," in which people can prepare answers to questions that the Selective Service would ask objectors in the event of a draft—can be found at www.mcc.org/us/co, www.mennonitemission.net/Serve/MVS/Pages/Home.aspx, and www.centeron conscience.org.

5. Daniel Mach, conversation with author, January 11, 2012.

6. *Employment Division v. Smith*, 494 U.S. 872, 1990.

7. *New York Times*, February 25, 2012.

8. *Hope v. Pelzer*, 2002.

9. R. Janzen and Stanton, *Hutterites*, 20, 295.

10. Ibid., 74.

11. Ibid., 299.

12. Kanagy, *Road Signs*, 127–128.

13. *New York Times*, February 28, 2011.

Bibliography

Government Records

Alcatraz, San Francisco, CA
Fort Leavenworth, KS
National Archives and Records Administration, College Park, MD; Kansas City, MO
National Personnel Records Center, St. Louis, MO
Park Archives and Records Center, National Park Service, San Francisco, CA

Manuscript Collections

American Civil Liberties Union, Princeton University, NJ
California Historical Society, San Francisco, CA
Center for Mennonite Brethren Studies, Tabor College, Hillsboro, KS
Freeman Academy Heritage Archives, Freeman, SD
Library of Congress, Washington, DC
Mennonite Church USA Archives, Goshen, IN
Mennonite Historical Library, Goshen College, Goshen, IN
Mennonite Library and Archives, Bethel College, North Newton, KS
Norwegian-American Historical Association, Northfield, MN
San Francisco Public Library, San Francisco, CA
Schowalter Oral History Collection, Bethel College, North Newton, KS
South Dakota State Historical Library, Pierre, SD
Tacoma Public Library, Tacoma, WA

Interviews

Bassiouni, M. Cherif. DePaul University College of Law, Chicago, IL

Hofer, Joe. Grandson of Joseph J. Hofer. Kyle Colony, Kyle, SK

Kleinsasser, Joe. Grandson of Michael J. Hofer. Kingsbury Colony, Valier, MT

Kleinsasser, Mary Hofer. Daughter of Michael J. Hofer. Miller Colony, Choteau, MT

Kleinsasser, Mike. Grandson of Michael J. Hofer. Kingsbury Colony, Valier, MT

Kleinsasser, Sarah. Granddaughter of Michael J. Hofer. Miller Colony, Choteau, MT

Mach, Daniel. American Civil Liberties Union, Program on Freedom of Religion and Belief, Washington, DC

Morens, David M. National Institutes of Health, Bethesda, MD

Rejali, Darius. Reed College, Portland, OR

Waldner, Katie Hofer. Daughter of David J. Hofer. Kingsbury Colony, Valier, MT

Waldner, Katie Jacob. Granddaughter of Joseph J. Hofer. Rockport Colony, Pendroy, MT

Wipf, Jacob. Miller Colony, Choteau, MT

Publications

Ansell, S.T. "Military Justice." *The Cornell Law Quarterly* V (1919): 1–17.

Baker, Newton. "The Embattled Democracy," December 12, 1917, *Frontiers of Freedom*. New York: Doran, 1918. In Daniel R. Beaver, *Newton D. Baker and the American War Effort*. Lincoln: University of Nebraska Press, 1966.

———. "Statement Concerning the Treatment of Conscientious Objectors in the Army," June 18, 1919, Newton Diehl Baker Papers, Library of Congress, Washington, DC.

Barry, John M. *The Great Influenza: The Epic Story of the Deadliest Plague in History*. New York: Viking, 2004.

Bassiouni, M. Cherif. *The Institutionalization of Torture by the Bush Administration*. Antwerp: Intersentia, 2010.

Beachy, Monroe L. "From Persecution to Acclaim." *Family Life*, April 1994.

Beadle, William. *Autobiography of William Henry Harrison Beadle*. Pierre, SD: State Historical Society, 1906.

Beaver, Daniel R. *Newton D. Baker and the American War Effort*. Lincoln: University of Nebraska Press, 1966.

Blakey, George T. *Historians on the Homefront: American Propagandists for the Great War*. Lexington: University Press of Kentucky, 1970.

Bowman, Rufus D. *The Church of the Brethren and War*. Elgin, IL: Brethren Publishing House, 1944.

Brock, Peter, and Nigel Young. *Pacifism in the Twentieth Century*. Syracuse, NY: Syracuse University Press, 1999.

Brock, Peter, ed. *"These Strange Criminals": An Anthology of Prison Memoirs by Conscientious Objectors from the Great War to the Cold War*. Toronto: University of Toronto Press, 2004.

The Bloody Theater or Martyrs Mirror of the Defenseless Christians, trans. Joseph F. Sohm. Scottdale, PA: Mennonite Publishing House, 1950.

Capozzola, Christopher. *Uncle Sam Wants You: World War I and the Making of the Modern American Citizen*. New York: Oxford University Press, 2008.

Castelli, Elizabeth A. *Martyrdom and Memory: Early Christian Culture Making*. New York: Columbia University Press, 2004.

Chambers, John Whiteclay, II. *To Raise an Army: The Draft Comes to Modern America*. New York: The Free Press, 1987.

Chatfield, Charles. *For Peace and Justice: Pacifism in America, 1914–1941*. Knoxville: The University of Tennessee Press, 1971.

The Chronicle of the Hutterian Brethren, vol. 1. Rifton, NY: Plough Publishing, 1987.

Clauss, Francis J. *Alcatraz: Island of Many Mistakes*. Menlo Park, CA: Briarcliff Press, 1981.

Coffman, Edward M. *The War to End All Wars*. New York: Oxford University Press, 1968.

Connelly, Mark, and David Welch, eds. *War and the Media: Reportage and Propaganda, 1900–2003*. London: I.B. Tauris, 2005.

Cooper, John Milton Jr., ed. *Reconsidering Woodrow Wilson: Progressivism, Internationalism, War, and Peace*. Washington, DC: Woodrow Wilson Center Press, 2008.

Correll, Ernst. "President Grant and the Mennonite Immigration from Russia." *The Mennonite Quarterly Review* 9 (April 1935): 144–152.

Cottrell, Robert C. *Roger Nash Baldwin and the American Civil Liberties Union*. New York: Columbia University Press, 2000.

Cramer, Clarence H. *Newton D. Baker*. Cleveland: World Publishing Co., 1961.

"'Crucifixions' in the Twentieth Century." Chicago: American Industrial Company, 1918.

"Desecration of the Dead by American 'Huns.'" Chicago: American Industrial Company, 1919.

Dick, LaVernae J. "A Noose for the Minister." *The Mennonite*, April 21, 1964.

Eaton, Joseph W., and Albert J. Mayer. *Man's Capacity to Reproduce: The Demography of a Unique Population*. Glencoe, IL: The Free Press, 1954.

The Encyclopedia of Cleveland History. Case Western Reserve University, Cleveland, OH. Available at http://ech.case.edu/ech-cgi/article.pl?id=HJC1.

Esslingler, Michael. *Alcatraz: A Definitive History of the Penitentiary Years*. San Francisco: OceanView, 2003.

Ewert, Jacob G. "The Martyrs of Alcatraz." *Gospel Herald*, October 2, 1919.

———. "Vier Hutterische Mennoniten im Militärkerker." *Vorwärts*, February 7, 1919.

Ferguson, Niall. *The Pity of War*. New York: Basic Books, 1999.

Ford, Nancy Gentile. *Americans All! Foreign-Born Soldiers in World War I*. College Station: Texas A&M University Press, 2001.

Fortescue, Granville. "Training the New Armies of Liberty," *National Geographic*, November–December 1917.

Foundations for the Future: A Commemorative Volume in Honor of Our 75th Anniversary. Cleveland: Baker & Hostetler, 1991.

Frazier, Ian. *Great Plains*. New York: Farrar, Straus and Giroux, 1989.

Friesen, John J., ed. and trans. *Peter Riedemann's Hutterite Confession of Faith*. Scottdale, Pa.: Herald Press, 1999.

Funk, Merle J.F. "Divided Loyalties: Mennonite and Hutterite Responses to the United States at War, Hutchinson County, South Dakota, 1917–1918." *Mennonite Life*, December 1997.

Gawande, Atul. "Annals of Human Rights: Hellhole." *The New Yorker*. March 30, 2009.

Gibbons, John J., and Nicholas de B. Katzenbach, commission co-chairs. "Confronting Confinement: A Report of the Commission on Safety and Abuse in America's Prisons." June 2006.

Godwin, John. *Alcatraz: 1868–1963*. Garden City, NY: Doubleday, 1963.

Gross, Leonard. *The Golden Years of the Hutterites*. Scottdale, PA: Herald Press, 1997.

Gross, Paul S. *The Hutterite Way*. Saskatoon: Freeman Publishing, 1965.

Grosser, Philip. *Alcatraz: Uncle Sam's Devil's Island: Experiences of a Conscientious Objector in America during the First World War*, 2nd ed. Berkeley, Calif.: Kate Sharpley Library, 2007.

Hallock, Dan. "The Martyrs of Alcatraz." *Menno-Hof Reunion* 14, no. 4 (Summer 2005).

Haney, Craig, and Mona Lynch. "Regulating Prisons of the Future: A Psychological Analysis of Supermax and Solitary Confinement." *New York University School of Law Review of Law and Social Change* 23 (1997): 477–570.

Harris, Frank. *My Life and Loves*. Secaucus, NJ: Castle Books, 1963.

Heaton, John L. *Cobb of "The World."* New York: E.P. Dutton, 1924.

Hershberger, Guy F. *War, Peace, and Nonresistance*. Scottdale, PA: Herald Press, 1944.

Hiebert, Peter C. *Feeding the Hungry: Russia Famine, 1919–1925.* Scottdale, PA: Mennonite Central Committee, 1929.

Higham, John. *Strangers in the Land: Patterns of American Nativism, 1860–1925.* New York: Atheneum, 1965.

Hilton, O.A. *"Freedom of the Press in Wartime, 1917–1919."* The Southwestern Social Science Quarterly 28 (1947): 346–361.

Hofer, Arnold M., and Kenneth J. Walter. *The History of the Hutterite Mennonites, 1874–1974.* Freeman, SD: Pine Hill Press, 1974.

Hofer, John. *The History of the Hutterites.* Rev. ed. Altona, Man.: D.W. Friesen & Sons, 1988.

Hofer, J.M., ed. "The Diary of Paul Tschetter, 1873." *The Mennonite Quarterly Review* 5 (July 1931): 112–127.

Homan, Gerlof D. "Americanism, Pro-Germanism, and Conscientious Objectors during World War I." *Mennonite Historical Bulletin* 55 (January 1994): 1–4.

———. *American Mennonites and the Great War: 1914–1918.* Waterloo, ON, and Scottdale, PA: Herald Press, 1994.

———. "The Burning of the Mennonite Church, Fairview, Michigan, in 1918." *The Mennonite Quarterly Review* 64 (April 1990): 99–112.

———. "Conscientious Objectors in Camp Funston, 1918–1919." *Mennonite Life* (December 1989): 4–9.

———. "A CO on Trial: The Court-martial of Amos M. Showalter." *Mennonite Historian* 17 (September 1991).

———. "Mennonites and Military Justice in World War I." *The Mennonite Quarterly Review* 65 (July 1992): 365–375.

Horsch, John. *The Hutterian Brethren: A Story of Martyrdom and Loyalty, 1528–1931.* Goshen, IN: Mennonite Historical Society, 1931.

Hostetler, John A. *Hutterite Society.* Baltimore: Johns Hopkins University Press, 1974.

Huddleston, Joe D. *Fort Lewis: A History.* Pierce, WA: Fort Lewis, 1983.

"Hutterite Brethren and War," *Gospel Herald,* August 9, 1917.

Hutterite CO's in World War I. Hawley, MN: Spring Prairie, 1997.

Jansen, Peter. *Memoirs of Peter Jansen: The Record of a Busy Life, an Autobiography.* Beatrice, NE: self-published, 1921.

Janzen, David A. "My Experiences as a Young Man of Mennonite Faith in World War I," Mennonite Library and Archives, Bethel College.

Janzen, Rod. *Paul Tschetter.* Eugene, OR: Pickwick Publications, 2009.

Janzen, Rod, and Max Stanton. *The Hutterites in North America.* Baltimore: The Johns Hopkins University Press, 2010.

Jensen, Joan M. *The Price of Vigilance.* Chicago: Rand McNally, 1968.

Johnson, Donald. *The Challenge to American Freedoms: World War I and the Rise of the American Civil Liberties Union.* Lexington: University of Kentucky Press, 1963.

Johnston, James A. *Prison Life Is Different.* Boston: Houghton Mifflin, 1937.

Jones, Rufus M. *A Service of Love in War Time.* New York: Macmillan, 1920.

Joseph, Ted. "The United States vs. H. Miller: The Strange Case of a Mennonite Editor Convicted of Violating the 1917 Espionage Act." *Mennonite Life,* September 1975.

Juhnke, James. "COs Caught in 1918 Version of Abu Ghraib." *Mennonite Weekly Review,* October 18, 2004, 6.

———. "John Schrag Espionage Case." *Mennonite Life,* July 1967.

———. "Mob Violence and Kansas Mennonites in 1918." *Kansas Historical Quarterly* 43 (1977): 334–350.

———. "Victories of Nonresistance: Mennonite Oral Tradition in World War I." *Fides Et Historia* 7/1 (1974): 19–26.

———. *Vision, Doctrine, War: Mennonite Identity and Organization in America, 1890–1930.* Scottdale, PA: Herald Press, 1989.

Kanagy, Conrad L. *Road Signs for the Journey: A Profile of Mennonite Church USA.* Scottdale, PA: Herald Press, 2007.

Kant, Joanita. *Gentle People: A Case Study of Rockport Colony Hutterites.* Brookings, SD: Prairie View Press, 2011.

Keegan, John. *The First World War.* New York: Vintage, 2000.

Keim, Albert N. *The CPS Story: An Illustrated History of Civilian Public Service.* Intercourse, PA: Good Books, 1990.

Keim, Albert N., and Grant M. Stoltzfus. *The Politics of Conscience: The Historic Peace Churches and America at War, 1917–1955.* Scottdale, Pa.: Herald Press, 1988.

Kellogg, Walter G. *The Conscientious Objector.* New York: Boni and Liveright, 1919.

Kennedy, David M. *Over Here: The First World War and American Society.* New York: Oxford University Press, 2004.

Kleinsasser, Amos, ed. *Our Journey of Faith: Hutterthal Mennonite Church, 1879–2004.* Freeman, SD: Hutterthal Mennonite Church, 2004.

Kohn, Stephen M. *American Political Prisoners: Prosecutions under the Espionage and Sedition Acts.* Westport, CT: Praeger, 1994.

Kraybill, Donald B., and Carl F. Bowman. *On the Backroad to Heaven: Old Order Hutterites, Mennonites, Amish, and Brethren.* Baltimore: The Johns Hopkins University Press, 2001.

Lane, Winthrop D. "The Strike at Fort Leavenworth." Reprinted from The Survey, National Civil Liberties Bureau, NY, 1919.

Laskin, David. *The Long Way Home: An American Journey from Ellis Island to the Great War.* New York: Harper, 2010.

Leatherman, Noah. *Diary Kept by Noah H. Leatherman while in Camp during World War I.* Rosenort, Manitoba, Canada: Prairie View Press, 1986.

Lehman, James O., and Steven M. Nolt. *Mennonites, Amish, and the American Civil War.* Baltimore: Johns Hopkins University Press, 2007.

Leighton, Morris M. *The Country about Camp Lewis.* Olympia, WA: Frank M. Lamborn, 1918.

Leisy, E.E. "The Martial Adventures of a Conscientious Objector," unpublished typescript, Mennonite Church USA Archives, Goshen, IN.

Lengel, Edward G. *World War I Memories: An Annotated Bibliography of Personal Accounts Published in English Since 1919.* Lanham, MD: Scarecrow Press, 2004.

"Letters from a Political Prisoner in a Military Hospital U.S.A." Chicago: American Industrial Company, 1918.

A Manual for Courts-Martial, Courts of Inquiry, and of Other Procedure Under Military Law. Washington: Government Printing Office, 1918.

Martini, John A. *Alcatraz at War.* San Francisco: Golden Gate National Parks Association, 2002.

———. *Fortress Alcatraz.* Berkeley, CA: Ten Speed Press, 2004.

"The Martyrdom of Joseph and Michael Hofer, 1918," in A.J.F. Zieglschmid's *Das Kleine-Geschichtsbuch der Hutterischen Bruder.* Franz Wiebe, trans. Philadelphia: Carl Schurz Foundation, 1947.

May, Mark. "The Psychological Examination of Conscientious Objectors." *The American Journal of Psychology* 31 (April 1920): 152–165.

McAdoo, William G. *Crowded Years.* Port Washington, NY: Kennikat Press, 1981.

McNutt, William Slavens. "Camp Lewis as Eastern Magazine Writer Sees It," *Collier's Weekly,* April 11, 1918.

Meigs, Mark. *Optimism at Armageddon: Voices of American Participants in the First World War.* New York: New York University Press, 1997.

Mendel, Jacob J. *History of the People of East Freeman, Silver Lake, and West Freeman from 1528 to 1961 and History of Freeman (continued 1958–1961).* South Dakota: Katie Gross, 1961.

Meryman, Richard S. Jr. "South Dakota's Christian Martyrs." *Harper's,* December 1958, 72–79.

Meyer, Ernest L. *"Hey! Yellowbacks!" The War Diary of a Conscientious Objector.* New York: The John Day Company, 1930.

"The Minute Book of the Committee on Exemptions of the Western District Conference 1917–1922," Bd. Ms. 110, Mennonite Library and Archives, Bethel College, North Newton, KS.

Mock, Melanie Springer. *Writing Peace: The Unheard Voices of Great War Mennonite Objectors.* Telford and Scottdale, PA: Pandora Press and Herald Press, 2003.

Moore, Howard W. *Plowing My Own Furrow*. Syracuse, NY: Syracuse University Press, 1993.

Moskos, Charles C., and John Whiteclay Chambers II. *The New Conscientious Objection: From Sacred to Secular Resistance*. New York: Oxford University Press, 1993.

National Civil Liberties Bureau. "Political Prisoners in Federal Military Prisons," American Civil Liberties Union Papers, Seeley G. Mudd Manuscript Library, Princeton University, NJ., November 21, 1918.

"Note on the Mennonites, Subsection 4," the Malone Report, Military Intelligence Division, War Department, Record Group 165, File 10902–18, National Archives.

Nussbaum, Martha C. *Liberty of Conscience: In Defense of America's Tradition of Religious Equality*. New York: Basic Books, 2008.

Ossewaarde, James. *Addresses on Patriotism*. Alcatraz, CA: Pacific Branch of United States Disciplinary Barracks, 1917.

Oyer, John S., and Robert S. Kreider. *Mirror of the Martyrs*. Intercourse, PA: Good Books, 1990.

Packull, Werner O. *Hutterite Beginnings*. Baltimore: Johns Hopkins University Press, 1995.

Peterson, H.C., and Gilbert C. Fite. *Opponents of War: 1917–1918*. Madison: University of Wisconsin Press, 1957.

"Political Prisoners in Federal Military Prisons." National Civil Liberties Bureau to Newton Baker, memorandum, November 30, 1918.

Porter, Katherine Anne. *Pale Horse, Pale Rider*. San Diego: Harcourt Brace Jovanovich, 1990.

Powell, E. Alexander. "Making the Makers of Victory," *Scribner's Magazine*, March 1918.

Preheim, Rich. "'He Will Be with Us Till the End.'" *Mennonite Weekly Review*, December 2, 1993.

Price, Jerry S. "History of the United States Disciplinary Barracks, 1875–Present." Student Study Project, Fort Leavenworth, KS, May 7, 1978.

"Record of the Trial of Recruits David J. Hofer, Michael J. Hofer, Joseph J. Hofer, and Jacob J. Wipf," Judge Advocate's Office, Ninety-first Infantry Division, Camp Lewis, U.S. Army, June 15, 1918, "Case Files of Conscientious Objectors Court-Martialed during World War I," MF MSS 171 a-b-c, Mennonite Library and Archives, Bethel College, North Newton, KS.

Rejali, Darius. *Torture and Democracy*. Princeton, NJ: Princeton University Press, 2007.

Rhodes, Robert. *Nightwatch: An Inquiry into Solitude*. Intercourse, PA: Good Books, 2009.

Richter, Anthony H. "Dakota-Germans and World War I." *Schatzkammer* 11 (Fall 1985): 57–66.

Rideau, Wilbert. *In the Place of Justice: A Story of Punishment and Deliverance*. New York: Alfred A. Knopf, 2010.

Riley, Marvin P. *The Hutterites and Their Agriculture: 100 Years in South Dakota*. Brookings: South Dakota State University, 1980.

Riley, Marvin P., and Darryll R. Johnson. *South Dakota's Hutterite Colonies, 1874–1969*. Bulletin 565. Brookings: South Dakota State University, 1970.

Roth, John D. *Stories: How Mennonites Came to Be*. Scottdale, PA: Herald Press, 2006.

Russo, Paul Gia. "The Conscientious Objector in American Law." *Religion in Life* 10, no. 3 (Summer 1941): 333–346.

Sawyer, Darrell R. "Anti-German Sentiment in South Dakota during World War I." *South Dakota Historical Collections* 38 (1976): 440–514.

Schell, Herbert S. *History of South Dakota*. Pierre: South Dakota State Historical Society Press, 2004.

Schlabach, Theron, ed. "Diary of a Conscientious Objector in World War I: An Account, by Jakob Waldner." *The Mennonite Quarterly Review* 47 (January 1973): 73–111.

Schultz Huxman, Susan. "Mennonite Rhetoric in World War I: Lobbying the Government for Freedom of Conscience." *The Mennonite Quarterly Review* 67 (July 1993): 283–303.

Shields, Sarah D. "The Treatment of Conscientious Objectors during World War I: Mennonites at Camp Funston." *Kansas History* (Winter 1981): 255–269.

Showalter, Richard, ed. *Nonresistance under Test*. Irwin, OH: Conservative Mennonite Board of Missions and Charities, 1969.

Smith, C. Henry. *The Coming of the Russian Mennonites*. Berne, IN: Mennonite Book Concern, 1927.

———. *The Story of the Mennonites*. 3rd ed. Newton, KS: Mennonite Publication Office, 1950.

Stoltzfus, Duane C.S. "Armed with Prayer in an Alcatraz Dungeon: The Wartime Experiences of Four Hutterite C.O.'s in Their Own Words." *The Mennonite Quarterly Review* vol. 85, no. 2 (April 2011): 259–292.

Stone, Geoffrey R. *Perilous Times: Free Speech in Wartime from the Sedition Act of 1798 to the War on Terrorism*. New York: Norton, 2004.

Stone, Harlan F. "The Conscientious Objector." *Columbia University Quarterly* 21 (October 1919): 253–272.

Strachan, Hew. *The First World War*. New York: Penguin, 2003.

Swan, Jon. "The 400-Year-Old Commune." *The Atlantic*, November 1972, 90–100.

Taubenberger, Jeffrey K., and David M. Morens. "1918 Influenza: The Mother of All Pandemics," *Emerging Infectious Diseases* vol. 12, no. 1 (January 2006).

Teichroew, Allan. "Mennonites and the Conscription Trap." *Mennonite Life* 30 (September 1975): 10–13.

———. "Military Surveillance of Mennonites in World War I." *The Mennonite Quarterly Review* 53 (1979): 95–127.

———. "World War I and the Mennonite Migration to Canada." *The Mennonite Quarterly Review* 45 (1971): 219–249.

Thomas, Louisa. *Conscience: Two Soldiers, Two Pacifists, One Family—A Test of Will and Faith in World War I*. New York: Penguin Press, 2011.

Thomas, Norman. *The Conscientious Objector in America*. New York: B.W. Huebsch, 1923.

———. "The Hutterian Brethren." *South Dakota Historical Collections* 25 (1950): 265–299.

———. *Is Conscience a Crime?* New York: Garland Publishing, 1972.

———. "Justice to War's Heretics." *The Nation*, November 9, 1918.

Thompson, Erwin N. "The Rock: A History of Alcatraz Island, 1847–1972." Historic resource study, Denver Service Center, Historic Preservation Division, National Park Service, 1979.

Tryon, Warren S. "The Draft in World War I." *Current History*, June 1968.

Tuchman, Barbara. *The Guns of August*. New York: Dell, 1962.

Ulmer, S. Sidney. *Military Justice and the Right to Counsel*. Lexington: The University Press of Kentucky, 1970.

Unruh, John D. "A Century of Mennonites in Dakota." *South Dakota Historical Collections* 36 (1972): 1–142.

Vischer, Robert K. *Conscience and the Common Good: Reclaiming the Space between Person and State*. New York: Cambridge University Press, 2010.

Vought, Hans P. *The Bully Pulpit and the Melting Pot: American Presidents and the Immigrant, 1897–1933*. Macon, GA: Mercer University Press, 2004.

Waltner, Edward J.B. "A 'C.O.' in the First World War," Freeman Academy Heritage Archives, 1942.

Ward, David, with Gene Kassebaum. *Alcatraz: The Gangster Years*. Berkeley: University of California Press, 2010.

Wiebe, David, ed. *The History of Hutterites*. Sponsored by Youth Secretariat, Colleges and Universities Affairs, Department of Manitoba, 1977.

Wilson, Woodrow. *Papers of Woodrow Wilson*. Edited by Arthur Stanley Link. Princeton, NJ: Princeton University Press, 1966–1994.

Work, Clemens P. *Darkest before Dawn: Sedition and Free Speech in the American West*. Albuquerque: University of New Mexico Press, 2005.

Wurtz, Andrew. "One Man's Encounter with Military Law," in *Hutterite CO's in World War I*. Hawley, MN: Spring Prairie, 1997.

Yoder, Joseph. "From the Director's Desk." *Menno-Hof Reunion* 14, no. 4 (Summer 2005).

Young, Gertrude S. "The Mennonites in South Dakota." *South Dakota Historical Collections* 19 (1920): 470–506.

Zacher, Dale E. *The Scripps Newspapers Go to War: 1914–18*. Urbana, IL: University of Illinois Press, 2008.

Zieger, Robert H. *America's Great War: World War I and the American Experience*. Lanham, MD: Rowman and Littlefield, 2001.

Zieglschmid, A.J.F. *Das Kleine-Geschichtsbuch der Hutterischen Bruder* (Philadelphia: Carl Schurz Foundation, 1947).

Index

Index

About the Author

Duane C. S. Stoltzfus is a professor of communication at Goshen College. He is the author of *Freedom from Advertising: E. W. Scripps's Chicago Experiment* (University of Illinois, 2007) and serves as the copy editor for *The Mennonite Quarterly Review*, a journal devoted to Anabaptist-Mennonite history, thought, life, and affairs. His articles have appeared in the *Common Review*, the *Indianapolis Star*, *Journalism History*, *Newspaper Research Journal*, the *New York Times*, and other publications. Before joining the faculty at Goshen College, he worked as a staff editor on the national desk at the *New York Times*.

Calvin Redekop, ed., *Creation and the Environment: An Anabaptist Perspective on a Sustainable World*

Calvin Redekop, Stephen C. Ainlay, and Robert Siemens, *Mennonite Entrepreneurs*

Steven D. Reschly, *The Amish on the Iowa Prairie, 1840 to 1910*

Kimberly D. Schmidt, Diane Zimmerman Umble, and Steven D. Reschly, *Strangers at Home: Amish and Mennonite Women in History*

Diane Zimmerman Umble, *Holding the Line: The Telephone in Old Order Mennonite and Amish Life*

David Weaver-Zercher, *The Amish in the American Imagination*